From Solidarity to Sellout

from SOLIDARITY

to SELLOUT

The Restoration of Capitalism in Poland
by TADEUSZ KOWALIK

Translated by Eliza Lewandowska

MONTHLY REVIEW PRESS *New York*

Library of Congress Cataloging-in-Publication Data

Kowalik, Tadeusz.

From Solidarity to sellout : the restoration of capitalism in Poland / by
Tadeusz Kowalik ; translated by Eliza Lewandowska.

   p. cm.

   ISBN 978-1-58367-296-9 (pbk. : alk. paper) — ISBN 978-1-58367-297-6
(cloth : alk. paper) 1. Poland —Economic policy —1990- 2.
Poland--Economic conditions —1990-3. Post-communism —Economic
aspects —Poland. I. Title.

   HC340.3.K6854 2012

   330.9438 —dc23

                   2012013104

Monthly Review Press
146 West 29th Street, Suite 6W
New York, NY 10001

www.monthlyreview.org

5 4 3 2 1

Content

PART THREE

LOOKING AHEAD / 251

Acknowledgments

This book is a kind of synthesis of my many publications about the systemic changes in Poland over the past twenty years. The list of people I am indebted to in writing it is long. Here I shall name only those of the utmost importance. I am most thankful to Warsaw's Literary Publishers MUZA S.A. One of its founders, Stanisław Stępień, commissioned the writing of this book, outlining its general contours. The publication was combined with setting up an inventive website (www.polskatransformacja.pl), containing many documents that are important for understanding the course of systemic changes in Poland during the past twenty years. Two other significant books on related subject matter are also being promoted at this time: *The Shock Doctrine* by Naomi Klein and *The Defeat of Solidarity* by the leftist U.S. political scientist David Ost (both books are presented in the website). All this has encouraged a kind of "coming out" of a niche current until now pushed to the sidelines (the Polish political scene is nearly entirely dominated by two right-wing formations). It is thanks to MUZA that my name is among the first six on the list of fifty authors most frequently quoted in books, according to the business newspaper *Gazeta Bankowa*. And in the commentary to this ranking, described as the only socialist among well-known Polish economists, which is stated as a matter of fact and without putting any blame on me for this.

The book was written at the Institute of Economics of the Polish Academy of Sciences, of which I am a member. The Institute has also financed a considerable portion of the translation costs.

The translation was done by Eliza Lewandowska, whose input has also been substantial in the preparation of the final version of this book, updated from the Polish version published in 2009.

Michael Yates has contributed greatly with his many remarks on how to improve the text not only in its language, but also in content matter, to adjust it to the English-speaking reader. With his questions and comments he has elicited the need for an "intercontinental" discussion about the various types of capitalism and the effectiveness of its reform.

Introduction

This book is designed as a critical analysis of the results of the Polish transformation—from a command to a capitalist economy—in the years before entry into the European Union (EU). My criticism is based on two interrelated premises: the new socioeconomic order is evaluated here not so much in terms of its economic growth rate and international competitiveness, as in its ability to employ labor and to satisfy the material and cultural needs of the main social groups. This is a radical criticism, one that should help formulate a program aimed at repairing the damages done by the transformation, or at least launch a program debate. I believe that EU entry, and especially the current world crisis, should provoke a general reassessment of the policy of systemic changes and a closer look at the different economic policies that exist within the EU, with an eye toward asking which of these might be applied in Poland so as to meet the needs of Polish society. The realization that the better choices available in 1989 have been lost should now serve to mobilize the Polish people to strive for a better life and social order. I shall return to this matter at the end of the book.

Hopefully, the main thesis of the book does not sound exotic today. In the mid-1990s, I described the Polish socioeconomic order as "one of the most unjust socioeconomic systems in Europe of the second half of the twentieth century," a perverse result of the Solidarity revolution, which I termed a bourgeois epigone revolution, a pale imitation of the original.[1] The U.S. political scientist David Ost published a book, *The Defeat of Solidarity*,[2] showing that the system created in Poland fails to meet even the basic criteria of liberal-democratic capitalism.

There have been many similarly radical opinions expressed recently. The following is one example.

Mieczysław Kabaj, who for over fifteen years worked for the International Labor Office in Geneva, writes:

> In the years 1990–2005 nearly 5 million workplaces were eliminated, while the working age population increased by more than 2 million. In effect, Poland has broken every disgraceful record: the employment rate has rapidly declined from 80 percent to 54 percent. . . . The unemployment rate (16 percent) is the highest among the OECD countries . . . we have the highest long-term unemployment rate—11 percent . . . the highest unemployment of young people, reaching 35–40 percent, the lowest entitlements (encompassing 13 percent of unemployed persons), and the lowest expenditures per unemployed person for active labor market programs.[3]

And sociologist Leszek Gilejko[4] fully agrees with this picture.

How is it possible that a country that has experienced the most massive worker movement in Europe (ten million members of Solidarity in 1980–81) could treat itself to such a system? I attempt to answer this question as someone strongly associated with this movement at its beginnings, and, in the eyes of some critics, to some extent, at least indirectly, co-responsible for it. For this very reason, this book cannot avoid a personal "stamp."

A Sage as Prime Minister
(Tadeusz Mazowiecki)

"Well, hello there, Tadeusz. I hear you're spreading the word that I have created the most unjust system in Europe." These are the words I was greeted with by former prime minister Tadeusz Mazowiecki (1989–90) in the vestibule of the building of the University of Warsaw. The occasion for this encounter was a conference of politicians and economists on the subject of Poland's expected accession to the European Union. It was attended by several former prime ministers and former and incumbent ministers. Mazowiecki was surrounded by flashing lights and television cameras. The broad smile on his face and the throaty but friendly voice suggested his gracious forgiveness for such "leftist excesses." He most probably had in mind the above-mentioned article about the bourgeois epigone revolution. Presumably, this demonstration of no hard feelings was supposed to mean that old friends are to be forgiven for even such an obviously untrue opinion. Which did not rule out a possible urge to maybe lightly mock, if not the author, then at least his opinions.

However, Tadeusz Mazowiecki is capable of going upstream, and so ten years later, notwithstanding the celebratory atmosphere spotlighting the Polish successes, he said at the University of Warsaw: "Had I known that unemployment would rise to 19 percent, I would have thought hard over the decisions on economic transformation."[5] If this is so, then there is nothing now that stands in the way of serious reflection over those and later decisions.

I became acquainted with Tadeusz Mazowiecki when we were members of the program committee of the semi-legal Society for Educational Courses in the years 1977 to 1979. And although earlier he had been an MP, I did not see a politician in him (even in one of the letters I wrote I saw in him "a sage with a gray beard" to whom a young person could turn for help with important existential dilemmas). I saw more of a sage than a politician in him also when, on August 22, 1980, I talked him into going to the Gdańsk Shipyard to help the strikers reach a compromise with the authorities. To me, he was more a public authority than a political strategist for negotiations. He asked why don't Geremek and myself go? Thus, eight days and some of the nights we spent with the strikers created particularly strong bonds, or so it seemed at the time. I thought that on a miniature scale this is how lasting cooperation is born above divisions, between a Catholic personalist and a chronic leftist.

These bonds survived the time of the first "Solidarity," though as opposed to that great experience during the August 1980 strike of the shipyard workers, I did not feel comfortable in the new movement. This was the main reason I declined two propositions made to me by Mazowiecki: to create, shortly after this strike, a research center for the new Trade Union and head it, and a couple of months later to serve as his deputy in the weekly *Tygodnik Solidarność*.

There is one matter that needs to be explained. Although I would return to the subject many times, I have never written that it was Tadeusz Mazowiecki who decided on the choice of systemic path, or "created" the existing socioeconomic order. Aside from the anti-sociological character of such an assumption, I did not ever say that his ideas turned out to be the causative factors. But I did emphasize the reluctance of the prime minister to look deeper into economic matters, which need not be something unfeasible for a layman with an education in law or history. Alas, he relied entirely on the opinions of experts. I expressed this best, I think, by using a metaphor. During the formation of the government team Mazowiecki would repeat that he was "looking for his Erhard"—the author of the social market economy in Germany—so I wrote that he wanted to go to Bonn for prescriptions, but his advisors bought him a ticket to Washington and Chicago instead.

The thing is, for a long time Mazowiecki did not realize that economic policy is more of an art than an activity based on science. Inevitably, advice and even expert opinions are highly diverse and have to be so, since they are determined by different axiological assumptions, interests, or even temporary fascination. And so he would say: "Economists tell me . . ." as if economists had the knowledge of an engineer concerning the endurance of a bridge. In this I rather saw the drama of a sorcerer.

I must admit, however, that to this day I am intrigued by the question that remains unanswered: how does an advocate of Emmanuel Mounier and Jacques Maritain (as someone once said), a walking code of moral values and in my eyes at the time the most outstanding Polish representative of the ideas included in *Laborem exercens* and *Sollicitudo rei socialis*, a humanist in every inch, reconcile his values with the fact that, in the country of—I repeat—the largest worker movement that twentieth-century Europe experienced, and which he served in an active way, such a glaringly unjust socioeconomic system emerged? A system that carries—next to the name of Leszek Balcerowicz, its architect—the name of "the first non-communist prime minister"? An explanation in this matter is owed by him and all of us who had the trust of millions of people at that time.

The Disillusion of "Solidarity"

For a time, among the post-communist countries, Poland appeared to be a hotbed of new, bold ideas, auguring a new systemic experiment for the future. Before long, however, it turned out that new ideas were to be replaced by old, imitative practice.

The ten-million-strong Solidarity movement of workers (1980–81) resounded with a strong echo throughout the world, leaving behind it the utopia of the Self-Governing Republic. The movement was not revived during the disintegration of the Soviet bloc, though it did seem that the "new socioeconomic order" outlined in the Round Table Agreements (spring 1989) was a pragmatic reference to this utopia. But it soon became clear that the "shock therapy" of 1989–90 was but a repetition of primitive capital accumulation. Lech Wałęsa himself sensed this paradox when on June 4, 1989, the night of the great electoral victory, he exclaimed: "To our misfortune, we have won!" As Hegel might have put it, it was history's cunning that made Solidarity's people the perpetrators of a return to nine-teenth-century capitalism.

The year 1997 could be seen as a time of Great Reflection. The constitution of Poland, drawn up with the great involvement of Tadeusz Mazowiecki himself and ratified by parliament, contained a catalogue of provisions foretelling the willful formation of a system referring to the best European models of the last half-century. The most important were:

> The Republic of Poland shall be a democratic state ruled by law and implementing the principles of social justice (art. 2). A social market economy, based on the freedom of economic activity, private owner-ship, and solidarity, dialogue and cooperation between social part-ners, shall be the basis of the economic system of the Republic of Poland (art. 20). Public authorities shall pursue policies aiming at full, productive employment by implementing programs to combat unemployment, including the organization of and support for occu-pational advice and training, as well as public works and economic intervention. (art. 65).

Many other provisions called for a high level of social security, public services free of charge, and respect for work and working people.

Nevertheless, neither the fundamental systemic assumptions nor detailed provisions served as the basis for government action. It was in the year of the constitution that the coalition of Solidarity Election Action (AWS) and the Union of Liberty (UW) came to power, with Leszek Balcerowicz in the lead and a program of reforms heading in exactly the opposite direction. Health care reform proceeded toward further commercialization and elitist privatization. But oddest of all was the capital-based pension reform. In place of the PAYG (pay-as-you-go) system, there were individual contributions forming two obligatory pillars: the state-run Social Insurance Institution (ZUS) and the Open Pension Funds (OFE). Strangely, the state made it mandatory to pay contributions to OFE that were administered by private Pension Fund Societies (Powszechne Towarzystwa Emerytalne). And because both the old and the new system had to

coexist for a long time, the state budget was burdened with simultaneously financing both systems. The costly and foreign capital–dominated OFEs thus became a source of quickly mounting public deficit
and public debt. When the current global crisis and fast growth of
debt inclined the government to move part of the contribution from
OFEs to ZUS, this was met with fierce objection on the part of the
strong, highly media-backed capital lobby group.

Two Americas in Poland

The events of Poland's economic transformation described herein are
closely interwoven with the United States, or with two kinds of
"Americas," so to speak. On the one side is the America of Ronald
Reagan and G. W. Bush, or, in the doctrinal sphere, of Milton
Friedman and F. A. Hayek. This presence, combined with the influence of the U.S.-backed International Monetary Fund (IMF), exerted
a strong imprint on Poland's system, particularly in the social and economic realms. Those who are only familiar with today's views of
Jeffrey Sachs will find it hard to believe that it was he (along with his
assistant David Lipton) who talked the Polish government into taking
a "jump into the market." The message given forth by this "America"
was captivating in its simplicity: commercialize, privatize, and deregu-
late as quickly as possible. It was the ideological (the great myth of the
American dream!), political, and economic presence of this "America"
that determined Poland's entry onto the path of capitalism fashioned
on the Anglo-Saxon model, perceived as a contradiction to the
Scandinavian (social-democratic) model or the German "social
market economy." The idealized myth of American liberal democracy
is best rendered by the election poster—today termed "megaposter"—
of the Solidarity opposition of June 1989, picturing a sheriff with the
caption "High Noon."*

*This was a direct reference to the well-known 1952 film *High Noon*, with Gary
Cooper and Grace Kelly.

On the other side is "the other America," in the words of Michael Harrington, an America that is weaker but increasingly visible. For a long time now, Poles have carried in their minds the highly idealized image of the America of Franklin D. Roosevelt and his New Deal, or the Great Society of John F. Kennedy and Lyndon B. Johnson.* Among contemporary institutions, the American ESOPs (Employee Stock Ownership Plans) gained great popularity in Poland, being supported by Reagan as well as by the "Polish pope" (the encyclical *Laborem Exerces*). This example also served as the basis for the rank-and-file movement toward employee companies, which in the 1990s became the most common form of ownership transformation (though legislation squeezed them into the stiff straitjacket of leasing, where they were quite openly combated instead of supported by the authorities). The social and economic mindset is slowly being molded by John Rawls's concept of egalitarianism and property-owning democracy (three of his major books have been published in Polish), and especially by the picture of American capitalism in the seven translations of recent works of Joseph Stiglitz.† These books have already contributed to an erosion of the myth of the Anglo-Saxon model of capitalism in favor of the more frequent reference to the Scandinavian model.

It is worth recalling that in the beginning of the systemic changes, in 1989, economists and politicians from "the other America" paid visits to the Polish authorities. The American economist and advocate

---

*Ironically, this was not without its impact on the favorable reception of the America of Ronald Reagan, or even of G. W. Bush. One could even suspect that the insane invasion of Iraq, in which Poland took part, was seen through the eyes of the old, just America fighting against German Nazism and Japan's aggression. Exotic politicians proposed that Poland join NAFTA, and that "Zbig" Brzeziński be made Poland's president. These reflect well a saying so popular at the turn of the century, that Poland has become or is trying to become the fifty-first state of America.

†Luckily, none of the micro- or macroeconomic textbooks of this author, written many years ago, has appeared in Polish. Thus Polish readers do not know the neo-Keynesian orthodox Stiglitz.

of participatory and market socialism, Thomas E. Wesskopf,[6] even succeeded in creating a group of experts offering free advisory services to Poland's government. Earlier, the Stockholm message of Joseph Stiglitz to the post-communist countries had also been taken heed of (more on this later in the book). But this was a time of neoliberals. Already in the 1980s Ira Katznelson (1996)* observed that many Solidarity activists were turning to neoliberalism. In his book, written in the form of letters to Adam Michnik, he tried in vain to talk him and others into the need for enriching liberal programs with socialist ideals.

The latter movement was a potentially important one as it ran parallel to a number of other trends of political and economic thought. Its characteristics included:

- it was close to the ideals of the Self-Governing Republic—the program of Solidarity of 1980–81, which had a chance to be reborn as a strong social movement; it would also have been easy to accept by the communist-oriented trade unions that appeared on the scene following delegalization of Solidarity during martial law;

- it was close to the highly social Swedish model that was popular in Poland, where in the 1980s Sweden cooperated with the Polish opposition, with support provided by the new emigrants from Poland;

- it also referred to the more modest Austrian model, popular in Poland as well and also supported by the new emigrants.

The existence of employee councils in state enterprises, established by the 1981 act, and the intellectual movement for employee participation would have made de-statization, or socialization of state property, much easier and less cumbersome socially than ordinary privatization. All these trends would have facilitated cooperation

---

*At that time still one of the leaders of New York's leftist New School for Social Research, which was helping the Solidarity opposition.

between people of diverse orientations: socialists, social democrats, Christian democrats, and social liberals.*

Certain questions come to the fore: How and why did the option we call social-democratic fail, bearing in mind, of course, the initial ideals rather than the parties that merely resort to this name? How is it and why is it that the Anglo-Saxon option has become dominant on the political scene and in systemic changes?

*I am not listing communists as a separate group here, since a great number of them had earlier resigned from their former (party) identification. Some even joined the ranks of laissez-faire market advocates.

PART ONE

Shock as Therapy

Sustainable development, and sustainable reform, are based on changes in ideas, interests, and coalitions. Let me repeat that *such changes cannot be forced.* Changes in ways of thinking often take time. That is why the approach to reform based on *conditionality* has largely failed. That is why the Bolshevik approach to changing society—forced changes from a revolutionary vanguard—has failed time and time again. The shock therapy approach to reform was no more successful than the Cultural Revolution [in China] and the Bolshevik Revolution.

—JOSEPH STIGLITZ, 2001

1. The Collapse
of "Really Existing Socialism"

More and more I tend to believe that the system that came into being in Poland after the Second World War is a lost cause in historical terms. It must be replaced with another one which simply is efficient. The question is, however, can this be done by the same people who had built the existing system? I have true reservations about that.

—Mieczysław F. Rakowski,*
Dzienniki, December 11, 1988

Alec Nove, the noted expert on the Russian and Soviet economies, once said, "The word 'socialism' is apt to produce strong feelings, of cynicism and hostility. It is the road to a future just society, or to serfdom. It is the next stage of an ineluctable historical process, or tragic aberration, a cul-de-sac, into which the deluded masses are drawn by power-hungry agitator-intellectuals."[1]

*At that time prime minister of the newly formed cabinet, the last "communist" cabinet.

It may come as a surprise to today's reader that barely half a century ago, for many scholars and politicians, the superiority of socialism was unquestionable as a system that is not only more just but also more efficient than capitalism. This seemed to be obvious to John Putnam, the American author of the book *The Modern Case for Socialism*, published in 1943. The table of contents gives an idea of the benefits that this system was supposed to bring: end unemployment; create hitherto unknown freedom; replace economic oligarchy with economic democracy; promote equality of opportunity, provide economic security for all; reduce inequality of income; create a free, democratic press, radio and cinema; eliminate the wastes of capitalist production, transport, marketing, commercial banks, and capital investment.[2] In the individual chapters the author describes in detail the waste existing at that time in the U.S. economy in each of these domains.

Similar pledges were also made in the beginning by the Russian Bolsheviks. They turned out to be illusory, however, which can partly be explained by the lack of corroboration for the Marxist theory of historical sequence in which socialism is the next stage following (developed) capitalism.

Such an understanding of socialism, as simply the opposite of capitalism, has currently been abandoned by nearly all parties of the socialist left. This came as a consequence of the negative experiences of centrally planned economies, where state ownership was predominant, with the market playing a subordinate role, and also as a result of new achievements in economic theory.

Really existing socialism (usually referred to as communism) at first appeared to be an effective form of modernizing the economy, particularly industry. This was thought to be true for both the centralized forms of planning (above all in the USSR) and the self-management version of Yugoslav socialism. However, even though the high growth rate in Yugoslavia was impressive enough in the beginning, massive unemployment remained an unresolved problem. In both versions, state ownership led to an overgrowth of bureaucracy that stiffened the whole system, in turn making it impossible to proceed beyond an extensive form of industrialization. Yet, even from such a narrow point of view, real socialism as a substitute for capitalism could pass the test only in the first phase, and even then only to a limited extent. As Polish economist Włodzimierz Brus said:

> Socialist modernization as we know it so far, seems to lack the capacity to generate a momentum of its own. Taking into account the relative backwardness of most of the countries in question, imitative development was to be expected for some time. But the degree of durability of imitation is extraordinary—except perhaps in the military sphere which we are not in a position to judge. More up-to-date technology—either imported or imitated in home production—must normally result in increased productivity; however, the modernization effect for the economy should be measured not by this result alone, but in the first place by the spill-over effect in spurring on home-grown technology and production innovation. This is hardly happening in the socialist countries, despite the supposed advantages in science and the education system, and in the abolition of commercial secrecy which was to ensure unhampered flow of information between fraternal firms, sectors and countries. Coupled with this is the inability to go deeper into structural modernization. Socialist countries have been relatively successful in developing traditional industries . . . but they have failed to show even a single case of leapfrogging into a comparatively new and promising field.[3]

The above reasoning was again repeated with the list of the "New Revolutionizing Products from the Period 1913–1957" presented by Hungarian economist and critic of command economies János Kornai.[4] Out of the nearly eighty technological innovations made throughout the world, the USSR was cited in only three instances (housing heating, underground coal gasification, and prefabricated housing construction). To this list can be added the invention of the laser, but only on an equal footing with the United States. Among the other countries of the Soviet bloc, only Czechoslovakia could boast of one invention (Kaplan's water turbines).* One cannot put the blame on scientists for this. According to the experts, as early as the 1920s Russian science was no worse than American science, while such disciplines as mathematics or physics were on a very high level even during Stalinist times. But the USSR's technological backwardness became ever more marked during the last decade of the empire, when the achievements of the IT revolution were quickly spreading all over the world.

Within the Soviet bloc, growth began losing momentum soon after Khrushchev's famous pledge from the early 1960s that the Soviet Union would catch up with the United States in per capita income within little more than a decade. The slowdown in growth affected the traditional branches of industry, and stagnation became more evident. In the 1970s and 1980s it became clear that apart from the military sector the economies of the socialist countries were not able to absorb and utilize the Western achievements of the IT revolution.

The stagnation phase merely confirmed the fall of the myth of the superiority of the Soviet model of social order over capitalism. The victorious Bolshevik Revolution of November 1917 had proclaimed the establishment of the worker-peasant state, which evoked much confusion throughout the world and in particular led to new divisions within the socialist movement. In fact, there were not that many workers in backward Russia. It would have made more sense to look for the revolution's driving force among the peasants, who in the first years obtained nationalized landed property. The revolution quickly degenerated, as had been predicted by eminent activists of the socialist movement, such as Rosa Luxemburg and Karl Kautsky. The revolutionary

---

*Kornai's list omits innovations in the military sector and those related to the "conquest" of space, where the USSR often was on par with, and at times on a higher level than, the United States (the launching of Sputnik in 1958). Concentration on these two closely related sectors led to negligence of the needs of civil sectors. Here it must be noted that in the Soviet political system the armaments sector was much more isolated from the civil sector than was the case in the United States, where the inventions of the former domain have been quite frequently adapted in the latter.

terror of Lenin and Trotsky gave way to blind Stalinist terror, which applied the Soviet type of Marxism to legitimize the system (later, during Brezhnev's times, called "really existing socialism").

Today, the Soviet model is widely regarded as a historically unsuccessful road to economic development. However, such a general conclusion does not tell the whole story. At the beginning of the last decade, a survey was conducted with the question: "When was life easier—in communist Poland or today?" More than 50 percent of the respondents preferred the old system and only 11.5 percent the existing one.[5] A similar trend can be observed in all post-communist countries. More than two-thirds of respondents have said that the system established in Poland after 1989 has had an unfavorable impact on their lives. Since that crucial year, more and more analysts are giving thought to both the advantages and disadvantages of the old system, recalling above all the existence of full employment and universal social security, even if of a low standard.[*]

Many socialists, Trotskyites, and social democrats have denied that this formation ever had any socialist character, going so far as to say that this was distorted or degenerated socialism. For a long time, however, it seemed that under favorable circumstances the system would evolve in the direction of democratic socialism. And the main obstacles to be overcome—according to the proponents of this theory—were not some imminent errors existing in the doctrine, but the obstinacy of the structured bureaucracy defending its own interests.

According to conservative economist Joseph Schumpeter, the Soviet Union came into being by a fluke. Yet this became an important historical fact in the formation of today's world. However, the implementation of communism in Central Europe and a good part of Asia, as well as its radiation to Third World countries, was already no coin-

---

[*]Naturally, the opinions vary greatly. It should be remembered, however, that even capitalism, with its long history, in theory and in practice, continues to be the subject of unending contestation, and the reasons for its origin are described in diametrically different opinions. It is therefore no wonder that the range of consensus of academic literature in the assessment of real socialism, or communism, continues to be narrow.

cidence. The fact that such a system could last for seventy years also bespeaks its longevity, albeit its existence was based on the strength of an open and secret machine of repression. But repression itself is not enough to maintain power. The process leading to the downfall of socialism revealed that the machinery of repression becomes powerless if societies in their mass reject the existing system.

Without going into an analysis of the causes that ensured victory for the Bolsheviks, followed by the spread of the Soviet system model to other countries, I shall dwell instead on the main features of a socialist economy, especially those that led to the ultimate collapse of the system. An assessment of economic categories cannot overlook the fact that the USSR under communist rule quickly became a military power alongside the United States, with a solid industrial base. And if one takes into account not only the Soviet Union, but the entire bloc, one cannot deny the considerable popularity of the system, extending well beyond the handful of its direct beneficiaries within the party or the power structures.

The most important attribute of really existing socialism was the combination of closely centralized and hierarchical political authority with state ownership of means of production.* This gave the political authority nearly absolute control over the economy. The all-encompassing planning, often called command-distributive planning, was bureaucratic in nature. During the time of the first five-year plans, the economy was subordinated to the buildup of the heavy and armaments industries. So long as the focus was on only a few economic tasks, with the mobilization (by way of political means) of unused raw materials and human resources, initially also by means of coercion, the system seemed to be working with relative effectiveness. Naturally, throughout its duration, the socialist economy (perhaps with the exception of that of Yugoslavia) became a semi-war economy, in the words of socialist economist Oskar Lange,[6] without much consideration given to the needs of con-

---

*Brus liked to call the monoparty power a "monoarchy" (as opposed to polyarchy), after the American political scientist Robert Dahl.

sumers. Work was made compulsory not only in principle, but it was also regulated by commands.

Later, following the period of the heroic plans, with the formation of a system that Kornai[7] calls classical, the state continued to determine the dimensions and directions of investment, as well as most prices and the interest rate. State actions also determined the general structure of consumption, and only within this framework did the state leave to the citizens the freedom to choose goods as well as their professions and place of work. The inflated economic plans gave rise to the trend of full employment, and often to employment overgrowth, which assuaged the social tensions resulting from the low efficiency of the economy. The "soft budget constraints" of enterprises (mainly the absence of a bankruptcy threat) were not conducive to cost reduction or to the introduction of innovation. In its various forms, the Soviet system was capable of evoking and mobilizing unused means of production (especially massive, open and hidden unemployment) and, thanks to this, of achieving a high national income growth rate. Even following correction of the much falsified official statistics, the GDP growth rate in the USSR was high during the first five-year plans. Poland's economy also developed relatively quickly until the 1960s. With the progress of industrialization, as the economy grew more complex, the initially fairly good results of extensive industrial modernization began to give way to greater chaos. On the other hand, in countries that had been industrialized earlier, the system had poor results from the beginning. This was true for both Czechoslovakia and the German Democratic Republic.

There is much truth in the words of the British economist Joan Robinson that, contrary to the predictions of Karl Marx, real socialism turned out to be not a successor of capitalism but rather a substitute for its earlier phase. However, even in the countries that had witnessed a certain growth as a result of imposed industrialization, its costs were very high. Probably the biggest expansion and overgrowth was seen in the position of party and state bureaucracy, in the formation of an all-encompassing staff *nomenklatura* (the bureaucratic elite enjoying special privileges) that controlled nearly all walks of social, political and economic life (the Yugoslav dissident Milovan Djilas [1957] called it the "new class").* It was this authority that precluded the necessary, and at times widely perceived and postulated, reforms, and also led to socialist reformers achieving much poorer results than they had expected. Often reformers became political hostages to the party and state machinery, devoid of any real power.

The Deceptive Calculations of Mikhail Gorbachev and Wojciech Jaruzelski

The increasingly bold reforms in the countries of Central Europe, especially in Hungary and Poland, mostly consisted of greater borrowing of systemic institutions from capitalism. While this did not adequately improve economic efficiency, it did serve to level out systemic differences. Brus called this "the progressing indeterminacy of socialism."[8] The process of implementing market elements into the economy led, at the same time, to the "commercialization" of the attitudes of the ruling elites and their loss of faith in the superiority of socialism, thereby to the erosion of any modernization mission. As soon as the most farsighted of the communist reformers began to realize that they would not be able to carry through more profound changes solely with the Party apparatus and state administration, they had to appeal to social groups beyond the party *nomenklatura*, which led to a change in the power status and finally to the collapse of the entire system.

The example of Mikhail Gorbachev is particularly illustrative and also dramatic. He understood the link of *glasnost* (openness) with *perestroika* (reconstruction). It was clear to him that without the support of broader public opinion he would not be able to break through the hard walls of resistance of the ruling bureaucracy. Gorbachev also

---

*A similar assessment was made by Jacek Kuroń and Karol Modzelewski—two young academics—in their widely known "An Open Letter to the Party" (1965) which they paid for with several years in prison.

believed in a "return to the sources," in drawing on the powers of recovery from the revolutionary tradition. All of this aroused the hostility of the corrupt apparatchiks who were scared to death of criticism, and in consequence launched an uncontrolled process that ultimately led to the disintegration of the USSR and the breakdown of the system.

Notwithstanding the many differences, a similar fate was met in Poland by General Wojciech Jaruzelski, for many years minister of defense, in the 1980s the first secretary of the ruling party, and subsequently the prime minister. He did not want the downfall of the socialist system, aiming instead at overhauling the system with the participation of the democratic opposition, which would be admitted to share power. This was the idea behind the Round Table Agreements in the spring of 1989 and the Contract Sejm with one-third of the seats being allocated to the opposition. The agreed-upon free election to the Senate resulted in the upper chamber being given to the opposition.

In the end, the settlements of the agreements were abandoned in favor of "shock therapy," that is, the implementation of a primitive form of capitalism, with its high unemployment, a high and deepening level of social exclusion, and very extensive and continuously growing income disparities. The Polish transformation went on to serve as a model for Eastern and Central Europe, resulting in deplorable effects for masses of people.

Communist China and Vietnam have drawn entirely different lessons from the defeat of the old systems in Eastern and Central Europe. The governments of those countries are commercializing, decentralizing, and then privatizing the economy, while letting in foreign capital. They are doing all this while control is retained by parties that still remain communist by name. For over thirty years now, the Chinese economy has been the fastest growing in the world, undermining the widely held belief that during transformation recession is inevitable.*

---

*Little noticed Slovenia was the only country of this region that managed to break away from the Polish syndrome (Mencinger, 2004), thereby disproving that only in backward China and Vietnam was gradual transition to a market economy possible.

However, many analysts maintain that economic expansion by itself, without political pluralism, freedom of the press, and so forth, is not viable in the long run.

In the minds of the Bolsheviks, as well as in the practice of real socialism, there were many ideas drawn from Marx and his successors.* This included first of all a deeply rooted aversion to the market and competition altogether, accompanied by an exaggerated faith in the art of planning, and in the last decades of existence of that system, in what has been called "comp-utopia." A similarly deeply rooted aversion to any private ownership was seen among Marxists, which went hand in hand with excessive faith in the potential of public or social ownership.

But was this social ownership? Probably the biggest pitfall of the fallen system was property controlled and managed by not so much an all-powerful as an omnipresent party and state bureaucracy. The political system ruled out the possibility of society having any influence on the basic directions of economic development, even to a limited extent, such as through the option of choosing among different programs during election campaigns.

Socialist Alternative to Soviet Communism

An evaluation of real socialism as a system of promised social justice and equality does not rate better than as a system bringing higher efficiency. The evolution of the economies of real socialism consisted of ever greater loans being drawn from the Western countries, more market elements being implemented, with less and less allegiance to the socialist principles. The recurrent question remains: Was it because socialism as such was bound to fall short of expectations entirely, or was it only the Bolshevik version (usurpation) that failed? Although the latter viewpoint seems to be more grounded, one cannot underestimate the lessons learned from the experience of the Soviet system version, important for socialist concepts in general.

*As correctly pointed out by Brus and Łaski (1989).

A reasonably mild, but also the most constructive form of criticism of Soviet socialism, formulated by the more conciliatory Marxists, went more or less like this: by industrializing Russia, and thus by creating a modern working class, the Bolsheviks, then Stalin, create the preconditions for socialism, and by the same token dig their own graves. With time, the working class will abolish the authoritarian system and enforce the transition to democratic socialism. This was, for example, the message of the book the leading Austrian Marxist, Otto Bauer (1936). For many years this reasoning was shared by the world-famous Polish economist Oskar Lange.* He created a truly alternative model of a socialist economy,[9] but did not deny the Bolsheviks their chances either. His (and Marek Breit's) credo was: "With great admiration we stand in the face of the cultural and moral greatness of the Russian proletarian and peasant revolution. . . . But let us remember that, in the long run, socialism is able to take root only as much as, aside from its moral achievements, it can show that economically it functions better than capitalism. . . . If the socialist economy were not to meet the hopes placed in it, then it would really not be worth the efforts and sacrifices that the working masses are bearing in the struggle for it."[10] If one passes over the glorification of the "cultural and moral" side of the Bolshevik Revolution, most probably due to lack of knowledge, the rest, referring to the economic sphere, sounds downright prophetic.

---

*Lange (1904–1965) liked to repeat the words of the renowned Russian economist Stanislav Strumilin that "Stalin dragged Russia out of its barbarity using barbaric methods."

2. The Neoliberal About-Face

The showy entry on the path of reversal to capitalism (at that time called market economy or the free market) contradicted the partly socialist, or syndicalist, program of the "Self-Governing Republic," ratified in October 1981 by the First Congress of the Independent Self-Governing Trade Union "Solidarity" (hereafter referred to as S.). Likewise, it contradicted the Round Table Agreements concluded in April 1989 and the declaration that followed several months later and that became an election platform for the Consultative Committee with Lech Wałęsa. The pivotal turn took place practically without struggle and without public disputes. How, then, did it happen that without any visible resistance, S. accepted (at least silently) the free-market orientation of the first non-communist government? And how could it be that the old government coalition from the days of the Round Table "handed over power" so readily?

Let us begin with S.

Many authors perceived S. in the years of its emergence, 1980–81, as a movement that was obsessively democratic, posssibly on the borderline of anarchism. The movement was said to skillfully combine decisiveness with readiness for compromises and unblemished moral purity. The name S. was justified by the extraordinary sense of responsibility for the working people as a whole, where workers were called to strike, for example, to defend the interests of underpaid teachers or doctors. Yet all this turned out to be frail and short-lived. Why so?

The massive and excessively easy exodus of the leading activists to government positions, which decapitated the unionist S., is not a satisfactory explanation and would require a political interpretation itself. Especially since S. was also deserted by activists with a worker background, among them people who had resisted corruption. Lech Wałęsa himself is a figure too controversial and ambiguous to serve as an example. But the new establishment also included such factory workers as the former leader of Wrocław's S., Władysław Frasyniuk, and in the beginning also the leader of the Warsaw chapter, the underground legend Zbigniew Bujak, in 1981 named as Wałęsa's competitor. When in the summer of 1990 the first split occurred within the ranks of S., it was Bujak who co-created a new party—the Civic Movement "Democratic Action" (ROAD—predecessor of the liberal Union of Liberty Party). Bujak claimed that a division into left and right made no sense, since both represent the middle class; that the government was managing very well with economic reform; and that the difficulty boiled down to "the immense psychological problem for entire human masses."*

Two key factors led to the change of character of S.: the martial law imposed on December 13, 1981, with the subsequent years of underground activity of the union, and the Round Table Agreements. Eight years of underground operation exerted a strong impact on S. First of all, the mass movement was transformed into a staff organization in which democracy was replaced with co-optation and nomination. Decisions were made by one man or arbitrarily within a small group, with no allowance for any critical or independent assessment of the

---

*More than a year later, Bujak radically changed his views. He acknowledged that the program was a bad one, not suited to the reality. In the book *Przepraszam za Solidarność* (Forgive Me for Solidarity) he made a reckoning, concluding that "this is not the Poland we were fighting for" (Bujak, 1991). This will not be the last total change of views of this activist. Several years later Bujak appeared at a Congress of the ultra-liberal Union of Liberty with Hayek's book in his hand.

strengths or weaknesses of the successive moves. The ranks were now to be cemented by loyalty, obedience, and discipline. Among the unionists acting underground, a new, combatant bond was formed, which in the future could easily turn into a "republic of buddies."[1] But probably the most important thing was that small groups of local activists were losing touch with the mass social base and became less involved in typical unionist problems than during the times of legality, instead becoming more absorbed with purely political issues. The unionist problems were taken up, as if in a natural way, by the employee self-management councils, reborn and tolerated by the authorities, albeit subjected to various restrictions.

The conditions of martial law and its repercussions in subsequent years were instrumental in making the illegal S. primarily an anti-system movement, adverse to the government and the system. Even activists who had been moderate in the past now had doubts about the feasibility of the reform of really existing socialism, or even of its cautious liberalization or the admittance of social pluralism. It was understandable that in response to the introduction of martial law, the illegal S. approved of the West's sanctions laid on Poland. What is more difficult to comprehend is the unwillingness to have them removed after martial law was repealed.* In addition, the new character of the leadership of Mikhail Gorbachev and the weight of his reforms were not understood adequately enough.

In his many declarations, Wałęsa regularly called for compromise and agreement, but many activists of the underground structures

---

*I had a personal experience in this matter. From spring 1981 to spring 1983 I was at the Wilson Center in Washington. Since before martial law I had been preparing the planned visit of Lech Wałęsa to the United States, I was often in touch with Washington's establishment. In the winter of 1983 the Americans were generally expecting that the S. leadership would take the initiative in the matter of lifting the sanctions. Cardinal Król of the Catholic Church also felt that they were primarily a blow to the Polish people. I relayed these opinions (through Bronisław Geremek) to Wałęsa. This did not bring about any change in his position. It was only the U.S. ambassador's later visit to Wałęsa (apparently on the instruction of Ronald Reagan himself, or definitely of his associates) that turned out to be decisive.

treated these pronouncements as merely tactical games with the authorities. Wałęsa was often criticized for them, at times with the most piercing accusations (later on even Adam Michnik would apologize to Wałęsa for them). It was the attitude toward socialism and socialist authority that led to the ultimate split of the old S. leadership into two conflicting factions. Those who remained unyielding to Wałęsa and his entourage included such regional leaders as Andrzej and Joanna Gwiazda, Marian Jurczyk, Seweryn Jaworski, Anna Walentynowicz, and, in the beginning, also Jan Rulewski and Andrzej Słowik.

Presumably the S. supporters, fed with anti-communist and "anti-Jaruzelski" literature, were suspicious of Wałęsa's tactics. This suspicion was skillfully fueled by the official propaganda, which underscored the privileged position of S.'s leader and the intellectuals surrounding him, supported spiritually and financially by the affluent West. It can be assumed with high likelihood that a significant portion of the old Unionist supporters eyed with suspicion the "collusion with the communists" at the Round Table. Especially since the increasingly liberal press was by then alarming the public about the "enfranchisement of the party *nomenklatura*," considered by some oppositional journalists to be the cheapest way of "buying one's way out" of the administration of the bankrupt system.[2] This enfranchisement was to be "political capitalism," as coined by the sociologist Jadwiga Staniszkis, who was severely rebuked for this by the Union's rank and file.[3] Sharing power with the opposition was in turn seen as opening the road to constraints on labor, to the advantage of capital.

Though it is true that the Round Table negotiations, relayed in detail by the media, showed a fundamental change of climate, they were also accompanied by the allegedly "conspiring" sideline meetings in Magdalenka, Wilanów, and in other government palaces, which suggested an elitist character of the agreements. The worker rank and file of S. ended up in the role of passive observers. This was in sharp contrast to the atmosphere of openness and many public controversies that characterized the 1980–81 period. Indeed, by now no one was turning to the workers themselves—the original cause of it all. Though the Round Table did include several worker activists, such as Zbigniew Bujak, Mieczysław Gil, Władysław Frasyniuk, and Alojzy Pietrzyk, a look at the minutes of the meetings clearly reveals their marginal participation. The most important of the settlements made, the "Agreement on Political Reforms," was signed by fifty members, of whom probably only Bujak could say about himself—I am a worker. Yet the "pro-worker" character was skillfully (loudly) played out by the other strong union, regarded as connected with the old regime, the National Federation of Trade Unions (OPZZ), headed by Alfred Miodowicz. The high turnout at the parliamentary election of June 1989 and its plebiscitary character (candidates from "billboards with Wałęsa" were picked by voters) could in part be the expression of a desire to eradicate the results of an accord made with a partner hitherto painted as a satellite of the "evil empire."

These as well as other circumstances resulted in the legalized S. gathering only one-quarter of the old number of its members (with a continued shrinking tendency), and of these not many from the intelligentsia. OPZZ, on the other hand, boasted that it had one-third of former S. members within its ranks. The negotiating weakness of S. was further worsened by the fact that while the crucial reform decisions were being made, it continued to be in the phase of organization, absorbed by the internal matters of the Union instead of by program issues. It was thus unable to perform as an independent force on the still very foggy political scene.

A disheartening factor was that S. now had its own people within the ruling administration, or even its "own government," whose members continued to frequently refer to the ethos and symbolism of the August 1980 strike and the resultant agreement. The cited styrofoam on which the new prime minister had slept with the strikers had been a symbol of the journey traveled together. But the political demobilization of S. as a trade union was at this point intended by Wałęsa. In public pronouncements, he stressed that the most urgent task was to carry out political and economic reforms and only later would the time come to deal with the Union in an intensive way. Obviously he feared that a legalized and reemerged S. would become too strong an organization. He even said this outright: "We won't catch up with Europe if we build a strong union that will decisively oppose the reform. Solidarity started these reforms and it has to help in accomplishing them."[4] This evoked surprise and the sharp reaction of his closest colleagues. Frasyniuk asked: "What is Wałęsa wagering on? I always thought it was on Solidarity, but today I hear it isn't."[5] Bogdan Borusewicz said: "As the person in charge of the estate on the verge of bankruptcy, that is to say the trade union, I am warning—let us not weaken it further. Especially now, when it is about to face very serious problems and it is the only significant political force."[6] And Jacek Merkel: "Today the union is weak and if we keep on repeating that we don't need a strong one, then this piano will fall apart."[7] On this occasion the activist unveiled how he sees the operation of changing the economic system: "What we have inherited from the communists is like a knot of tangled up threads— it won't do to pull out each one separately. . . . This knot has to be cut by a single stroke. This will most certainly be done by the government. It will address the union with the question, how much can you bear, how much can the people bear? And we will answer that they can bear it or that they can't."[8]

However, none of the opponents could be convincing so long as they were unable to describe what kind of new socioeconomic order could be backed by S. A model that might serve well could be the Swedish socioeconomic system, which was formed with the large participation of the trade unions (not long ago as many as 90 percent of workers belonged to trade unions in Sweden), and the successive social democratic governments enjoyed their strong support. It is thanks to this that the Swedish economy, one of the world's most stable, "caught up with Europe."

During this time, an overpowering role was played by the concept of S. promoted by the leading intellectuals/politicians, as a political and economic "omnibus"—a synthesis of "formerly competitive orientations." This is the S. that Adam Michnik wanted at the time: "The collection of principles of Solidarity comprises Christian ethics and an open association with the values of the Catholic Church; the national tradition of the fight for freedom, independence and tolerance; the obstinate battle for social justice and emancipation of the working world; for truth in the world of political conflicts and rationality in the world of economic decisions."[9] Earlier, however, together with British political scientist Timothy Garton Ash and Hungarian oppositionist Janos Kis (1989), Michnik had appealed to the West for help in the construction of the new social order based on "law and order, on a free-market economy, on pluralism." It is hard to imagine that any social movement could exist capable of creating a catalogue of such contrasting values.

Understandably, such declared free-market conservatives as Stefan Kisielewski or Piotr Wierzbicki warned against S. as a trade union. Wierzbicki felt that "the unionist origin and character of Solidarity constituted its accursed stigma and fettered its wings when it tried to become the vanguard of reforms reaching the foundations of the current system."[10] Yet similar lines of thought were expressed by former activists of S., for example, Andrzej Celiński, secretary of the National Commission of the legal S., who even before the formation of the government of Tadeusz Mazowiecki warned that "the factor blocking changes is turning out to be the strength of the working class of manufacturing industry, especially as it has its [parliamentary] representations."[11]

Toward a Free-Market Philosophy

In 1993, there was much talk about the book by Karol Modzelewski *Dokąd od komunizmu?* (Where to from Communism?), which contained a political assessment of the fruits of three years of implementation of the Balcerowicz Plan. One of the main observations of the author was:

> To this day I am under the impression of the ease with which the elites singled out by the worker movement turned around 180 degrees, abandoning the values until now regarded as the primary cri-

terion of socioeconomic policy . . . such an abrupt change of point of
view, this extraordinarily easy transformation of unionists into liberals, shows a lack or rather absence of the sense of loyalty to the
social base of the movement. . . . That is why I feel shame.[12]

Modzelewski confines this "abrupt change" mostly to the roaring
year of 1989. However, many facts indicate that this pivotal turn
took place earlier and was well pronounced on both sides of the
political scene already in 1987. Here are two such cases. The U.S.
political scientist Ira Katznelson and his university* collaborated for
years with democratic opposition circles in Poland and other countries of Central Europe, supporting them in various ways. When,
after years of absence, he once again arrived in our country (May
1987), he was struck by the radically changed attitude: the rejection
by the Solidarity opposition of the "Self-Governing Republic" program in favor of conservative liberalism, which people began calling
neoliberalism. He gave the following account of a social gathering in
the apartment of sociologist Aldona Jawłowska (which may have
been organized specially for him): "At the meeting there was a crowd
of about thirty key representatives of the Polish opposition—among
them were the editors of *Krytyka* and *ResPublika* . . . and the leaders
of Solidarity." Following the talks, conducted "after a long evening
with much drinking," he concluded: "Your† acceptance of liberalism, not only as an alternative for the party-led states of your
region, but also for the revisionist Marxism of the sixties, with which
you were once associated, was enthusiastic and full of involvement. .
. . You rejected any concept of an 'intermediate way' between the
capitalism of the West and the socialism of the East, acknowledging
that in the current circumstances it is an illusion."[13] While the guest
did observe certain differences in viewpoints, he had the impression
that Karl Popper's *The Open Society and Its Enemies* and Friedrich

---

*The New School of Social Research, now New School University.
†Katznelson's book is written in the form of letters to Adam Michnik as representative of the opposition.

Hayek's *The Road to Serfdom* "had become the basic political texts for the entire movement."*[14]

Even more penetrating remarks were expressed by yet another observer, also "foreign" in a way. This was the account of philosopher Andrzej Walicki, who came to Poland after a six-year sojourn in Australia. His observations concern not one, but a whole series of events:

> When I came to Poland in May 1987 . . . the Polish intellectual scene turned out to be different than I had expected. The liberals were no longer treated as oddballs, unimportant lunatics or, at best, a handful of crazy intellectuals, propagating in a provocative way ideas that were maybe interesting, but that did not fit the country's reality. They became the most dynamic intellectual group, located in the best strategic point, pushing aside other groups to defensive positions. Proponents, or at least sympathizers of liberal ideas were visible nearly everywhere and greatly contributed to the change in the general intellectual climate. . . . Obviously, this process was the result of the new political circumstances, created by the general amnesty for political prisoners of September 1986, the pragmatic implementation of the policy of the communist authorities and finally . . . of the increasingly perceptible influence of the reform actions of Gorbachev.[15]

Walicki also took note of the publication of *Karta Prywatnej Przedsiębiorczości Gospodarczej* (Charter of Private Economic Enterprise). The Charter postulated a permanent place for the private sector, praising private enterprise and unrestrained competition "as the most effective way of mobilizing human energy, releasing ingenuity

*As for me—who talked for several minutes, I was then involved in the edition of the works of Oskar Lange and Michał Kalecki and described myself as a leftist social democrat—I was treated as an absolute exception by Katznelson. At that time he was dean of the Graduate Department of New York's New School of Social Research and he proposed to me a trimester of lectures on the subject of the great Western debate around capitalism and socialism, which I was able to take advantage of only two years later.

and initiative, making people disciplined and responsible."[16] He devoted much attention to the conservative-liberal views of Mirosław Dzielski and Bronisław Łagowski, of whom the latter propagated these ideas while being a member of the Polish United Workers' Party (PZPR),* which for Walicki was an indication of the progressive erosion of the official doctrine and of the differentiation in attitudes within the establishment. He was deeply impressed by the meetings of sociologists with deputy prime minister Zdzisław Sadowski. "The deputy prime minister talked about 'enterprise,' 'competition' and 'profit' as universal economic categories, applicable also in the socialist economy—which was of course tantamount to complete rejection of Marx's view that these are strictly historical categories, specific for the capitalist system. . . . An amusing paradox was . . . the fact that a member of the communist establishment [was defending] the liberal postulate of independence of economics from politics."[17]

In a sense, both Katznelson and Walicki lift from at least some of the union leaders the accusation that they had betrayed their own base at the moment of exchanging their places in the union and opposition for those in government, parliament, and business. Modzelewski analyzed the evolution and change of character of S. before martial law and in the years of illegality, but he did not notice that in the second half of the 1980s it was not S., not the worker movement in general that made up the direct base of the oppositional elite, but what some called the "alternative civil society." It was composed not of the reactivated S. deprived of its intellectual "head," but mainly the part of it that had survived martial law and the years that followed. This was the rich publishing-cultural network, various new groups aspiring to the role of political parties (such as the nationalistic Confederation of Independent Poland, Young Poland), the semi-legal seminars and clubs (the "Flying University") that continued the work as the Society for Educational Courses of the 1970s.

---

*It is interesting that Łagowski dates the formation of his conservative views, mainly under the influence of Raymond Aron, back to the 1960s (Łagowski, 1996).

At this point one should also name some of the opposition activists who had found financial support in the rapidly developing private sector, which gave rise to economic societies. Already on January 1, 1989, one declaration, "Minimum zmian" (Minimum of Changes) was published by Economic Action, associating several regional economic societies. This minimum was quite substantial, as it included repealing rationing of production factors and liberating prices of production and consumption goods, and even of some public services, setting the interest rate at the market level, withdrawal of the state from the banking system, and many changes in the organization of the economy. And all this was to be done at once—"within half a year."

As can be seen, in early 1989 there were already manifestations of views anticipating the shock therapy that was put forward more than half a year later by Jeffrey Sachs and Stanisław Gomułka. These declarations were accompanied by the emerging rudiments of the new economic group, for which the free market concept served a functional purpose. Not only the old official *nomenklatura*, but also these new groups turned in the direction of the state sector for enfranchisement. In the material economic base, conditions were developing for the common interests of both groups, "above divisions" of a purely political nature.

A separate place belongs here to Kraków's liberal, Mirosław Dzielski. Given all the reservations one may have against his exaggerated faith in the free market—he was against state intervention, even with regard to agriculture and housing construction—it must be said that his economic and political views were original. Dzielski wanted to build capitalism "from below," locally, not against authority but by way of its acquisition. "As regards political activity, our group—as opposed to other oppositional groupings—for years has been practicing something that can be called local politics. We believe that the economic changes in Poland are essential now and that these have to be big changes. In economic matters you cannot frown upon authority even when in all other matters you have different views. It is a question of *raison d'état*. For this reason we have always tried to build a bridge in the direction of the people of authority in Kraków."[18]

It appears, however, that the establishment of the government of Mieczysław F. Rakowski (1988) and his first laws and reform plans appealed to the Kraków conservative. Praising the new prime minister for his dynamism and courage, he added that he had to be even bolder if he wanted to avoid confrontation with the nation. "In politics being right is not enough. In Poland many people do not understand the government, do not trust it even if it takes the right steps. For this reason the prime minister needs to show a grand gesture that would shake Poles, that would awaken not only their trust, but would awaken their loyalty. Such a gesture can only be the enfranchisement of citizens."[19] Moreover, he felt Rakowski's success was conditional on the breaking up of groups that represented "social interests . . . by means of decisive political moves." Naturally, in the circumstances of those days, this breaking up would mean that repressive, or possibly coercive, means were to be used.* In other words, what Dzielski was suggesting to the government was to corrupt society by means of enfranchisement. According to the Kraków liberal, "There is no democracy without people who own something and are responsible for it."

The activists of S., on the other hand, were trying to prove that healing the economy should begin precisely with democratization. In this respect, a characteristic polemic took place between S.'s economist Ryszard Bugaj and Daniel Passent from the weekly journal *Polityka*. Bugaj called for a return to the Gdańsk accords, that is, to introduce social pluralism as a prerequisite for market-oriented development. The idea was to have "more democracy" in the public sphere. Trade unions and NGOs would operate beyond the control of party and state authority.[20] Passent,[21] in turn, clearly saw that S. was not only a trade union, but also a political movement. He wrote that "Messrs. Bugaj and Geremek, and the whole Western world after them, are playing possum and consider this to be e.g. merely innocent union pluralism . . . they offer dialogue and covenant with someone they are proposing suicide to and are surprised that the administration has no desire to sit down to the table over this proposition." He also

---

*Semilegal workplace committees of S. were already reemerging.

referred to the writings of Dzielski, according to whom, "The time has now come for economic liberties. Democratization ought to proceed inasmuch as it is essential for the implementation of economic reforms."[22] It was obvious that Dzielski considered S. to be mainly a political movement.

The Meanders of the Authors of the "Self-Governing Republic"

Let us reconstruct the socioeconomic imagination of the "mind" of S. shortly before the Round Table and the turning point that occurred in late summer of 1989. Historians are in a privileged position in that they have at their disposal the records of the bargaining proceedings from late autumn 1988, when negotiations were already under way prior to the historical meeting of the ruling administration with the opposition. I have in mind here material from the conference in Radziejowice, organized under the auspices of the Polish chapter of the Club of Rome, which gathered twenty-five historians, sociologists, jurists, political scientists, and economists. Later on, seven of them were to take part in the Round Table negotiations, with the main addresses being delivered by the "mind" of S.: Tadeusz Mazowiecki and Bronisław Geremek. Other speakers included Jan Józef Lipski, who talked about the program of the Paris monthly *Pobudka* and reflected on the association of socialism with the national issue; Tadeusz Kowalik ("Prywatyzacja czy gospodarka mieszana"— Privatization or a mixed economy); and Włodzimierz Wesołowski ("Jednostka a sfera polityki w koncepcjach socjalistycznych"—The Individual and the sphere of politics in socialist concepts). An active role in the debate was also played by Adam Michnik. Only the fourth, most important person was missing—Jacek Kuroń.

What, then, was the ideological and program mindset of these leading intellectuals who were about to embark on negotiations that were to change Poland in such a radical way? Although the conference was opened by Geremek's introduction, outlining "Dylematy socjalizmu w XX wieku" (The Dilemmas of Socialism in the Twentieth Century),[23] closer to the urgent problems of the day was the address of Mazowiecki, titled "Spotkania chrześcijaństwa z ideami socjalistycznymi i kontrowersje między nimi" (Encounters of Christianity with Socialist Ideas and the Controversies between Them).[24] It was he and not Geremek who emphatically formulated the problem of—as he put it—reorientation of the opposition from the struggle against "something" to a struggle "for something." His speech could thus constitute a point of departure for concrete program considerations. Mazowiecki, editor of the monthly Więź, carried out an analysis of the process of the rapprochement of Christian and socialist ideals. The most important point of his address was the contention that S. forms an ideological triple synthesis: "A convergence of the values and traditions discussed here can be found in the Polish 'Solidarity' movement. Such a convergence is no doubt a very important experience. I would name here three groups of different traditions integrated within the 'Solidarity' movement: national independence, Christian ideas, and the socialist tradition."[25] He made it clear that in the Union program of the Self-Governing Republic (1981) "we did not dare" to refer to certain traditions of socialism, but only to the worker movement traditions, solely due to the "communist usurpations" associated with this notion.

Whereas Mazowiecki did point out that he was not sure whether this "very important experience" of rapprochement of Christianity and socialism could be sustainable, he nevertheless honed this matter in a touching way. He observed that despite the reprimands S. received from John Paul II, there was still a prevalence in it of efforts to "throw out the red" over the struggle "for something, for certain values." This was what "disturbed and hurt" the speaker. Calling for a return to the ethos of social justice in the formation of the post-totalitarian society, he tactfully but decisively objected to a "certain oppositional conformity that seemed to set aside the problem of social sensitivity as an integral component of its own tradition." In reference to class struggle, he observed a rapprochement of the Christian and socialist trend: the Church did not realize "the consequences of objective class divisions," although it strongly objected to class struggle as "an organized method of social transformation" that led to hatred and inhuman consequences. Socialism, on the other hand, had rejected the concept of dictatorship of the proletariat in favor of evolutionary transformations with the observance of democratic procedures. It became "a certain pragmatic method of operation in the sphere of politics and in resolving social issues."[26] Referring to the French theologian Jacques Maritain, he saw Christians meeting non-Christians in social activism and in joint execution of certain social projects. This is how the circles close to *Więź* understood the attitude toward anti-totalitarian socialism. Poverty and exclusion as well as an organized battle against these became "an area of shared concern of Christians and socialists." In the end, Mazowiecki called for the recognition of religion as an autonomous value, as this would be of "significance for resolving today's problems." He had in mind that Christianity would designate the borderlines for human expansion and ambition, which problem, arisen from the traditions of nineteenth-century rationalism, had according to him been overlooked by socialism.

The speaker's theses did not meet with understanding in the debate, particularly among those who were to play a decisive role in politics later on. Adam Michnik summed up the speech by saying that it was "an account of a situation where a certain identity has come to an end and nobody knows what next."[27] A future minister in Mazowiecki's cabinet, Marcin Święcicki, observed that in the face of the disproportion between the affluent North and the poor South, the concepts of Willy Brandt and the Swedish Social Democrats contradict the neoliberal orientation. However, afterward he said, apparently with a feeling of disappointment, that "in Poland it would be very difficult to introduce the economic principles of neoliberalism ... [which was difficult even in Reagan's America or Thatcher's England]. The people in Poland are permeated with socialist ideals, but they do not realize this."[28]

Bronisław Geremek gave a whole list of reservations, but notably without once referring directly to Mazowiecki's idea of a triple synthesis of S. And he referred to Maritain only to recall the latter's words about an essential delay of clocks in the Church. "The nineteenth-century debates over the issue of pauperism suddenly encountered the arguments of representatives of the most conservative Christian thought with the most aggressive socialist thought."[29] Jan Józef Lipski, chairman of the reemerging PPS (Polish Socialist Party) and later senator, did indeed notice that "John Paul II . . . is constantly calling for a third path to be found. . . . And I think that it is here that there is a chance for such Christianity to meet . . . with the socialist tradition,"[30] but at the same time said that in the place of "a longing for unity" he would recommend pluralism. "Instead of union, I would always prefer diversity, which is a prerequisite for any social movement."[31]

For some participants, Geremek's introduction was a surprise. Let us return to Geremek's speech at the start of the conference and the discussion over it. The most important aspect seems to be the professor's reflections on the state as a whole and on the welfare state, as well as the mutual relations between liberalism and socialism. Without negating a socialist orientation toward democracy, the speaker primarily emphasized the statization so deeply rooted in the socialist movement. "European socialism generally appears to be overshadowed by the Jacobinist tradition, the same that was led to hypertrophy by the communist movement."[32] He bitterly denounced the recent Congress of Austrian Socialists. Their "program concept evolves around state institutions and when it tries to define a third path between capitalism and communism, it perceives it primarily in the development of the state's social functions."[33] Consequently, he highlighted this problem in his summing up. It is the liberal tradition that renews socialism, "in accordance with the principle: the less of the state, the better, because then there is more room for actions of the people, their groups."[34] Geremek rejected the welfare state, which usually coincided with faith in the benefits of the free market. "I have this feeling that today's socialist movements . . . have problems with the ideology of the welfare state. Because once again there appears the problem of expropriation of people from decisions on their own fate. Right now the liberal polemic directed against the welfare state arises among others from socialist circles and from circles governed by Christian thought. This is why I believe that in the renewal of socialism there can be a future for the thesis on the essential significance of self-organization of people."[35] Geremek did not notice that, for example, the Swedish welfare state was the result of pressure from "self-organizing" employees, followed by the multitier cooperation of the authorities with the trade unions.

The reactions of the discussion participants varied. Krystyna Kersten said: "We are on the battlefield of norms, values, principles, political systems, social movements."[36] Jerzy Holzer, on the other hand, wondered: "Is there any sense in referring to socialism? I am nonetheless convinced that this is not a pointless issue."[37] Wojciech Lamentowicz criticized that in the speech "the analysis of the socialist tradition is mainly concentrated on the Bolshevik thread,"[38] and Ryszard Turski pondered whether "socialism today is only a rubble heap of ideals."[39] Tadeusz Kowalik felt the speech "is unfair in the evaluation of socialism and in the placement of Bolshevik thought."[40] Ryszard Bugaj asked: "Can there be a reckoning with the entire socialist tradition by treating it as a cohesive tradition?"[41] Looking from a distance, perhaps most important was what Adam Michnik said: "I agree with the statement that today we don't know what socialism is as a postulate. In becoming involved in criticism of the world of institutions, we know today what we don't want, but not what we do want."[42]

Beneficiaries of the System Interested in Its Demise

In the excellent book *Obraz robotników polskich w latach 1945–1989* (Picture of Polish Workers in the Years 1945–1989),[43] nearly unnoticed by the mass media, the author, practicing "social history," gave an interesting explanation of the downfall of the old system. According to him, there appeared inside the establishment symptoms of auto-destruction, and it is mostly to its people that we owe the corrosion of socialism:

> The system collapsed because for various reasons, also understandable ones, it was abandoned (betrayed?) by its initial beneficiaries and

sentries. For people of the economic *nomenklatura* of the Party and—
though probably on a smaller scale—of the party apparatchiks, with
the passing of time the system would become a straightjacket that was
becoming less and less comfortable as incomes rose. . . . The managers, and particularly the economic elites were drawn to solutions
patterned after the West, in the hope for a future secured for themselves and their families after becoming independent of the political
authorities, which could erase the career of a director at any moment,
and after acquiring and multiplying appropriate assets.[44]

Słabek supports this hypothesis with three factors. The first factor,
though certainly not the most important, yet according to Słabek
"astounding" and providing much food for thought, was that in the
election of June 1989 the S. list was backed by as many as 80 percent
of the employees of embassies, foreign service posts, and construction
projects. This was despite the fact that these people to a large extent
owed their careers to the authorities of communist Poland. According
to the author, this was an expression of a turn to the right, as the other
S., "unlike the one prior to martial law, was already quite widely
known as a rightist organization."[45]

Another factor was the rapid growth of the private sector in the
second half of the 1980s, and especially the establishment of companies on the basis of the resources of state enterprises, leading to the
enfranchisement of the *nomenklatura*. The following are data that
even today may astound with their scale of public acquiescence to this
dishonorable practice:

Just before the establishment of the government of Tadeusz
Mazowiecki, there were about 3,000 companies operating in the
country, of which the overwhelming majority (75 percent) were
formed on the basis of 1,700 large state enterprises. As many as 44
percent of directors of state enterprises co-creating these companies
were at the same time their bosses. Every fourth, and in early 1994
nearly every third head of a company, had been a director, every for-
tieth an important party "apparatchik," and every eighteenth a director

of a voivodeship office. Almost all others had been lower-rank managers (managing officers, chief accountants). According to the findings of public prosecutor inspections, only a small portion of these companies (20 percent) conducted publicly useful operations. The heads of companies in particular (their co-owners) gained wealth at the cost of the people.... From 1990 the enfranchised groups included an increasing number of Solidarity activists. Nevertheless, a distinct prevalence still seemed to be held by members of the old establishment who underwent radical political change.[46]

These (and other) factors incline Słabek to pose the rhetorical question: "the 'communist' elites set fire to their own home?" And he replies that this is what in fact happened: "They consistently acted to their own advantage, in accordance with their own, albeit changing interest. The interest was changing and so they also made haste to reorient themselves to fit the image of these new times they had undoubtedly dreamt about."[47] It is no wonder then (and this is the third factor) that the central administration became so easily reconciled with the lost election of June 4, 1989. Słabek quotes Jerzy Urban, who had experienced "the biggest shock" when at the meeting of the Politburo of the Central Committee of PZPR (the Polish United Workers' Party) the electoral loss ("massacre") did not evoke even the slightest discussion. This was most probably—writes Słabek—the outcome of the "distrust among those assembled in the moral sense and chances of their activities, missions."

A Middle Class from Pocket Diaries

For Słabek, the key to understanding what happened in 1989 lay in the enfranchisement of the *nomenklatura*. This was a topic consistently overlooked, particularly by the left side of the political scene, to its own disadvantage. If the methods of this enfranchisement had been seriously analyzed earlier, many subsequent corruption and favoritism scandals could probably have been avoided.

However, Słabek exaggerates when he writes that in public discussion these issues have been and continue to be "totally absent, because they are inconvenient for all political groups, although for different reasons in each case."[48] First and foremost, one must not forget that the whole galaxy of intellectuals from the opposition defended head-on the process of enfranchisement of the *nomenklatura* as the simplest form of "buying yourself out," or as the best way of keeping capital inside the country. May I cite several such opinions. Back in 1988, Aleksander Paszyński observed: "One can acknowledge that from the moral point of view, this is an ambiguous phenomenon, being a sign of corruption both ways, but in terms of destruction of the system the effect is visibly one-sided . . . the inconsistent reform acquired unexpected—but dynamic—support from the sidelines."[49] According to Ernest Skalski,[50] the self-enfranchisement attitudes "should be nourished and tended." He was even disturbed that this was a historical opportunity that could be wasted "due to the wrath of the people." Jadwiga Staniszkis, in turn, in her address at the Employee Self-Management Forum, presented a similar concept of "accelerated" transition to political capitalism of a "primitive accumulation of capital." She praised enfranchisement because she believed that otherwise the *nomenklatura* capital would escape abroad. Even after some time she continued to be surprised that she had found no acceptance, and one employee self-management activist accused her of unethical glorification of theft, reminding her that "an academic title obligates to ethical values."[51] She interpreted this as a penchant for empty gestures in lieu of argumentation.

The development of enfranchisement with state property divided the jurists. Some bent the law on a massive scale to make everything appear legal, others, such as Professor Teresa Rabska of Poznań University, demanded in alarming cases that the previous status quo be reinstated in the name of elementary social justice, with the application of "all legal means, including extraordinary appeal."[52] Hubert Izdebski, law professor at Warsaw University, in turn, as well as Jerzy Dyner and Henryk Szlajfer, tabled an anti-enfranchisement bill to the authorities. This was accompanied by a warning that the increasingly common method of "money grabbing" may prevent the formation of a healthy market and gaining support for the "multi-sectoral economy model."[53] However, the new government did not take up this legislative effort, as most probably it favored this form of emerging capitalism as the lesser evil. Even Jacek Kuroń did not back the new bill, believing that the existing legislation and open tendering procedures would suffice to eliminate any anomalies.

Kuroń would often refer to the clientelism and corruption at the outset of Polish capitalism as an attribute determining its shape. He expressed this most clearly in the book *Siedmiolatka czyli kto ukradł Polskę* (Seven Years, or Who Stole Poland),[54] where he outlined the results of the operations of both the "old" *nomenklatura* as well as the newly developed one existing within the structures of the political and economic authority. Recalling the beginnings of this form of operation of the party-state *nomenklatura* in the late 1980s, he concluded: "But these were the beginnings of the gigantic transfer of wealth that took place literally before our very eyes. Together with the slogan 'get rich' and its general turmoil, wild privatization was unleashed. It will probably never be possible to count how much money was lost by various state enterprises whose bosses entered into contracts with *nomenklatura* companies of acquaintance, bringing losses to the enterprises, but immense fortunes to the companies. . . . Fraud was evident, but the law turned out to be helpless here."[55]

For Kuroń this was at any rate part of the mechanism of the formation of the middle class, in methodology similar to the process of formation of the new state authorities. The first non-communist administration was formed in such a way that the closest colleagues of the prime minister searched for names of friends in their pocket diaries.

This method was continued for the subsequent months and years, when it was necessary to staff banks, companies, voivodeships, embassies and the state media. . . . The Polish middle class emerging from the first version of post-communist capitalism did not gain its positions through the market. For a great portion—or at any rate for those who acquired great fortunes—it was not the free market that turned out to be the most important, but pocket diaries. And so if this group is in fact defending anything, it is these pocket diaries—the connections, arrangements, quotas, government orders, limits, customs barriers, monopolies, thanks to which it gained its current position. This is the Polish drama.[56]

Kuroń had no doubts that this was "a phenomenon of key significance for the development of Polish democracy and the market economy."[57]

3. A Brief Compromise:
The Round Table

The historical significance of the Round Table Agreements in initiating the path toward peaceful transfer of power cannot be overstated. Such a turn of events had never been thought possible by analysts and observers either in Poland or abroad. Yet here a model of peaceful systemic changes was created that could be applicable also to other former communist countries or even to the whole world.

This book, however, focuses on the socioeconomic aspects of Polish transformation. Within not even half a year, Poland performed "a leap to a market economy," using as a model the theory of F. A. Hayek and Milton Friedman and the practical applications of Ronald Reagan and Margaret Thatcher. By doing so, it silently abandoned the program for a "new economic order" as settled in the Round Table Agreements. An economist's perception of the Round Table is different than that of a political scientist. It is essential to show those elements of the agreements and accompanying and subsequent events that doomed compromise in economic matters to a short-lived existence. And looking from this point of view, the context of the Round Table negotiations (lasting from February to April 1989) was perhaps more important than the agreements.

The preparations and talks leading up to the Round Table continued, with varying fortunes, from August 1988.* On August 25, at a meeting of the Politburo of the Central Committee of PZPR, the theses of Lech Wałęsa, considered as moderate, were examined after being relayed by Andrzej Stelmachowski.[1] The chairman of S. postulated consent for the creation of workplace sections of S. The first bilateral contacts were established within several days. In the selection of documents called *Okragły Stół* (Round Table), published by Krzysztof Dubiński (1999), the list of meetings opens with a memorandum of talks dated August 31, between Interior Minister General Czesław Kiszczak and Lech Wałęsa, Bishop Jerzy Dąbrowski, and Stanisław Ciosek, and of the meeting on the same day of Kiszczak with the Chairman of the National Council of PRON (Patriotic Movement for National Rebirth), Jan Dobraczyński.[2]

Less than three weeks later, the cabinet of Zbigniew Messner was dismissed and a new, radically different government was appointed, headed by Mieczysław F. Rakowski. One of the first spectacular moves of this government was the decision to shut down the Gdańsk shipyard. This assault on the "cradle" of S. was bound to provoke a violent reaction by the opposition, thereby delaying the efforts of Kiszczak and Ciosek. The key issue, not only on the opposition-authorities line, but also within the authorities themselves, was the legalization of S. (which I shall not be dealing with here).

There was one noteworthy event, considered by Władysław Baka[3] to be a sign of "crossing the Rubicon." The first and no doubt decisive step toward changing the position of the governing party in this matter occurred during the two-part 10th Plenum of the Central Committee

---

*Still earlier developments open the five-volume edition of documents and material of this historical event (Borodziej and Garlicki, 2004). The first is a memorandum addressed to the incumbent First Party Secretary, General W. Jaruzelski, from Kazimierz Barcikowski, concerning the meeting of September 13, 1986, with Jan Strzelecki, who was asking about the possibility of talks between the administration and the opposition. Strzelecki suggested that he could encourage Tadeusz Mazowiecki to do this, from which Barcikowski deduced that Strzelecki was an informal messenger of the future prime minister.

of PZPR. On December 20, 1988, Prime Minister Mieczysław Rakowski took, as the author writes, "the bull by the horns." Rakowski posed many questions concerning the legalization of S. in such a way that their logic would have been very difficult to deny. Let me cite only two of them. "In generally large work establishments there are currently over 200 organizations and founding committees of 'Solidarity' operating openly or half-openly, although illegally. If in the coming months several hundred new ones are created, what should we do? Ignore them? Fight them down with administrative measures, in accordance with the law?" The prime minister also wanted to know whether it was true that "in conflicting situations it is not uncommon for a director to secretly negotiate with the establishment's activists of 'Solidarity' to stave off these conflicts. Why is this so? Is it merely an understandable attempt to have 'peace and quiet' or is it awareness of the true power status. . . . "[4] According to Baka, Rakowski was also to have said: "The time has come for the whole party to answer the question whether we can cope by ourselves with the immense challenge that Poland faces, or should we act together with a constructive opposition which after legalization would also assume part of the responsibility?"*[5]

These and other questions were answered in the second part of the plenary meeting, convened nearly a month later. The statements of comrades were for the most part decidedly negative, combined with a general attack on the supreme administration, accused of opportunism and even betrayal of socialism. Only a motion for a vote of confidence, combined with the threat of resignation of six members of the Politburo along with the party first secretary and the prime minister, finally paved the way for the Round Table.

But Rakowski took "the bull by the horns" mostly in another area—in government and parliament. The very composition of the government, no doubt formed by Rakowski alone, already came as a shock for many observers in Poland and abroad. Ireneusz Sekuła, a

---

*I cannot find these words in the text published by Borodziej and Garlicki (vol. 1, 2004), but they reflect well the contents of Rakowski's dramatic speech.

businessman, was made deputy prime minister and Mieczysław Wilczek, a well-known and wealthy entrepreneur, by the standards of the time, became minister of industry. Advocates of radical reform also included another deputy prime minister, Kazimierz Olesiak, who quickly became known as a consistent proponent of freeing food prices and apparently of the free market in general, and also the minister of finance, Andrzej Wróblewski, earlier involved in talks with the International Monetary Fund concerning assistance for Poland. Thus composed, the government began to energetically move toward profound reforms.

A manifesto of the free-market economy was first of all the Law on Economic Activity passed by parliament on December 23, 1988, and the accompanying (but more cautious) Law on Economic Activity with the Participation of Foreign Parties. Below are several absolutely innovative provisions of the former law, which came to be known as the Law on Economic Freedom:

> The undertaking and conducting of economic activity shall be free to all on an equal-rights basis. . . . Within the scope of their economic activity, economic entities may perform operations and actions which are not forbidden by law.
>
> An economic entity may hire employees in an unlimited number and without the agency of employment organs. An economic entity shall be entitled to associate, on a voluntary basis, in organizations of economic entities. Economic entities, regardless of the type of ownership, shall be subject to public liabilities under equal terms and shall make use of bank loans and supply of production means. Undertaking of economic activity . . . shall require . . . entering this in the economic activity records.

These provisions were accompanied by a very modest list that included barely eleven areas in which starting activity required a license.

I am recalling the content matter of this law before it was crammed with numerous added regulations that block economic activity and are a real nuisance for those who are starting a business. Obviously, this initially unusually liberal law for those days was more of a vision or blueprint of the free space for economic operations than an offer for its realistic application. If implemented, it would have still been constrained by many other regulations and administrative creations, not to mention the all-powerful party *nomenklatura*. It is also true that in its original, unchanged form the law was so radical that it would have had little chance of surviving for long.

These two laws were followed, or were to be followed, by many other important statutes. For example, in late January 1989 the Banking Law was passed, patterned on—as Baka writes—Western European models. This was the beginning of Sekuła's abundant package of reforms. The main idea of this package was expressed in the introduction to the two laws referred to, published as an appendix to the then "government" newspaper *Rzeczpospolita*. It was said that the principles of the laws were to be "very similar to those in force in places where commodities are commodities, prices are prices and money is money."

The Round Table—Disputes and Settlements

These circumstances led to the weeks of Round Table negotiations, with the participation of dozens of opposition activists along with high Party and government officials.

The Round Table settlements that I consider to be the most important are those that pertained to reform of the political sphere, which created the framework for economic reforms. Both the declared general principles and the specific provisions concerning organizational and institutional changes were of importance. The "Agreement on Political Reforms" contains the following general principles: political pluralism, freedom of speech, democratic appointment of all representative government organs, independence of the courts, and a freely elected strong local government with full rights. These were constitutional settlements *par excellence*, auguring a radically changed Constitution. Among concrete provisions, an important matter was the time and character of parliamentary elections and the acceptance of trade union pluralism, which signified the legalization of S.

For the concept of economic transformation, an extremely important, though quickly broken, general political settlement was that "both sides are ... deeply convinced that essential reforms of the state should take place—in accordance with the national *raison d'état*—by evolution. The evolutionary way of implementing changes could be threatened by actions that are too radical or the doings of conservative opponents of reforms."[6]

The second important settlement was the "Agreement on Social and Economic Policy and Systemic Reforms." On the face of it, the fragment titled "The New Economic Order" would seem to be the most important. However, other sections are also noteworthy, although perhaps a little too detailed, since the possibility of transferring power to the opposition had not yet been taken into account. There are many provisions there that with another transformation concept would be important for the transitional phase. These provisions concern: the living conditions of the people, inflation and equilibrium of the economy, protecting society against negative impacts, protection of labor and employment, and state debt issues. Of primary importance here are the provisions concerning protection of labor and employment, and particularly the systemic principle of full employment, written out into ten settled upon and two contentious points. All these detailed settlements distinctly show that the participants of the agreement had no such thought in mind as a "leap" into a market economy. On the contrary, evolutionary changes were taken into account, while declarations calling for fast systemic change were exceptions.

In the course of the Round Table negotiations, unlike at the political "table" where two opposing parties were seeking a compromise, the economic "table" talks were conducted by economists who had evidently more in common than what they might disagree about. A co-chairman from the "coalition-government party" was Warsaw University professor Władysław Baka, a long-term Party official of the Central Committee of PZPR (Polish United Workers' Party) and at the same time for many years government plenipotentiary for economic reform. He was thus not only directly involved in reforms but also well acquainted in practice with the conservative resistance of both the Party machinery and the government organs. In addition, he was a specialist in monetary-banking matters, which was unquestionably one of the weakest elements of the economy of really existing socialism. This reserved, unusually courteous and quiet man was at times described as "an apparatchik who has nothing of the apparatchik in him."

His Solidarity-oppositional counterpart was Witold Trzeciakowski, professor of the Warsaw School of Economics, a high-class foreign trade expert, well acquainted with Western writings, an entrepreneur and manager in the first years after the Second World War. He was associated with the primate and the episcopate, did not belong to any political party, and possibly never had any particular hopes relating to socialism, but he did not evade activity in Party and government undertakings aimed at reforming the system. He was no radical and tended to display reticence, mildness, and gentleness in interpersonal contacts. From the 1944 Warsaw Uprising he carried out a sense of great responsibility and fear of blameworthy but uncontrollable defeats.

The role of co-chairmen inclined them to present opposite standpoints, at least in the beginning, but in character and as economists they resembled each other. At the first meeting of the team for economy and social policy (February 8), each set different frameworks for a future compromise. Baka presented the reforms as a continuation of the plan of consolidation of national economy of Rakowski's government and talked about "a system of operation of the economy based on monetary-market economy logic, which must replace entirely the administrative-command economy logic."[7] Trzeciakowski defined the aims of reform in a different way. For him "the new order in the economy should be based on a demonopolized market, on the principles of freedom of management, freedom of citizens to associate . . . on a pluralistic structure of ownership leading to the elimination of nobody's ownership, on broad rights of employee self-management in state-owned enterprises, having rights relieved of the restrictions imposed by the law of 1982; it is necessary to depoliticize the system of management." He also spoke of breaking with continuity: "The collapse of Polish economy, its immense indebtedness, the impoverishment of the people, the rising inflation leading to economic chaos and the contamination of the natural environment—these are the results of the existing system's order. This order must be rejected."[8]

Probably because joint actions had not been coordinated, Ryszard Bugaj of the S. side read out a declaration that, compared to those of the co-chairmen, sounded unusually minimalist. Following the statement that "we cannot accept" the government program in its present form "as the basis of consensus in economic matters,"* he proposed that a certain temporary minimum be sought.† He declared: "Taking into consideration the dramatic situation in the country, we nevertheless acknowledge the need to seek a pragmatic compromise of an interim nature. The suggestions of corrections and supplementation put forward by us are designed to ensure more favorable conditions for the start of market reform, for guaranteeing the essential minimum of protection of living conditions of the people and making progress in the removal of particularly pathological economic phenomena."[9] He did not explain, however, what the market reform would be like.

---

*Rejection of the government documents as the basis of the negotiations was the result of a tactical maneuver in the new situation, as it appeared that the authorities were more intent on reaching an agreement than the opposition. To recall, a year earlier, Bugaj, in a text written jointly with Andrzej Wielowieyski, declared, under certain conditions, of course, support for the second stage of reform of Messner's cabinet, which had a much more modest scope than the propositions and first measures of Rakowski's government. Counteracting a "masochistic satisfaction" due to the authorities' lack of success, the authors declared: "Independent circles should do everything possible to prevent failure of the currently undertaken changes. Given the whole risk involved with supporting changes currently put forward by the authorities, there seems to be no alternative more favorable for the country's interests." (Typescript of theses, without title, for use in internal discussion of the opposition, written "on the threshold of 1988," p. 11, emphasis as in original.)

†These and other statements I cite until further notice from the transcript (in my possession). The five-volume edition of documents of the Round Table is a selection, unfortunately. Some of the statements have been omitted, or given in abbreviated form.

One may wonder whether this quite modest proposition resulted from the poor preparation of Bugaj himself and of the leaders of S., from an inability to quickly communicate with other activists, or from an estimation that the current situation makes reflections over an alternative model unproductive, or even utopian. To this day, Stefan Bratkowski recalls with bitterness that "all appeals for preparation in the event of freedom were treated with irritation in the group of Wałęsa's Civil Committee of 1986–89, or even with rudeness full of irritation."

It was only in the second meeting (February 13) that a serious debate began. Its basis was the long and fundamental program statement made by Deputy Prime Minister Ireneusz Sekuła, the chief driving force of reforms in Rakowski's government. The four months of operation of the new government were summed up with the general message: "We have already begun the implementation of radical market reforms. Help us . . . "

Sekuła considered the plan of consolidation of the national economy to be the "leading document" and focused on what he described as "turning things right side up." Out of the several hundred decisions, he listed: lifting rationing of gasoline and coal; elimination of allotments for automobiles; being allowed to keep passports at home that are valid all over the world; preparations to lift meat rationing. He also forecast statutory decentralization of central and local administration. According to him, the most important move was repealing more than half of the legal acts and the announcement of the further diminution of their number, but he devoted the most attention to "very far-reaching, radical systemic changes." Apart from the numerous, already passed laws, with the Law on Economic Freedom in the lead, he also named a package of laws tabled to the Sejm. Altogether, the new laws were to create a "critical mass" making changes "irreversible and complex." Mentioning a law on the National Bank of Poland and a banking law, he announced the formation of commercial banks, a foreign exchange law, and the rules for financing state-owned enterprises. He extensively explained why the current government was preparing bills in such haste, even at the price of their quality.

Sekuła explained how he understood the three fundamental slogans repeated by the ruling authorities: freedom, equality, competition. The meaning of the first slogan can be found in the Law on Economic Activity. Equality was to consist of equal treatment of economic entities of all ownership forms, both in obtaining loans and in the system of taxation, the regulation of which, due to the range of the changes, required time. Competition was "reduction of the redistribution function of the budget, shrinking of centrally financed imports, creation of conditions where the production (and) employee assets may be transferred, allocated to where they can be used more effectively, with greater profitability through bankruptcy or liquidation of inefficient economic entities."[10] The government arrived at the conclusion, he continued, that in order to balance the market and curb inflation it was necessary to create conditions to stimulate the economy, which could only be achieved through "the fastest possible introduction of a market economy wherever this is possible and as quickly as this is possible." With this as a guiding principle, the government proposed to "radically introduce a market economy in the entire agro-food complex."[11]

As the bill on consolidation contained special government powers that were questioned by the S. activists, Sekuła explained that this time the idea was not as in the past to discipline economic entities but to create instruments for "radical implementation of economic reform, to overcome barriers and difficulties that slow down this process of implementing reforms, and to create conditions for its acceleration."[12] In the end he expressed support for a social accord, "allowing more time to radically implement economic reform."[13]

A discussion followed. Cezary Józefiak focused on pointing out the discrepancies of government economic policy, and particularly of the systemic projects. He criticized the proposition to liberate food prices as another example of artificial fragmentation of the scope of market economy implementation. "Expansion of the scope of isolated markets is proposed rather than integration of economic processes through mutually connected markets. . . . And in my opinion this is very dangerous."[14]

Unexpectedly high criticism came from Jan Mujżel, according to whom the consolidation plan "is not a satisfactory program of a) radical change of the structure and economic status of an enterprise, b) implementing the market system as the mechanism of allocation, c) social protection of the work force, d) democratization of economic relations."[15] In systemic terms, two postulates of Mujżel appear to be the most important: transformation of state-owned enterprises into employee companies and distribution of the assets of state firms on commercially preferential terms or free of charge.*[16] It is interesting that even the otherwise pragmatic Jan Mujżel became euphoric over the speed of the systemic changes. He commented about the declaration of the new government to have a "7-year transitional period" in the following way: "We couldn't have accepted such an approach without convincing reasoning. It would have hardened in people a feeling of hopelessness, and would have moved reconstruction of the system, improvement of efficiency and overcoming of the crisis into a more distant perspective."[17]

The discussion led to the crystallization of a concept of far-reaching free enterprise in the economy and its privatization. Was this already the embarkation on the path to capitalism? The declarations of Minister Wilczek and Janusz Beksiak leave no doubt that in their opinion, and most probably also that of Cezary Józefiak, this was the only realistic solution. There are two postulates, however, that make one hesitate to give such an interpretation: the creation of employee companies and the expansion of employee self-management in state firms. But the obvious aim—more or less deliberate—was in the direction of some kind of hybrid formation, a mixed economy, which was expressed in the final settlements concerning the new economic order.

---

*Tomasz Stankiewicz referred to this when he postulated that for a point of departure the statement of Minister Wilczek could be adopted. Wilczek "would prefer—as Stankiewicz said—that only 50 percent of the enterprises be state owned." (Ibid., 72.)

The New Economic Order

The first sentence of the consolidation plan, concerning the implementation of a new social order, suggested that it was more of an indication of the way in which this objective might be achieved: "Transformations leading to the new economic order comprise first of all." After this pronouncement, six general principles were named, as follows:

- development of employee self-management and participation;

- unfettered formation of the ownership structure;

- development of market relations and competition;

- elimination of remnants of the command-distributive system and limitation of central planning to the formulation of state economic policy, exercised by means of economic instruments;

- a uniform financial policy toward enterprises;

- subordination of the mechanisms of management-staff selection in enterprises to the criterion of professional competence.

The implementation of these principles, expounded in detail in many speeches, was to signify the crowning of the new economic order, created "as quickly as possible, not later than by the end of 1991."[18] Did this magic date signify a "leap" into the new order, which would contradict the principle of evolution proclaimed in the agreements? This question cannot be answered explicitly. The new order can be understood as a system in which the declared principles are respected. If, for example, a freely formed pluralist ownership structure was assumed, then a long-term process of its formation was taken into account. Although plans to create a stock exchange in early 1991 are curious. There would have to have been quite a number of firms already in existence and ready to be listed.

In establishing the time frame for implementing the new order, an important fact was that each principle was furnished with a protocol of differences between the Solidarity-opposition and coalition-government parties; therefore subsequent negotiations were expected to take place in the future. The first difference was of a general character and concerned the attitude to the government platform of negotiations. The Act on Certain Conditions of Consolidation of the National Economy was regarded by the opposition as contradicting the deliberations and settlements of the Round Table. The government, on the other hand, defended this act as facilitating reform actions. This matter would resurface in discussions many times. The act was passed by the Sejm on February 24, which was more than two weeks after the Round Table negotiations had started, yet such an important document had not been settled with the opposition. The criticism of the law was so sharp due to the justified belief of opposition activists that the government placed the Round Table participants before accomplished facts, which in their opinion foreshadowed a disregard for all of the results of the negotiations. But the paradox was that ultimately the settlements were rejected (in the economic part) not by the existing coalition of the authorities, but by the future Solidarity-led coalition. Another question arises here: If all these principles had been meticulously implemented, then would a new socioeconomic system have come into being that would be socially desirable and at the same time adequately efficient?

With this in mind, let us take a look at a certain elaboration of the listed principles. In as many as nine points, the issues of employee self-management and participation are discussed, in which the most important are:

- reducing by half the number of enterprises in which by the 1981 law the director is appointed by the founding body;

- the right to the establishment of a nationwide initiative of employee self-management;

- guaranteeing the influence of representatives of employee councils on the activity of companies to which the enterprises belong;

- introduction of employee participation in private firms that employ more than one-hundred persons.

Equally extensive were the settlements concerning the formation of a "pluralist ownership structure," which encompassed a constitutional guarantee of such a structure, the establishment of the National Property Fund, "with powers to control state assets (including sale under statutorily defined principles)," tendering as the principle of leasing state firms, the creation of legal foundations for the establishment of employee companies, and regulations concerning bankruptcy. Essential changes were also announced to allow for competition. The professional character of the management staff of enterprises would be ensured through mandatory competition and other procedures of public oversight, although here the coalition-government party permitted only mention of the negative standpoint regarding *nomenklatura* practices.

The innocent-sounding subsection, "Overcoming the Debt Barrier," contained a description of opening the economy to the world, with hopes expressed for the infusion of foreign capital. Consent was even pledged for the adjustment program of the International Monetary Fund.

The First Swallows of the "Leap" into Capitalism

Looking at the Round Table Agreements in terms of a comparative analysis of economic systems, two concepts can be distinguished. The first is the implementation of an economy based on cooperative, social-democratic principles that encourage a mixed economy, with considerable employee participation and a full-employment policy. This would bring the planned social order closer to the Austrian and Swedish models. The second is based on privatization in the form of joint stock companies, opened to global competition, the development of the stock exchange, and the desire to cooperate with the International Monetary Fund, combined with acceptance of what was then called the Washington Consensus along with its well-known conditionality principle (providing assistance under certain conditions).

The first concept accentuated the protection of employee rights and the living standard of the people. Its weakest point was the decision on 80 percent wage indexation, which on this scale would make it harder to halt the galloping inflation. The weakness of this provision became apparent when Rakowski's government freed food prices from controls. The representatives of S. practically accepted it, requesting only that a more detailed program be presented and that they be consulted on the implemented solutions. It was decreed, for example, that "the scope and form of these actions [demonopolizing agriculture]—appropriately harmonized with the assumption of introducing the free market in food economy—shall be consulted with the representatives of trade unions and other organizations of farmers."[19]

The other concept called for sacrifices and would be a shock that would carry the danger of unforeseen consequences for the standard of living and employee rights. It was not certain yet which of these concepts would be victorious. The matter became clear after just a few weeks, and late in the summer decisions were taken that determined the victory of the Anglo-Saxon version of capitalism, built through shock and sacrifice. Examples are not hard to find.

One of the results of the Round Table was the establishment of the Consultative Committee to supervise and monitor the implementation of the concluded agreements. The committee acknowledged as evident the continuation of the rule of the old government, which, it could be assumed at that time, was given a mandate from the opposition to implement the new economic order. The committee did not survive the parliamentary election of June 1989, as the pluralist parliament had much better instruments for performing the tasks imposed on it. Three sessions of the committee were held, but the main topic consisted of attempts to diminish the effects of the electoral defeat and especially to salvage the candidates from the national list, that is, the entire leadership of the old system.

Two weeks after the election, there was also a meeting of the economic team of the committee, the only one held by it. The several-dozen pages of minutes of the meeting provided a major insight into the views of the economists of both sides in the new post-electoral situation. From this transcript, it is worthwhile to note two matters that would be of primary significance in the coming months.

During the Round Table negotiations much attention was devoted to the issue of liberating food prices, as advocated by deputy prime minister K. Olesiak. As I have said, the opposition economists did not reject this concept, but demanded a detailed cost estimate; in other words, this operation should be well prepared so that it would be least painful for the people. A good portion of the negotiations on indexation evolved from these apprehensions. The opposition did not obtain any concrete answers in this matter. All the while inflation was gaining momentum, and wage growth outpaced price movements and productivity, meaning there was more and more money that could not buy anything.

At a meeting of the Committee, Olesiak no longer had to convince anybody about the operation of liberating prices itself; he even had to explain why this had not been done earlier. One of the reasons he gave was the difficulty in reaching agreement at the Round Table. Ryszard Bugaj, on the other hand, criticized him (and the government) that due to the policy of negligence, "all the taps with money have been turned on," as a result of which the budgetary deficit was growing rapidly.[20] Yet despite this, in an act of desperation, he consented to this concept. What's more he informed the committee that he even tried to persuade the leadership of NSZZ "Solidarity" that "there is in fact no other way but that we have reached some sort of compromise, which may be difficult but must be accepted."[21] Now he asked the deputy prime minister, "Why didn't you request [the union—presumably] to solve this matter?"[22] The liberation of food prices came into force on August 1 and was accompanied by heated disputes. The day before the Sejm had passed a law, imposed by the

S. caucus, on full price indexation to offset the effects of introducing a free-market system.* The decision of the government encountered the strong objection of Władysław Baka, member of the Politburo and secretary of the Central Committee of PZPR, who for this reason resigned from both positions (in the end, he remained in the Politburo at Rakowski's request). Baka, who had long opposed Olesiak's ideas, evaluated the law "on the spot" as totally contradicting the letter of the Round Table Agreements. "With its implementation there will be an immense inflow of 'empty money' and deepening of the already glaring wage disproportions, destruction and breaking up of the market till the end, intensification of inflation, etc. Without any doubt, no government will be able to exercise its power any longer, having this law 'on its shoulders.' It is obvious that in the thinking of the architects of this law, that is, the leadership of 'Solidarity,' its passing is to play the role of 'a nail in the coffin' for the government created by the coalition hitherto in power (PZPR, SLD [Democratic Left Alliance], SD [Democratic Alliance])."[23]

Another matter that the economic team devoted much attention to was the prospect of accepting the adjustment program of the International Monetary Fund (IMF). The meeting was attended by Finance Minister Andrzej Wróblewski, who had already conducted negotiations with this institution both as minister and earlier to that. He informed the rest that the IMF had changed its attitude toward Poland as a debtor to a more favorable one, which can be seen in the reduction in the IMF's pressure on our country to meet debt payments. During an unofficial visit in early June, the IMF experts set three conditions under which the IMF could offer a bailout: absolute reduction of domestic demand, broad restructuring of the economy, including the methods of its operation, and "external balance," which would enable debt repayment.

---

*One may ask what Rakowski had in mind when he decided on this operation on the day before the planned dismissal. The Sejm accepted the dismissal of Rakowski's government on August 2, and Baka gave as one reason for refusing to take up the post of prime minister the unfortunate implementation of a free-market economy.

Although the transcript contains mistakes and it is not always clear who said what (Andrzej Wróblewski or Andrzej Topiński), it includes very sharp words against the general (customary) demands of the IMF.* For example, there was talk of "very strict monetary-credit policy" and "very drastic interest policy." A reminder attributed to Topiński was that in Bolivia, as a result of applying the IMF program, already "with the first try, 17 tin mines were shut down out of 20. Overnight."[24] Wróblewski said: "The key issues at this moment according to us are . . . working out this adjustment plan and deciding on what we are really capable of swallowing."[25]

True, Bugaj asked twice how rigid the IMF's position was. True, Marcin Święcicki warned that "they [IMF] can say yes, we are giving you those 10 bn, here you are, there is only this one small condition, that the living standard, shall we say, real wages, [have to] fall by 15 percent, you have to shut down so and so many factories, you have to raise some interest rates or other . . . would it not be necessary therefore . . . to underscore the exhaustion of the people with the crisis."[26] True, Trzeciakowski warned that the approach to the IMF's conditions would be two-way: "The bloody tyrant, the minister of finance, who stifles the living standard, and on the other side the heroic Bugaj who defends the standard." But even he, a cautious and sensitive person, expected that "within this duel some compromise will be reached."[27] In the end, however, there was no mention of the stipulation in the Round Table Agreements that "such a program [of adjustment of the IMF or other] shall not lead to a decline of consumption per capita, and moreover shall ensure its average annual growth of about 2 percent."[28] Naturally, looking back on those days one can say that such expectations were too optimistic, but it is all too obvious that the settlements written into the agreements were forgotten quite easily even by their original authors.

---

*A very essential statement is attributed to Topiński. He was not minister of finance, however, so he could not have said: "I generally, already as minister of finance . . . " (213–16).

A much more important example of the departure from the Round Table Agreements, in my opinion, is the so-called appeal to the West, unfittingly called the Trzeciakowski Program. We know the most about the creation of this program from Jacek (now Jan Vincent) Rostowski who said in an interview four years later for *Życie Gospodarcze*: "In July 1989 . . . in Brussels, a meeting was held, chaired by Prof. Witold Trzeciakowski and gathering experts and 'Solidarity' activists who were to prepare an outline of the economic program of the trade union as the leading opposition force in Poland. The idea was to draw up a vision of economic changes in Poland. I was invited to this discussion as one of the foreign experts. . . . There was an interesting collection of names there. Next to Jerzy Milewski, as host in the Brussels office of 'Solidarity,' there was also Jan K. Bielecki, Jacek Merkel, Andrzej Milczanowski, Zdzisław Najder, Tomasz Stankiewicz, Jerzy Thieme. On the second day Jeffrey Sachs came from Warsaw."[29]

Unfortunately, I have only the first version of this four-page "program." The document carries the name "International Assistance Program for Poland," with an annotation in the right-hand corner: "Draft Brussels, 11 June 1989," and at the end is written: "Gdańsk . . . June 1989." Prof. Trzeciakowski and the Gdańsk people went to Brussels with this very program.*

It was addressed in particular to the International Monetary Fund, the World Bank, the Paris Club (Poland's creditors), and a similar London Club of commercial banks. Assistance was to consist of a loan of 10 billion U.S. dollars, suspension of our foreign debts, and assistance in restructuring the economy. The crucial part of the document, titled "Conditions for Assistance," sounds sensational. A radical shift in the settlements of the Round Table was made. It is a fragment of such great importance, that it is worthwhile to quote it in full:

*I think that I received this document from Trzeciakowski, with whom for a certain time I shared an office at the Institute of Economics of PAN (Polish Academy of Sciences). I remember how unwilling he was to talk about this subject. But it could be that because of this interview of Rostowski, he emphasized that this was not a program, but an appeal, and in an appeal you use arguments that the addressee wants to hear.

1. For this program to be implemented, the suspension of all debt repayments to the Soviet Union until 1994 would have to be renegotiated.

2. The granting and acceptance of any and all new credit must be approved by the Senate.

3. Assistance should be conditional on the authorities of the People's Republic of Poland being required to limit inflation and to balance this economy, particularly regarding:
   a) balancing the state budget over the next two years,
   b) discontinuing, as of next year, the financing of state expenditures by way of increasing the money base,
   c) an end to the granting of automatic credit to economic units,
   d) elimination, as of next year, of excess investment demand.

   If unemployment occurs during the implementation of the anti-inflation program, it will be necessary to introduce measures envisaged in the Round Table Agreement, and particularly the program of retraining of workers which would need to be supported by IMF and World Bank funds, as envisaged in point B.4 above.

4. Conditionality relating to economic reforms should include above all programs agreed to at the Round Table, particularly:
   a) elimination of administrative allocation and rationing of goods, services, and financial resources,
   b) expansion of the autonomy of state-owned enterprises,
   c) elimination of unprofitable enterprises,
   d) formation of an anti-monopoly agency independent of the government by the end of 1990, and the introduction of stricter anti-monopoly laws,
   e) creation of a securities stock exchange at the beginning of 1991,
   f) the initiation in 1989 of a program setting out the speed and extent of the privatization of state property (including the means of production), in accordance with the Round Table Agreements,
   g) the achievement, over a period of time, of at first internal and subsequently full convertibility of the zloty.

   Monitoring of the implementation of this program on the Polish side, and of the fulfillment of conditionality associated with it, will be vested in the Senate of the People's Republic of Poland as the democratically elected representative body of the nation that is legally entitled to supervise external relations.[30]

Whereas there is reference three times to the Round Table Agreements, and the announced reforms do not stand in direct contradiction to them, all the essential items that would differ from typical IMF stabilization programs are missing. The following were ignored: the postulate of full employment, the matter of indexation, employee self-management, employee companies, and concern for not lowering the living standard of the people. Even entrusting supervision duties concerning the famous conditionality principle did not contradict the agreements, in which it was stated that "the Senate . . . will exercise essential supervision, in particular with regard to human rights and legality and socioeconomic life."[31] "Socioeconomic life" is a very broad concept. However, placing the Senate in matters so significant and important as the change of system, entrusting supervision not to the whole parliament, but to a chamber where only one representative of the old system was sitting, could create the impression that the opposition wants to be the privileged part of the administration, which has the right to control and criticize, but does not assume shared responsibility for decisions.

There is no information, alas, on how the final version of the appeal looked and what it contained. On the basis of Rostowski's accounts, one can assume that at the Brussels meeting there was a prevailing desire to reject the Round Table Agreements. Asked by a reporter whether they "were not in some way constraining," Rostowski replied: "Of course, and the idea was mainly to withdraw from these agreements." And to the question on the attitude to the appeal of Trzeciakowski—the author and signatory of its economic part—he answered straight out: "The professor often pointed out the discrepancy of our ideas with those agreements. But the general consensus was that we must resign from these settlements, as they are anachronistic and sooner or later they will slow down economic growth."[32]

Yet the cited appeal was not the most vivid example of the withdrawal from the Round Table Agreements. One could list many myths that arose around the agreements. One is the view that the issue of privatization was "absent" at the Round Table. This is what the Warsaw-Oxford scholar Piotr Jasiński says.[33] Also, according to Cezary Józefiak, "The discussion about the ownership structure did not come about."[34]

Perhaps the furthest from the facts was when Jacek Żakowski announced that the authorities "at the economic table did not give away even a fingernail."[35] Similarly untrue was Geremek's comment on Żakowski's indictment: "This came as a certain surprise to us. It was a painful surprise, because we attached great importance to economic reform. . . . It was in the economic sphere that the results of the 'round table' were the most disappointing. In fact we managed to carry through only our concept of wage indexation." On reading these words, one can at best assume that the head of the S. faction in parliament did not remember only a year later what had been settled in the agreements.

To end the matter of the myths surrounding the Round Table, may I also observe that the program of liberation of food prices as of August 1, 1989, that is, by Rakowski's government, encountered a similar fate. Clearly not familiar with the course of negotiations of the Round Table, Żakowski asked: "Was this decision the last chord of Party reform, or an intentionally placed political bomb that was to tear down the already anticipated government of the existing opposition?" And Geremek answered: "I think that the aim was to precede the reforms announced by us. After all, we talked a lot and loudly about introducing market mechanisms, we repeated that we have to decisively depart from distribution and commands. The authorities heard this. too. They knew that these are popular slogans and they decided to take them over. Except that we never proposed to the people such mad leaps, diving into the market head on and with closed eyes. . . . Rakowski with Olesiak simply ordered marketization; in other words practically liberating food prices overnight, and the prices shot upward."[36] Geremek did not know or ignored the fact that the program outline was ready by early 1989 and became the subject of intense debate during Round Table negotiations. The operation of liberating prices was described with approval by the chief advisor of Mazowiecki's cabinet: "Marketization of food prices as of August 1, 1989—a correct decision envisaged at the Round Table, a big step in the direction of a market economy, which decision we did not repeal."[37]

4. From Gradualism to "Jump"

Apart from the abundant document archives mentioned in the Preface and my conversations with Stanisław Gomułka, we have at least three more testimonies by witnesses of the events described in this book. The earliest is the book by Waldemar Kuczyński (1992), exceptional in its openness and sincerity. Then there is the reticent, milder account of the markedly self-controlled Leszek Balcerowicz, *800 dni. Szok kontrolowany* (800 Days of Controlled Shock) (1992), and two books by Jeffrey Sachs (1993, 2006). Economic issues are also dealt with in a book by the head of the Citizens' Parliamentary Committee, Bronisław Geremek (1990), which displays an uncritical attitude toward the radical Sachs-Beksiak concepts but is sometimes misleading because of lack of knowledge in economic matters.

The roles of each of these individuals were distinctly different and hence their varying viewpoints. Balcerowicz and Gomułka worked directly on the program of what came to be known as the Balcerowicz Plan and were its co-authors. Sachs would visit Poland briefly many times, and his main role was to create a favorable background for the great jump. His general concept of jumping into the market, and also his tendency to exaggerate or go to extremes, turned out to serve a function, making other radicals appear more reasonable. As we shall see, Stanisław Gomułka in particular benefited from this. Sachs's position is also tainted with propaganda and a kind of self-promotion. The fact that his views have undergone a pivotal change also undermines his credibility. There are times now that he appears to be closer to St. Francis than to Balcerowicz. And yet he feels no need to explain the old prescriptions he had for Poland from the standpoint he holds today. All this when even the heads of the International Monetary Fund and the World Bank have managed to show more self-criticism.*

Against this background, Kuczyński's book, in many places revealing a great writing talent, is a rare gift for economic and political historians. When the author was writing the book he believed that the Balcerowicz Plan was, in spite of everything, a success and the best solution, and that made it possible for him to disclose the surrounding conflicts. He was certainly best positioned for this, being not only a confidant of the prime minister, as he described himself, but also his loyal friend, so that toward the economic dictator he could act, in turn, as an arbiter and, in a sense, his superior in rank. He was not directly responsible for the concrete form of the economic program and so could retain his position as observer. Naturally, Kuczyński's book is one-sided: he defends the actions of Mazowiecki's team and is deeply convinced that the "jump" to a market economy was a historical necessity. But he does show respect for the facts, including the uncomfortable ones. And of all the writers mentioned, he is the only one who gives such fine portraits of Mazowiecki and Balcerowicz.

The Welfare State of the Future Confidant

Following a seven-year sojourn, Kuczyński returned from Paris, where he had been engaged almost solely in Polish matters, mainly of an economic nature. He had been learning the French language from

*Prof. Kazimierz Łaski informed me that during Sachs's stay in Vienna he had asked him on what grounds he believed in 1990 that the transition to a market economy was possible within six months. Sachs was surprised and said he didn't recall ever saying such a thing.

scratch, which in a way predestined him to devote himself to Polish issues. Earlier he wrote a book published underground, *Po wielkim skoku* (After the Great Leap)* (Oficyna Wydawnicza "Nowa," 1980), which brought him considerable acclaim, and even the highly prestigious private award of Czesław Bobrowski,† equivalent to several average monthly wages. The book analyzed Edward Gierek's attempt at an unfortunate speeding up of industrialization with the support of Western loans. This leader of the ruling party had earlier worked for some years as a miner in France, and had an idea for Poland's controlled openness to the West. Many new plants were created in the 1970s, unfortunately manufacturing outdated goods, burdening the economy with an immense and rising debt when efforts to radically increase exports failed.

Kuczyński quite regularly commented on Polish economic matters on Radio Free Europe. He wrote about these topics for the Parisian *Kultura* and *Aneks* and so returned quite knowledgeable in Polish affairs.

Toward the Polish emigrant as well as the domestic opposition, however, he showed a certain reticence. Earlier than others he noticed the landmark character of Gorbachev's moves and their liberal implications for Poland, especially after the 1986 amnesty. He was close in this to Mazowiecki, who then was seeking conciliation with the authorities. He became friends with the future prime minister in 1981, while working for the weekly journal *Tygodnik Solidarność* (he was deputy to Mazowiecki as chief editor). But at the time of his return, were both aware of the differences in views caused by the seven years of absence?

We know that Mazowiecki's hypothesis from the late 1980s was that the S. movement was a near-perfect triple synthesis of efforts toward national sovereignty and the ideologically similar aspects of Christianity and socialism. And what was Kuczyński returning with?

---

*Under this title, published by Monthly Review Press in 1986.

†Legend ary figure among Polish economists, founder of the Central Planning Board and the First Three-Year Plan, sacked in the process of "Stalinization."

In his book, he would write that to break from the communist economic system, "what was needed was a liberal team, distant from the left movement, even from the part originating from Solidarity. . . . It was a time of liberals."[1] In another place he even says that he is no "fan of liberalism," but that this was a time for it. Yet he behaved like an advocate of neoliberalism, for many years writing for the weekly *Wprost* a commentary titled "Rozmyślenia monetarysty" (Reflections of a Monetarist), although earlier he had not given the slightest hint of being a monetary specialist. Free-market thinking made him, as chief of the economic advisors of Prime Minister Buzek, speak out against greater outlays for science in Poland, stressing that in this area Poland was doomed to an imitative development of science, a position that would subsequently alienate the academic environment against him.

If we assume that this fascination Kuczyński had for monetarism came later, then there is something distasteful in the words "I am no fan of it, but since this is a time for it. . . ." The only thing that could justify such an attitude would be the desire to merge the slogans of liberalism with "non-liberalism." But he did not reveal such a desire.

The notion of liberalism itself calls for certain clarification. This was not a time (*Zeitgeist*) of liberals in general, but of such free-market conservatives as Ronald Reagan in practice and Milton Friedman and Friedrich A. Hayek in theory. Not only American liberals associated with the Democratic Party, but also the multihued European social and political liberalism originating from John Stuart Mill, and especially from John Rawls, Bruce Ackerman, and many others, were in sharp opposition to Reaganomics from the very beginning. Kuczyński may not have been aware of this. What was it he knew for sure, then? First of all, that in front of his very eyes the socialist government of François Mitterrand suffered a bitter defeat, which forced him to appoint a rightist, free-market government, for years dooming him to difficult cooperation with successive right-wing cabinets (the famous *cohabitation*). Second, some of Kuczyński's declarations indicate that he was not simply an uncritical proponent of free-market capitalism, but it is not clear if he was critical toward the rightist economic policy at that time, not only in France but also in other great Western countries—the United States, Great Britain, Germany—as well as toward the prevalent free-market trends within the European Economic Community. But his reserve with regard to the old and new emigrants and what he wrote about the welfare state and the inspiring role of socialist ideas could have been the reason Mazowiecki believed he was persuading an ideologically close activist to return and work with him.

The following are several of the most emphatic of Kuczyński's statements, notably addressed mainly to Polish extreme liberals. The most clearly outlined credo can be found in the article "Kłopoty z socjalizmem" (The Trouble with Socialism),[2] where he takes a firm stand in rejecting really existing socialism, and even perceives signs in Poland's documentary literature indicating that matters are progressing in this direction. At the same time he recognizes the need for the inspiring ideas of socialism and social policy. He connects the postulate of the elimination of real socialism only to the so-called relations of production. And he adds a strong declaration that could have become a guiding principle for the Polish transformation:

There is no reason, however, to extend this postulate to embrace socialism as an inspiration for a whole range of social policies, or ways of distributing goods, known mainly from the experience of Western "welfare states" or "protective states." In this role it can demonstrate great achievements and remains applicable, while those welfare states, despite the criticism they have recently been subjected to, and despite the elimination of various overly protective schemes, are doing quite well. . . . And so, these are not inactive ideas typical in a period of a certain slowdown, and then only where things have been overdone. But this certainly did not happen in Poland. In view of this, *it is astonishing to see the enthusiasm with which our liberal opposition . . . is attacking the ideas of a welfare state. . . .* There is no reason why a return to the economic mechanisms typical for the West would require an explicit declaration of preference for Friedman over Keynes, or American capitalism over Swedish capitalism.[3]

And in a more pronounced tone:

> The return to capitalism of the Polish economy will not mean that along with it there will be a definite end to the historical role of the socialist formation, and especially the left movement, which is what liberal proselytes sometimes suggest. On the contrary, the experience of "socialized" European capitalism proves that the market and private economy offer a favorable groundwork for carrying out many ideas of the socialist movement, including the idea of public authorities partly steering the economy.[4]

In addition, some of Kuczyński's formulations resemble certain enunciations made by Mazowiecki concerning the rapprochement of the opposition and socialism. "It would be fitting and maybe realistic to *bring the perspectives somewhat closer together, getting rid of remnants of utopian thinking by one of the sides and, if one may say so, of a 'restoration extreme' by the other.*"[5] Also, he emphasized that a return to capitalism is a task "for an entire era" and not "a method of leaps and rebounds," which could have been for Mazowiecki an indication that here a man with views very similar to his own was returning to Poland. The question is, though, what made Kuczyński the *porteparole* of the great leap into unfettered capitalism, the spokesman—as he himself writes—of a "restoration extreme"?

Stanisław Gomułka—from Capital Mini-Market to Shock Margaret Thatcher–Style

Nothing can more fittingly describe the Polish adventure, called shock therapy, than the imported Thatcher-style shock concept. It was brought to Poland by London School of Economics professor and advisor to Balcerowicz, Stanisław Gomułka, who from the beginning had been monitoring the Polish socioeconomic transformation.

Gomułka was not unwilling to cooperate with the government of Mieczysław Rakowski, assuming the role of an independent expert.

He prepared the first expert analysis, "on the commission" of Finance Minister Andrzej Wróblewski, in July 1989. Its title was "Jak stworzyćrynek kapitałowy w Polsce i jak wykorzystać ten rynek do reformy systemu własności" (How to Create a Capital Market in Poland and How to Utilize This Market to Reform the Ownership System).* In light of subsequent publications, and especially Gomułka's later role in formulating the program of economic transformation, this is an extremely important analysis, as it reveals that still in midsummer of that year he had been an advocate of the evolutionary concept of introducing a market economy and privatization.

He proposed to start creating the capital market with the establishment of five to ten agencies of Bank Inwestycyjno-Handlowy (BIH), with a stock structure, and the transformation of one hundred state-owned enterprises into joint stock companies. The shares of these enterprises would be evenly divided among this BIH network. The technical part of the idea is not important, whereas the general assumptions and the time perspectives are so different from the proposals that were steadfastly associated with his name that it is worthwhile to describe them.

To begin with, Gomułka takes as fact the existence of concentrated state ownership, although he notes that this makes it very hard for state enterprises to make decisions without heeding the political circumstances. His proposals merely aimed at creating the conditions in which "enterprises out of necessity state owned would behave like, or nearly like, private ones." Moreover, over the first five to ten years, they would remain state firms. Even the partial (*sic!*) privatization of BIH would be postponed until later. He provided for a certain role to be played by the National Property Fund envisaged in the Round Table Agreements. Whereas he felt that for a realistic valuation of enterprises market prices would be needed, he limited his postulate significantly, writing that "control of prices should be abandoned for enterprises entering the capital market." He did not rule out the participation of

---

*The eleven-page typescript with handwritten corrections made by the author (Gomułka, 1989a) is in my possession.

representatives of employee councils in supervisory boards, which would raise the interest of employees in the firm's good condition. The whole undertaking was to be modest and encompass not more than half of one percent of those employed outside of agriculture, since it was only such, and only partial at that (!), that purchase of shares would be possible, given the level of domestic capital.

Caution, moderation, and the toned-down character of the plans become even more striking when these propositions are compared with the government document "Założenia programu gospodarczego na lata 1989–1992" (Economic Program Guidelines for the Years 1989–1992), published in the daily *Rzeczpospolita* in July 1989. Rakowski's team had already postulated the general commercialization of state-owned enterprises, treating this as an introduction to privatization, far-reaching market economy, radical reduction of the quantity of money in the economy, and a profound restructuring of enterprises, combined with bankruptcies and unemployment. The author of one of the first histories of this period would evaluate the content matter of this document as "nearly entirely concurrent in the basic aims and methods with the program later implemented as the Balcerowicz Plan."*[6] In writing his analysis, Gomułka most probably was not familiar with this document. Otherwise, he would not have allowed himself to be outpaced so much in his radicalism.

Barely one month later, in mid-August, he would write in an entirely different tone:

Poland needs competitiveness to service debt, and it needs unemployment to create competitive labor markets to produce greater mobility, discipline and the control of wage inflation. The Polish economy clearly requires a surgical operation to remove the outdated and inefficient industries. A similar operation in [Great] Britain in the

---

*This is the view shared to this day by the main architect of this document, former finance minister Andrzej Wróblewski, who publicly said that he was happy that Balcerowicz implemented his plan. (Public statement of the minister at the meeting of May 19, 2009, in the Mokotów House of Culture.)

early 1980s led initially to much higher unemployment and an improvement only later. The interesting question is whether a Solidarity-led government will be capable of conceiving and implementing such a Thatcherite policy.[7]

This is the conclusion of an article published in the British daily *The Guardian* (August 19, 1989), titled "Shock Needed for Polish Economy" with the added caption reading "Free Market Cuts Jobs before Business Revives." Gomułka wrote this article the day before his arrival in Warsaw, together with Jeffrey Sachs and George Soros (with whom he had been in close contact since April—more about this later). From now on, he would be persuading successive Polish governments to endorse the implementation of Thatcher-style schemes. With the exception of Grzegorz Kołodko, he advised many finance ministers and also the president of the National Bank of Poland (NBP). Even in this last assignment, his role was more significant than merely as an "internal" advisor. Needless to say, he was much better prepared for the role of advisor than his Harvard colleague.

Gomułka graduated in physics from Warsaw University. After obtaining a master's degree, he abandoned physics for economic studies at this university, where he shortly became an assistant to Oskar Lange. His tutors also included Michał Kalecki and Włodzimierz Brus, but the student soon became more radical than they. In the early 1960s, acting under the wings of the Socialist Youth Union, he criticized really existing socialism from the position of orthodox Marxism, with a pro-worker and anti-bureaucratic orientation. In the West such views were often classified as Trotskyite. In Poland, however, this term has negative connotations. In 1965, he helped Jacek Kuroń and Karol Modzelewski write an extensive program that served as a basis for "An Open Letter to the Party." Its authors were imprisoned for this, accused of preparing to overthrow the system, and their advisor was banned from working with students and was expelled from the university.

As a result of the anti-Semitic *dintojra* (mock court) of March 1968, he was imprisoned for several months. Following his release, the

Gomułkas decided to emigrate, making use of the Jewish background of his wife, Joanna. After spending one year in Denmark, Stanisław obtained a lectureship at the London School of Economics, where he worked until retirement. (It is worth noting that in this school the pervading mood in economics was closer to the American mainstream than to the leftist university in Cambridge.) During this time he maintained contacts with the Polish March 1968 emigrants and with dissidents in Poland, though he was critical toward the first S.

It is not easy to reconstruct the further evolution of his views, but certain points are nonetheless clear. In the early 1970s, he was unusually positive toward Edward Gierek's policy of modernization. In 1977, he was very critical of Włodzimierz Brus's book, *Uspołecznienie a system polityczny* (Socialization and the Political System),[8] thereby opening an exceptionally interesting debate. Participants included the leading intellectuals of the post-March emigration: Leszek Kołakowski, Maria Hirszowicz, Aleksander Matejko, and somewhat later the author of the criticized book.

In Gomułka's intellectual development this was a significant step in the direction of a new identity. He tried to see real capitalism and real socialism with the eyes of a neutral observer—a believer in the systemic convergence theory that was quite popular at the time, expressed in the title of the treatise: "O czynnikach ekonomicznych w demokratyzacji socjalizmu i socjalizacji kapitalizmu" (On Economic Factors in Democratization of Socialism and Socialization of Capitalism). The main hypothesis was that socialism would undergo processes toward a free-market economy and "capitalization," while capitalism would undergo "socialization," that is, would be increasingly regulated and socialized.

Returning after ten years to this polemic on the invitation of the underground magazine *Dwadzieścia Jeden*, Gomułka almost predicted the pivotal turn of the USSR in the direction of a market economy. His polemic partner Włodzimierz Brus, on the other hand, continued to seek something intermediate, adopting as his point of departure the beautiful essay by Kołakowski, "Jak być konserwatywno-liberalnym socjalistą" (How to Be a Conservative-Liberal Socialist).

Gomułka's first major treatise with typically Sovietological content and form was the study "Specyficzne systemowe przyczyny kryzysu polskiego lat 1980–82" (Specific and Systemic Causes of the Polish Crisis, 1980–82).[9] It must have been noticed, since only two years later he became a consultant for the IMF for reform in Poland. That was when his views most probably crystallized around Thatcherism, along with what became known as the Washington Consensus a few years later, and in practice what appears as the structural adjustment programs of the IMF. From then on, Gomułka was loyal to his views to the extent that he was not closely involved in any types of capitalism other than the Anglo-Saxon kind, or in any transformation models other than those preferred by the IMF. His interest in the Chinese-Vietnamese path was limited to the issue of the symbiosis of authoritarian rule with a market economy.

The Plans of George Soros

It is interesting that one of the first authors who hastily made their way to Poland with their plans was the financier George Soros. Between the end of March and December 1989, he presented as many as five different program versions. Not waiting for the outcome of the final round of talks of the Round Table, on March 24, 1989, he presented the document titled "International Economic Assistance for Poland." This brief (two-page) proposal expressed equal concern over stabilization of money and internal economic reforms and over what he called the "restructuring" of the Polish foreign debt.

Soros emphasized the inextricable connection between the above three components, which was supposed to be organizationally expressed in the establishment of a special agency to manage state enterprises turned over to an equally special organ, called a trust. But the agency was to deal with debt rescheduling as well. It would also have the power to sell these enterprises to both domestic and foreign buyers. Soros stressed that it would be independent, though foreign advisors would take part in managing it. He understood the independence (here quotation marks may just as well be used for this word) of the central bank in a similar way. The wording Soros employed is so original that it is worth quoting it: "Foreign advisors would also participate in running the central bank and controlling the domestic money supply. This would give the central bank the independence needed to carry out a successful monetary reform. Monetary reform would, in turn, be made possible by a reorganization of the international debt and a reduction in debt service payments."[10]

A detailed program was to be drawn up by an international task force composed of representatives of "all interested parties." This probably meant the participation of representatives of Poland, foreign creditors, and the IMF, which usually realigned economies to enable them to repay debt, or at least to service it regularly.

How would Poland benefit from this and what kind of assistance would be given? Apart from this "independence," such an arrangement would provide professional expert advice for Poland, and Poland in realistic time limits would demonstrate its reforming assertiveness, providing justification for the involvement of the West in the process of reform. Soros also proposed certain direct and tangible benefits in the form of a three-year moratorium from the Paris Club (representing debt drawn or guaranteed by state creditors) and a low and fixed interest rate, at the level of, for example, 3 to 5 percent. Only after the moratorium period would the Paris Club decide whether the actions of the agency were satisfactory and convert the debt into privileged shares in the agency.

We do not know the reaction of the people who received this program. The programs that followed were much more extensive and seriously altered. Dated June 8, 1989, "A Plan for Poland" dealt with economic problems in a more comprehensive way. The essential components of the program remained, and in particular: the concept of establishing the agency along with its powers, foreign advisors, the moratorium of the Paris Club, and the low interest rates. The included alterations can be divided into two groups.

First, Soros perceived the potential sensitivity of Poles and the Polish state authorities to the issue of sovereignty. And again, the following words of his should be recorded in history's annals: "The [liquidating] Agency would be established by the agreement between the Polish government and the governments represented by the Paris Club, subject to the approval of the Polish Parliament, so that it would not infringe on Polish sovereignty. Its independence from domestic political pressures could be assured by the fact that the foreign lenders may not accept the eventual exchange offer if they are not satisfied with its work."[11]

The second part of the proposition also showed an important change of position. Probably for the first time the term "Big Bang" appeared. This is at any rate Soros's idea of the stabilization program: it would assume the form of a Big Bang, consisting of sudden removal of price control subsidies and pegging the zloty to the ecu (predecessor to the euro) at a realistic rate. The social consequences would not have to be particularly painful. It is doubtful whether his contention that real wages need not fall was compatible with his general concept.

In general, on account of the one-time repeal of subsidies and price controls, this was a proposition for radical reform (Big Bang), but with some elements of social protection and certain financial assistance. Soros sent out his plan to several people from countries that played the most important role in the Paris Club, to deputy prime minister Ireneusz Sekuła in the cabinet of Mieczysław Rakowski, Finance Minister Andrzej Wróblewski, and to Bronisław Geremek, one of the leaders of the Solidarity opposition. He also noted that his propositions had raised much interest both in Poland and in Western countries. The government of Poland, as well as Solidarity, signaled that they would readily start informal discussion under the auspices of the Soros-founded Batory Foundation in Warsaw. Moreover, a trilateral meeting was suggested within a short time, first in London, then in Warsaw.

Both meetings did take place shortly, although not in the planned form. On April 28, a semi-social lunch gathering was held in Oxford, organized by Professor Zbigniew Pełczyński and attended by, apart from the organizer, Włodzimierz Brus, Stanisław Gomułka, and George Soros. According to Gomułka's account, the debate focused mostly on Soros's plan and on the next meeting, in Warsaw. Struck by

Gomułka's critical remarks, Soros invited him to his home in London, where another version of his plan was worked on. Probably no account written at the time has been preserved either from the lunch or from the work on the new version.

The meeting in Warsaw was not held under the auspices of Soros's Batory Foundation, but at the Ministry of Finance. Soros, who earlier had been meeting with deputy prime minister Ireneusz Sekuła, this time invited three experts and financed their trip. These were Stanisław Gomułka, Jeffrey Sachs, and former IMF staff member David Lipton. Most probably, the basis for discussion was the new version of Soros's plan, dated June 8, 1989. In terms of the concepts concerning stabilization, perhaps the most important new element was the proposal to freeze wages for half a year.*

The meeting was preceded by a letter of Finance Minister Andrzej Wróblewski, expressing the desire to carry on further discussion. This extensive, three-page letter of May 23, 1989, was devoted nearly entirely to the character and manner of establishing the agency, the capital market, pegging the zloty to the ecu, the moratorium, converting debt into shares in state enterprises and the sale thereof, and the powers of the Paris Club.[12] He did not, however, touch on the issue of the Big Bang with regard to prices, subsidies, and unemployment together with its social safety net. Could it be that a member of the formally "communist" government accepted in advance such a radically shocking proposal? As we shall see, such a speculation is not too distant from the somewhat later documents of the ministry.

Both Soros and Wróblewski were in favor of a discussion with a group of experts. The Warsaw meeting, however, was held after the

---

*The June meetings with the minister of finance and other meetings were probably the peak moment of Soros's involvement in the Polish transformations. Later on, the lead was taken up by Gomułka and Sachs. Soros drew up two more versions of his plan: one dated August 31, 1989 (Soros, 1989d), and the second, "A Plan for Poland—Stage Two," dated December 19, 1989. Soros returned to the essentially unchanged concept of restructuring (or rather privatizing) state enterprises in association with foreign debt. He postulated the announcement of a similar plan directly after the implementation of the stabilization program.

June 4 election, that is, in a much different political situation. The question is, why did it take place at the Ministry of Finance and with the participation of probably its entire management, with the chief in the lead? It is not unlikely that the initiator of the change of venue was Minister Wróblewski himself (and maybe even the whole government) who began to hurry with the preparation of reform. Unfortunately, I do not have at my disposal any minutes of the discussion, and the only information available is from the extensive talks I had with Gomułka.[13]

Two important documents emerged from this meeting. The first was the proposition of Stanisław Gomułka for the creation of a capital market, commissioned by Wróblewski and elaborated and described above. The second was titled "Założenia programu gospodarczego na lata 1989–1992" (Assumptions of the Economic Program for the Years 1989–1992) and was prepared at the Ministry of Finance and accepted by the government, then published in the daily *Rzeczpospolita* in July 1989.

In the summer of 1989, the political situation in Poland was changing at a fast pace. As of August 1, food prices were liberated, this being the last decision of the old government and the old system. Now the IMF and the World Bank threw themselves with new energy into matters concerning the Polish economy. Soros's plans became too general by their nature, and by autumn of that year premature, since two matters now came to the fore: the budget for the coming months and the budget for the year 1990, combined with systemic changes.

Dariusz Rosati's Leap Forward without Unemployment or Lowered Living Standards

One of the extreme proponents of a free-market economy was Dariusz Rosati, advisor to Prime Minister Rakowski. Shortly before the parliamentary election, he outlined a concept that was concurrent not only with the forthcoming Balcerowicz Plan, but also with the more radical proposals of Beksiak's group. He postulated "liberated prices and—

please use bold type here [he requested]—liberated wages, and also: lowering tax burdens," fluid interest rates balancing supply and demand, a capital market, currency convertibility, foreign competition, and opening up to privatization.[14] The market transformations were to last one to two years.

What is very characteristic is that in two points these proposals differ greatly from what Rosati would be writing several years later. In June 1989, he assured us that the whole operation did not and should not lead to lower incomes and a lower standard of living (he made a point of this several times). Declaring himself to be in favor of the bankruptcies of inefficient enterprises, he assured that "it is not hard to get a job in Poland, we have no threat of serious unemployment." He explained his optimism in the matter of not lowering the living standard by saying that "people will be manufacturing what it pays to manufacture and will receive decent pay for this." And so, he advocated the prompt bankruptcy of inefficient firms, "by way of stopping credit."

Rosati played no greater role in constructing the Balcerowicz Plan because he was connected with the previous system. It is all the more interesting that later he would become one of the enthusiastic supporters of shock therapy, together with the very high social consequences of such an operation, as seen clearly in his book *Polska droga do rynku* (The Polish Road to the Market). Here is his most general view:

> Two basic social groups—hired workers and individual farmers—in the first stage of reform bore the highest cost. . . . Reduction of the share of hired workers in the global incomes of the population by one-third, and of individual farmers by more than half, explains the violent erosion of public support for the radical market reforms in the first stage of the transformation. . . . The increased share of the remaining incomes reflects the dynamic development of the private sector. These incomes comprise both income from individual economic activity and income from property—profit, capital shares, income from stocks, bonds, bank investments, real estate. The social group making use of this income, in the beginning small, is growing very rapidly, becoming the core of the middle class.[15]

Let us add that in the general income of the population, in the years 1990–93 the share of this social group rose—according to the numbers he cites—from less than 7 to nearly 17 percent, that is, by two and a half times.

In his description of the events that ultimately led to this result, Dariusz Rosati produces numerous critical remarks about the Balcerowicz Plan and its execution. It was he who "immortalized" (after the daily *Trybuna Ludu*) the following statement made by Leszek Balcerowicz during the hearing by the Sejm committee: "It's now or never—you have to close your eyes and leap down, not checking the water on the bottom or the height of the precipice. The choice is only whether this is a leap with short preparation or completely unprepared."[16] He treated this declaration as an expression of "neophyte enthusiasm and determination."

It is interesting that from the point of view of the political economy of the transformation, Rosati ultimately acknowledged the social effects of this leap. Namely, efficiency had been achieved at the price of egalitarianism.

The mechanism of this choice is simple: improvement of efficiency requires increased income disparities and, the other way round, ~~Scandinavia?~~ reduction of income inequalities as a rule entails lowered economic efficiency. . . . Economic liberalism, which is necessary to launch effective market mechanisms, and the implementation of the principles of a welfare state are thus to a certain extent incompatible. . . . Increased efficiency can take place in conditions of given, limited resources only at the price of essentially increasing the income disparities.[17]

For him, such reasoning suffices not only to explain the collapse of real socialism but also to express support for a free-market economy as being more efficient than a social market economy.[18] According to him, the great delusion lies in the fact that most of society wants both greater efficiency and a higher standard of living.

I am deliberately not referring to the opinions of the "neophytes" directly involved in the implementation of the Big Bang, or the closest advisors, but to a representative of the part of the elites that still calls itself left-wing. Rosati's position illustrates that in this matter an understanding above divisions was formed. The faith in the inevitability of something in the way of primitive capital accumulation as an inseparable part of the transition to a market economy was then an integral part of the imagination of the political and economic elites. It was a faith devoid of any evidence.

Rosati is loyal to this view at the price of ignoring the new approach to the strategy of industrial modernization of two successive deputy chiefs of the World Bank, formerly the bastion—next to the IMF—of Washington orthodoxy. While resorting to the extensive research of his predecessor, Michael Bruno, the deputy head and chief economist of the World Bank, Joseph Stiglitz, explicitly rejected the alleged incompatibility of efficiency and equality. And here are the conclusions he drew from the experiences of the East Asian "tigers": "Historically, the development process has been characterized by marked increases in inequality (the Kuznets curve). . . . East Asian economies, on the other hand, were able to achieve rapid growth without an increased inequality . . . the redistribution of income contributed to political stability, an important factor in creating a good environment for domestic and foreign investment."[19] Rosati is an enlightened man (former minister of foreign affairs), having worked for many years in the Geneva agency of the United Nations specializing in foreign trade. He did not have to wait for Stiglitz's enunciation or the similar, earlier remark of Michael Bruno. There were many reasons to reflect on the Japanese, Taiwanese, Korean, or Scandinavian developments and to pose the question: How did it happen that these countries, while preserving considerable egalitarianism, have effectively joined the club of the most affluent countries of the world? The American economist David Gordon has listed the indicators in Table 4.1.

It is remarkable that all indicators, without exception, both economic and social ones, have turned out to be more favorable for countries with a social market economy (cooperative) than for countries based more on a free market and open class conflict. Japan, for example, started an accelerated modernization march by radically

Table 4.1: Cooperative and Conflictual Economies (1973–1989)

INDICATORS	COOPERATIVE	CONFLICTUAL
Productivity growth, business sector	1.9	1.1
Productivity growth, manufacturing	3.4	2.2
Investment share of GDP	14.2	10.8
% change, capital-labor ratio	3.3	2.2
Inflation rate, GDP deflator	5.8	8.0
Unemployment rate	3.7	7.6

Source: Gordon, 1998, p. 196.
NOTE: These are unweighted averages, obtained from annual averages for a given group of countries. In the first group of countries Gordon included Germany, Japan, Norway, and Sweden; in the second, the United States, United Kingdom, and Canada.

reducing income (wages) and property disparities (*zaibatsu* expropriation, agricultural reform). Sweden by no means paid for its egalitarianism with lower efficiency, as it moved to the lead (next to two countries with a similar system—Denmark and Finland) among the knowledge-based economies in the world.

But Rosati overlooked not only the new world developments. He ignored the wealth of data concerning his own country. He mistakenly assumed that before 1989 Poland had an extremely egalitarian economy. In the second half of the 1990s, he had access to many publications that showed that Polish income disparities at that time were greater than the disparities in the Scandinavian countries, Japan, and India, and were more or less at the level of the Federal Republic of Germany, Belgium, and the Netherlands. And so the causes of poor efficiency and the "disintegration" of the system of real socialism did not lie in excessive pressure—as Rosati writes—to ensure social justice.

Jeffrey Sachs

During the emergence of the concept of a "jump" into a market economy, on the stage of Polish changes there appeared a young professor from Harvard University, Jeffrey Sachs. He created quite a stir as architect of the economic stabilization program for Bolivia. His role in the Polish transformations was not as significant as he himself described in the book *Poland's Jump in a Market Economy* (1993) and in the chapter devoted to Poland in his book *The End of Poverty* (2006). The IMF is mentioned in his books from time to time, but not once in connection with work on the Balcerowicz Plan. From what he writes, one has the impression that the plan was nearly entirely his own creation and that of his disciple and fellow worker, David Lipton. But undoubtedly he did play a great role in "injecting" in many Polish politicians the idea of a sudden jump into the market.

In early 1989, most probably during the Round Table negotiations, a messenger of the Polish embassy in Washington, Krzysztof Krowacki, was sent to Sachs. He suggested a visit to Poland to discuss the problems of reforms. Sachs refused, saying he might come in the future on the condition that NSZZ "Solidarity" was legalized. When the Round Table Agreements foretold the legalization of the union, he began visiting Warsaw, usually with his assistant and friend, David Lipton. These visits were paid for by the American billionaire George Soros.

The first time Sachs was present in an essential debate on reforms, two weeks after the parliamentary election of June 4, 1989, is not noted in his books. It was the debate at the Ministry of Finance, which he attended together with Soros, Lipton, and Gomułka, on the invitation of the incumbent minister, Andrzej Wróblewski. Possibly at that time,* together with Lipton, perhaps also with Stanisław Gomułka (whose presence Sachs notoriously fails to mention), he held talks with the leading activists of the democratic opposition. The description of these talks given by him offers an excellent insight into how in certain conditions grand ideas are born that may change the course of events. I shall present them in the way that Sachs does, toward the end pointing out the difficulty in determining certain dates.

Sachs (along with Lipton) had the first talk with Bronisław Geremek, trying to convince him that the opposition should take the reins of the economy and decide on a jump into the market. According

---

*Sachs is not accurate when he locates these talks in July.

to the accounts of Sachs, Geremek first reacted in a negative way, favoring instead the concept of stimulating reforms by the Senate committee. In the end, however ("after several hours" of persuasion), he was to say: "I feel terrible after this discussion because I think you're right. Maybe we don't have a choice."[20] And he suggested that both have a similar talk with Jacek Kuroń.

The part of the account referring to the talk with Kuroń is questionable, and it can be presumed that in Sachs's memory two different meetings melted into one. But first, here is how Sachs describes it. The talk (through an interpreter) lasted several hours; from the beginning Kuroń showed a full understanding of Sachs's ideas. And although the meeting extended late into the evening, the Americans gave way to Kuroń's insistence to write the program for the morning of the next day. They went to the office of the daily *Gazeta Wyborcza* and there, on the office computer, created a fifteen-page document overnight. "It was the first time, I believe, that anyone had written down a comprehensive plan for the transformation of a socialist economy to a market economy. It briefly touched on the question of trade, exchange rates, price liberalization, convertibility of the currency, stabilization, industrial policy, debt cancellation, and a bit on privatization, which was the area of greatest uncertainty. Our proposal was for a dramatic, quick transformation to a market economy—a leap across the institutional chasm. "[21]

The Americans presented the main points of the ready program also to Michnik, who repeatedly said that he was not an economist and did not understand "these things," but several times he wanted to make sure whether they felt its implementation was realistic. Ending the conversation, he said: "Okay, then, you have filled in the last piece of my puzzle. I've known what to do politically. Now you tell me that there is an economic strategy as well. In that case, we're going to go for government."[22]

The talk with Lech Wałęsa went off even less well. They were talked into going to see him by the three earlier interlocutors. When Sachs wanted to get to the essence of things, Wałęsa said brusquely: "I didn't come here for an abstract discussion; I want to know how we get banks into Gdańsk,"[23] and following brief efforts by Sachs to stick to the main topic, he again asked for help in drawing in the banks. Sachs left, "perplexed and dismayed."

The above account is not exact on some issues. Sachs passes over the fact that he and Lipton drew up not one but two radically different plans. The first was still addressed to the old authorities and revealed that the idea of a sudden jump into the market was not born in Sachs's mind right after the June election, victorious for the Solidarity opposition. In the second half of August, the weekly *Gazeta Bankowa* published a two-part article by Sachs and Lipton titled "Program stabilizacyjny dla Polski" (Stabilization Program for Poland), informing readers that it was a summary of the text that came into being "following their visit [to Poland] in June this year." The article is extremely interesting, as there is no talk of a sudden jump into the market, or about S., which should assume responsibility for the economy and its reform. On the contrary, many parts suggest an evolutionary pace of change that sounds minimalist, as if the authors publicly declared their willingness to help the existing authorities. The following is the decisive fragment, in my opinion:

> There are two reasons why most probably full implementation of a market system in food economy would not succeed this year. First, stabilization concentrated on "sensitive" prices could presumably lead to a storm of protests, as had been the case in the past. . . . Second, even if the protests did not undermine the effects of the taken measures, the system of state-owned enterprises would take care of that. . . . What is needed is a stabilization program conforming to the economic and social conditions. Poland should not mainly rely on growth of "sensitive" prices, but also examine other roads leading to the goal.[24]

Consequently, Sachs suggested five "elements," focusing not on a jump into a free market of prices, but on the currency exchange rate, external support, partial privatization (for example, of apartments), "small controlled rises of prices of goods and services"(!), and a social accord with the trade unions.

In my belief, this document is of utmost importance. It shows that only a few weeks earlier Sachs had been inclined to accept the role of advisor to a government in which the hitherto existing opposition would not take part. We do not know when the views of this American became more radical. In a similar way, the other advisor to Leszek Balcerowicz, Stanisław Gomułka, had at first been reticent. At any rate, the change of concept concerning transformation, from a program of cautious stabilization to a jump into the market, bespeaks its political character and not the alleged economic necessity of selecting the shock therapy, as would be declared afterward.

The other plan of Sachs and Lipton, in the form of a computer printout, is in the private archives of the documents of Stanisław Gomułka. It is dated—and this is important—August 5, 1989. Thus it came into being exactly one month after the publication of the well-known article of Adam Michnik (1989), "Wasz prezydent, nasz premier" (Your President, Our Prime Minister). By that time, Sachs did not need to convince Geremek, and certainly not Kuroń or Michnik, for the opposition to take over power. And so the American is relaying talks with Geremek and Kuroń that took place at a different time.

Sachs's program became "a political and documentary hit"[25] only three weeks later, when its assumptions were presented to the deputies and senators of S., gathered in the Sala Kolumnowa in the Sejm (on August 24—the day Tadeusz Mazowiecki was appointed prime minister). *Gazeta Wyborcza* backed him with two successive articles that had the symptomatic titles: "Czy Sachs powtórzy sukces Grabskiego?" (Will Sachs Repeat Grabski's Success?)* (August 23, 1989) and "Plan Sachsa" (Sachs's Plan) (August 24, 1989).

The scenario could be fitting for a film: on the podium there sat the Republican U.S. senator Robert Dole with his wife (also a Republican politician), while alongside Jeffrey Sachs sermonized for over one and a half hours. The excessive simplicity of the jump and the self-confidence of the speaker made a bad impression on the audi-

*Władysław Grabski (1874–1938), author of the successful monetary reform of 1924.

ence. Skepticism toward the program was expressed later by ministers: Jerzy Osiatyński and Marcin Święcicki, and even Stanisław Gomułka. According to the account of a journalist in *Życie Gospodarcze*: "Only MP Jacek Kuroń, who began by saying that he knows little about economics, acknowledged without reservation that everything points in favor of Sachs's program."[26]

Kuroń was enraptured by Sachs (probably the same can be said about Geremek and Michnik) because, as K. Modzelewski put it, "he gave simple answers. This could be presented in an understandable way. Jacek could do that. . . . Back in 1981. . . Jacek Kuroń wrote that the sacrifices required to overcome the crisis will not be accepted by the people unless it is under the influence of a psychological shock. . . . Such a government was created and it adopted a liberal concept, also as a psychological shock."[27] This is reaffirmed by the dialogue that ensued between Bugaj and Kuroń, who were listening to Sachs's tirades. Kuroń recalls: "Rysiek said, 'What nonsense this guy is saying!'" And I replied: 'I don't know much about that stuff . . . but listening I know that this scheme has political value. . . . The program can be economically better or worse. But it must have political value, that is to say, you present such a program to the people, and they understand what you have said and will support it. If you obtain this support and can maintain it, you can do the strangest things.'"[28]

The only economists who from the beginning publicly backed Sachs's program were Aleksander Paszyński and Marek Dąbrowski. Dąbrowski explained his support in a similarly desperate way as Kuroń. Though he conceded that the patient may not survive this "major surgery" (the people may revolt), he asked nonetheless, "Is there any other therapy that offers better chances for survival?"[29]

An indirect polemic was waged with Sachs and Kuroń by Jan Lipiński. Declaring himself to be in favor of a transition to a market economy, he argued that this cannot be done "in conditions of such profound lack of equilibrium and such high inflation" and added: "It's as if during a fire you renovate a house or rebuild it."[30] Equally critical remarks were made by Marcin Święcicki: "This is undoubtedly an inspiring vision, presented in a persuasive way, of a radical transition, a leap into a land full of market freedom. Its total radicalism is evidenced in that it does not acknowledge any social or economic constraints. . . . This resembles prescribing an immediate draconian cure to a seriously ill patient . . . without carefully examining what the patient is suffering from. The risk of decease is therefore high."[31] Disapproval of Sachs's ideas was also expressed by the editors of *Życie Gospodarcze*, as can be seen in the article of the deputy chief editor, Karol Szwarc, under the meaningful title "Radykalnie czy na oślep" (Radically or Blindly),[32] rejecting the "jump into market" option.

5. Great Systemic Choices

When analyzing the great leap from real socialism to capitalism, we cannot overlook the historical context of this event. This was not only a period of ordinary technocratic transformation of one system of economy into another (described as the natural succession of the free market after the disintegration of the command-distributive system), but something much more important. There were also intense changes in the social structure, of which the most important was the radical shift of part of the wealth from the poor to the rich, shoving aside certain social groups and elevating others. There was shock, disappointment, and paralysis for the former, but thriving prosperity for the latter.

What is particularly disturbing is that the perpetrators of these profound changes came from the intelligentsia, from people who were sensitive to social problems, not to mention the worker-Solidarity roots. At that time, I thought people with such views made up the overwhelming majority. No doubt, there were some neoliberal neophytes here and there. But it was not they who set the tone. The anxieties of the intelligentsia have been probably best rendered by Jerzy Jedlicki. In an interview in early September 1989 for the weekly *Wprost*, objecting to the ideas of the free market extremist

Janusz Korwin-Mikke, of returning to nineteenth-century capitalism, Jedlicki wrote: "It is easy to say: we are throwing everybody into deep water, some will survive, others will drown. But how to do this—and what for? It is easy to imagine what the social consequences of this would be. In the quest for civilization's opportunities, we should not lose those social achievements that it was so hard to gain." Several days before the appointment of Mazowiecki's government, Jedlicki warned against adopting the American model, pointing out the "immense areas of social poverty and pathology" in New York, and turned to Europe for good examples: "Out of the European countries closer to us, a point of reference can be found in medium-sized countries where there is organic growth, combining economic efficiency with a sensibly organized system of social security, self-governance, avoidance of extremes. Naturally, it is hard for us to decide whether the most applicable for us would be the Swedish, Austrian, or other schemes."[1]

Yet when the American model "won," with few exceptions the social liberal intelligentsia became silent on these matters, probably in the name of the newly defined solidarity with colleagues in the government. Even those who saw the dearth of democracy had a ready excuse for it. In the words of Marek Belka, "The government of Mazowiecki was in a way 'dictatorial.' It offered a certain program for the people, which was accepted—after all, there was no place to retreat. Behind us there were only queues and vinegar on shop shelves. There was no alternative; therefore the new system was given to us, or—if you will—imposed on us. It was a dictatorship of experts."[2] This is how one of the successors of Balcerowicz sees the problem of systemic choice. And it took only fifteen years for Belka to forget that the program was carried out half a year after the liberation of food prices. Sound criticism did come, but from the outside, from Western intellectuals, including many liberal economists.

My belief is that the Big Bang (or shock therapy, as the Balcerowicz Plan was sometimes called) was not necessary. It revealed a neophyte faith that the main decision makers and their advisors had in the free market, facilitating the adoption of the standard prescription of the

International Monetary Fund, which ignored the specific circumstances of an economy emerging from real socialism. At the close of 1989, even the shock measures designed to stifle inflation had weak realistic grounds, since inflation had mostly been the effect of government decisions (sudden liberation of food prices) and was quickly falling by the end of the year. The monthly rate of inflation was 54 percent in October, 23 percent in November, and 18 percent in December. Oddly enough, the experts who suggested that Poland "leap" into the market earlier had been propagating views that had more to do with evolutionary changes, showing no sign of the radicalism that was to come.

The fate of the "leap" concept was primarily determined by the opinions of Tadeusz Mazowiecki, Waldemar Kuczyński, and Leszek Balcerowicz—the triad that was to have a decisive influence on the shape of what has been dubbed the Balcerowicz Plan. A great cushioning role for this plan was provided by Jacek Kuroń. At this point a little more needs to be said about these actors, especially for the benefit of younger readers.

THE PRIME MINISTER. When in the late summer of 1989 Tadeusz Mazowiecki was looking for an economist who would be responsible for the economy in the government, he would say that he was looking for his "own [Ludwig] Erhard." Later on, this analogy reappeared often and became especially more meaningful in 1992 when L. Balcerowicz received the Ludwig Erhard Foundation award. In simple reasoning, Mazowiecki had to sacrifice his values on the altar of the good of the country. A frank explanation was given by the conservative Aleksander Hall: "[Mazowiecki] aroused my great respect, because although his social sensitivity and enchantment with workers rather inclined him to follow the thinking of Ryszard Bugaj, he nonetheless decided on Balcerowicz's program, which was in contradiction to his sensitivity, but good for Poland."[3]

In the beginning, this was simply incomprehensible to me. But now, after many readings, I am inclined to believe that Mazowiecki, never much interested in economics and not understanding it, made a

"Columbus mistake" of direction: he was looking for a model in Bonn, but was given prescriptions from Chicago and Washington, which following brief hesitation he accepted, then attempted to rationalize. In this he was helped by the throngs of defenders of the Balcerowicz Plan and those who criticized him mercilessly. He made this mistake unaware of the consequences of his choice, and when he spoke up for a *social* market economy, he found no support from the economists closest to him. L. Balcerowicz often made ironic remarks about the adjective "social," whereas Kuczyński treated this term as a purely verbal concession. And entangling nearly every social discourse in the logic of the media made both positions look like a game of flirting with a different portion of public opinion. But even from available documents one can discern the divergence in views between the prime minister and his economists.

If one were to trust the accuracy of Kuczyński's accounts, then Mazowiecki sought and found in Leszek Balcerowicz not so much an Erhard—a creator of a social market economy—but more of a proponent of a free-market economy who would have the courage to push through radical reform.* Here is how he remembered the words of T. Mazowiecki, addressed to the future deputy prime minister and minister of finance: "I need my Ludwig Erhard. We are going to fight against inflation and put the economy on a normal, free-market foundation. Would you care to accompany me in this work?"†4 Those who speak of free-market foundations as normal usually have in mind the Anglo-Saxon economic model, known for its modest share of "welfare state" and very limited state intervention in the economy. This contradicts Kuczyński's earlier views, but fits well into his later outlook, for many years presented in the weekly *Wprost*.

---

*If Mazowiecki really did have in mind only the 1948 monetary reform of Ludwig Erhard, he would have referred instead to Władysław Grabski, the very popular architect of the successful Polish monetary reform of 1924.
†This conversation is recalled in a similar way by Leszek Balcerowicz: "The prime minister began by saying that he is looking for his Ludwig Erhard. What he had in mind was a person who, like Erhard in postwar Germany, would undertake to carry out a radical reform of the economy" (Balcerowicz, 1992, 10).

Not much is known about the views, nor about the economic intuitions of Mazowiecki. The free market does indeed appear in his speeches, but not linked with social market economy in a reflexive way. His older writings, style of thinking, the frequently manifested sensitivity of a humanist (being an admirer of the personalism of Jacques Maritain and Emmanuel Mounier), the ideological line of *Więź*, which he had created and continued to edit, the later withdrawal from the Union of Liberty Party he had headed, additionally preceded by the public denouncement of the narrow "budgetary" policy of the Union of Liberty chairman, Leszek Balcerowicz—all this shows that at the decisive moment of choice, he had (and maybe still has) a poor knowledge of Erhard's achievements, but with that name associated something more than price-monetary reform and in economic matters depended on the opinions of his economic advisor, Waldemar Kuczyński. The sensitivity of a humanist must have lost when confronted with a professional.

Obviously, Mazowiecki did not anticipate the social consequences of the Balcerowicz Plan, yet years later he would still write about them as if they came as a complete surprise to him. In an interview given to Polish journalist Teresa Torańska he said, for example:

It was hard for me to imagine that large enterprises would begin to fall. At a certain moment, in early 1990, after legislation implementing the market economy entered into force, my friend and advisor Waldemar Kuczyński said to me: "What's going on, they should be falling and they're not!" That's how it looked in the calculations of an economist. That inefficient enterprises have to fall. I got goose pimples. I knew what this could mean. . . . For me it was a great moral dilemma. After all, regaining sovereignty was possible thanks to the strikes of the big enterprises in 1980. It was they who made "Solidarity" possible. I was hoping that the start-up of the market economy would be balanced with a social policy.[5]

Even after many years, Mazowiecki does not realize that it was no economic calculation at all but the calculation of this specific economist, or rather those surrounding him. At the same time, he isolated himself from other economists who were alarming the supreme authorities that the dramatic consequences were easy to foretell and historical necessity did not predetermine them at all.

THE ECONOMIC DICTATOR. The choice of deputy prime minister for economic matters and minister of finance and other cabinet members was determined by many chance factors. For different reasons, the following professors turned down the offers. Witold Trzeciakowski did not accept the march to the free market. Cezary Józefiak, by contrast, determined his consent on the guarantee of the prime minister that he would back the painful but necessary measures leading to this market. Władysław Szymański, professor at the Warsaw School of Economics (formerly SGPiS), also refused, during talks held twice with Tadeusz Mazowiecki. Other candidates had also been approached in vain, including professors Janusz Beksiak and Witold Kieżun, both from the Warsaw School of Economics, and Janusz Gościński from the University of Warsaw. The final choice fell on Leszek Balcerowicz.

Balcerowicz had been little known to the general public. In economic circles he had earned a good name as the inspirer and head of an informal group that in 1981 drew up the most professional—though distant from radicalism—program of economic reforms. He loosely cooperated with S., mostly with the Network of Large Enterprises, but as he was busy with his research work, he did not really take part in opposition activity. He received the proposition to enter the government at a time when he was getting ready for a longer stay in England as lecturer at a university in London of lesser rank. He had never steered a large group of people and his interests were limited to pure theory, even when he wrote about reforms.

To the surprise of many, his talent and above all his character turned out to be of a high order. His career as an economic politician was based on his steadfast adherence to his principles and persistence in the execution of adopted conceptions. After only two years, he became one of the best-known, though controversial, figures in the world, respected by some, loathed by others.* One of his friends said about him: "For Leszek material goods are not important. He is a deeply ethical person. He places very high demands on himself and on others; while he was in government he could have easily arranged this or that, helped his friends by signing something or other. But he never did things like that; you could not take advantage of knowing him to arrange any gain."†6

*The following two press information titles illustrate this controversy: "Balcerowicz przed Trybunał?" (Balcerowicz before the Tribunal?) (Gazeta Wyborcza, August 9, 1991) and "Balcerowicz kandydatem do Nobla" (Balcerowicz a Candidate for the Nobel Prize) (see Krajewski, 1991). And when after two and a half years he was leaving the government posts, the authors of the biographical sketch titled "Odejście tyrana" (Departure of the Tyrant) (Eysymont et al. 1992) wrote that society accepted the opinion disseminated by his enemies, who criticized him brutally. According to them, Leszek Balcerowicz was destroying the Polish economy, being a traitor, swindler, dictator, monetarist, suppressor of the people, an enemy to peasants and small businesses. Naturally, the sketch was written by supporters of Balcerowicz. In private talks, obstinate individuals cannot resist pointing out that he obtained his apartment and car voucher when he was working for the Marxism-Leninism Institute of the Central Committee of PZPR.

†A brief explanation is due here. Balcerowicz in 1989–91 was a non-Party professional devoted to reforming the economy who was reticent with words and promises and avoided politicking. But he always had difficulties in acknowledging, even partly, the reasoning of polemicists. This was also observed by Adam Michnik, one of his most adamant admirers: "I admire him, agree with him, but at times it seems to me that he presents his reasoning in such a way as if his adversaries consisted only of idiots" (Michnik, 1993). Younger readers know a much changed politician, not only an economic one. Assuming the lead in the Union of Liberty (in which he was called MacIintosh), and particularly participation in the 1997 parliamentary election campaign, altered Balcerowicz, who took on the style typical for American politicians, dependent on the media, with a continuous smile on his face and—unfortunately—inclined to make easy promises. Nearly all of his ideas were associated with promises of improving the lot of flood victims, raising the living standard of all citizens, mass creation of new jobs and even doubling the national income within a decade. In polemics he applies the epithet of populism in an extremely instrumental and demagogic way. Most of his commentaries appearing every other week in *Wprost* were not of a high order and were often tainted with plain politicking. And so, even his colleagues more and more often speak of his "political wearing out."

With what economic views did Balcerowicz enter the government and to which views did he remain loyal? His early works stood out for their high discipline of reasoning and his propensity for defining and systematizing concepts. Toward the end of real socialism, shortly before taking office as deputy prime minister and minister of finance, he published a monograph, *Systemy gospodarcze* (Economic Systems; published by SGPiS, 1989). In a sense, this was a pioneering book in Poland, even though the manner of presenting the issues in the book was highly affected by the collapsing system.

In comparative studies, Balcerowicz showed extensive knowledge, including about the various types of capitalism. In the 1980s, he leaned more and more in the direction of its free-market version. In his book he elaborated on the various mechanisms of coordination of the economy and—more broadly than in many Western textbooks—on the problem of ownership, basing his discussion on the neoliberal theory of property rights. What is noticeable is the complete absence of an analysis of the issues concerning division of income and assets, equality and inequality, or—as they say today—distributive justice.

Of great importance for Balcerowicz's later activity as an economic politician was the character of his earlier criticism of the system of real socialism. The study "Spór o pojęcie celów społecznych" (Dispute over the Concept of Social Objectives) contains apt critical remarks about the political economy of socialism, where the frequent referral to the "general interest" was a cover-up for the interest of the authorities. The basis of his criticism was a general rejection of the very notion of "society's objectives." The latter notion, in his opinion, would make sense only "in an unreal world of abundance of goods called communism. In the real world this notion is empty."*[7]

Balcerowicz also made great efforts to compromise—like the term "social interest"—the adjective "social," employed, for example, in the model of the West German market economy. Such a standpoint was

---

*It is interesting that later, when S. supported him, he praised it as a movement that did not express self-interest and in which society's objectives were a high priority (Balcerowicz 1991).

bound to lead him to extreme individualism, a negation of the role of the state as a general social institution, with only the interest of the authorities being important. Balcerowicz does not write this outright, but his reasoning resembles a lot the well-known view of Margaret Thatcher, that there is no such thing as society (and thus it does not exist). He rejects the very notion of social justice and often simply avoids this subject. For example, interviewing him as a deputy prime minister, Adam Michnik asked: "You know better what is better for the people?" Balcerowicz replies: "Not the prime minister but the market knows best."[8] According to him, it is not the division of wealth that determines the strength of votes on the market, but the effectiveness of competition.

Such an understanding of the market leads Balcerowicz to a total repudiation of state intervention in the economy and of state ownership. Observation of various countries suggests to him that "many imperfections ascribed to the capitalist economy result from the fact that there is not enough capitalism there. There is too much state intervention, protectionism, regulation of market access, licenses, a strong position of the trade unions and political instability."[9] Efficient capitalism is a system that is a fully private market, unspoiled by state intervention.* Balcerowicz expressed very strong criticism against the welfare state, and especially its proponents. In a speech delivered to the Polish Business Council, he said: "If we look at Poland, we can see that as a result of blocking many reforms—we have much greater burdens than Sweden, Denmark, Germany or France when they had a similar per capita income as ours. . . . An expanded social state is the

---

*In this respect, Balcerowicz is like Milton Friedman, who in September 1990 advised Polish politicians to draw on models not from contemporary America, infected by socialism, but from the America of a hundred years ago. But Balcerowicz went even further. While pressing for faster privatization, he also warned not to sell cheap to foreigners. He said in an interview: "It would be a mistake . . . when a large portion of basic production means of a given country is in the hands of foreigners, this is politically unacceptable in the long run. Remember: foreigners are not going to invest in Poland to help Poland, but to help themselves" (Strzelecki,1990).

result of bad and immoral policy. Its proponents and creators have no right to display moral superiority over those who oppose them. On the contrary, they deserve moral condemnation."[10]

Balcerowicz's knowledge, of course, remained theoretical, abstract, and distant from real economic policies. This is most probably what Marek Belka, one of the later economic chiefs, had in mind when he wrote about the success of the Polish transformation: "It is a real coincidence that in 1989, at the head of the economy stood a man with an unprecedented persistence, with a gift for organizing people and—if you pardon me—little knowledge about economic and social processes. This allowed him not to see the difficulties and to press forward. He simply did not know that he was doing the impossible."[11]

THE ANESTHESIOLOGIST. The appointment of Jacek Kuroń as minister of labor was one of the most spectacular (maybe even shrewd) staff decisions of Tadeusz Mazowiecki. A legend of the democratic opposition, well known outside of Poland, co-creator of the Workers' Defense Committee (KOR), at the time one of Wałęsa's three candidates for the office of government chief, and after the ultimate election of Mazowiecki he became one of the main actors on the new political scene. He could have certainly become dangerous for the authorities if he had been outside the government. Most probably he did not become prime minister because he was perceived (particularly in conservative Church circles) as a leftist. It was not yet known that he would be ready to suspend his leftist views when the foundations of the "market economy" were being created.

For the first time, Kuroń's radically new views were manifested when he enthusiastically embraced Jeffrey Sachs's ideas. But unlike the amazingly optimistic arguments Sachs used, he explained the need for a desparate jump: "I was sure that in fact there was no other way. The people are impatient, angry and an attempt to keep up things as they are will lead to a total breakdown. A leap should be made and we are not prepared for it. I knew that this is suicide, and also that I conned them into this government. . . . I didn't think that I would be minister for longer than two or three months." And further on: "Since no one succeeds with a planned economy and manual steering ... then all the more is it impossible to implement the idea that it can be further steered, taking on additionally the burden of its planned transformation into a free-market economy."[12]

Kuroń had three incarnations, so to speak. As minister of labor he tried to draw up an ambitious social policy program. But the sudden and unexpected deep breakdown of the economy dispersed any hopes for such schemes, and the ministry he was managing could only act as a fireman putting out fires. However, Kuroń seemed not to understand this and said that the people had rejected his good proposals. As a social activist he initiated and propagated the development of self-help social organizations. The free meals for the homeless and the poor initiated by him (Kuroń's soups called *kuroniówka*) were supposed to encourage the formation of self-help and charity organizations. He himself established and partly financed the SOS Foundation. And finally, as the anesthesiologist,* he commented on current events in weekly television chats, which were greatly popular among viewers. These chats were filled with compassion for people who were suffering because of the shock therapy. In the beginning, a large portion of viewers believed in the reasoning that "for things to get better in the future, they now have to suffer and that generally speaking . . . there could be no other policy."[13] But in the second half of 1990, Kuroń became the target of harsh attacks. With stark sincerity he recalls how during his visits to factories he sensed the lack of acceptance among the workers: "They all believed that Wałęsa will come soon and make everything all right. . . . None of these people, apart from school teenagers, understood a market economy, capitalism. They only explained to me that . . . if I paid them more, everything would be all right."[14] If, however, one agrees with the criticism formulated by the advocates of the theory of Michał Kalecki (e.g. Kazimierz Łaski and Amit Bhaduri) that the drastic fall of output was mainly caused by the excessively radical reduction of consumer demand, then these ordinary

---

*This is how I referred to him during one of the conferences, and Kuroń readily accepted it.

people were closer to the truth than Balcerowicz and Kuroń. These wage demands of the individual interest groups could not only reduce the discomforts of the workers but also mitigate the drop in output.

Here I must add that of the "four actors," only Kuroń had the guts to reassess his views. He not only returned to his leftist beliefs (in 1993), he also took on part of the blame for the defects of the transformation: "The defeat of 'Solidarity' took place because the state authorities chosen from within it, instead of taking the lead in a mass reconstruction movement, acted above the people. Above their heads a statist-technocratic program was pushed through, which shoved the majority into a movement of leftist claims, being more radical the greater the costs of the fall of communism."[15] He was convinced that in the years 1989–93 there occurred a "destruction of the 'Solidarity' movement by the government and the administration."[16] Later, he would often say that the great loss of the workers, the gravediggers of the old system, gave him sleepless nights.

Mazowiecki—Sachs—Beksiak

We know from Kuczyński that Mazowiecki had an aversion to the domineering Jeffrey Sachs:

> He did not trust a man who did not know Poland, its reality, and yet had such pronounced views. But he had in mind not so much the advertising campaign around the "shock" and Sachs, as the actions originating from the OKP (Citizens' Parliamentary Caucus). . . . The group of Polish economists that had been working for some time with Sachs was formed into the Economic Rescue Team toward the end of August. This team, headed by Janusz Beksiak, was entrusted by the OKP Presidium . . . with the preparation of the concept of the program of stabilization and systemic transformations. . . . He was afraid of any hasty economic actions, and in this case a ready-made letter to the Monetary Fund's chief was shoved in front of him. This letter was supposed to be sent on behalf of the prime minister by the head of the

Economic Rescue Team and was to be taken [to Washington] by Sachs and Lipton. Mazowiecki did not yield to these pressures.[17]

But above all, Mazowiecki did not yield to Sachs and the OKP when he refused to allow Kuroń to be imposed on him as deputy prime minister and probably Beksiak as minister of finance, which was what Sachs, according to Kuczyński, wanted.* On the commission of the OKP head, Bronisław Geremek, Beksiak's group prepared and published a report that proposed total withdrawal of the state from the economy; a market economy was to come into being spontaneously. There were to be no price regulations and no building of a new system by the state (constructionism). This merely confirmed the extreme, uncompromising laissez-faire policy disclosed by Beksiak at the Round Table. At any rate, the signatures under the report, of Jan Winiecki and Stefan Kurowski (who later entirely changed his views), spoke for themselves.

Mazowiecki could thus think that he had gotten rid of or neutralized the extreme radicals. Also, what happened afterward—the months of intensive work and the involvement of many experts of the IMF and the World Bank—could for an economic layperson create the impression of the correct turn in the direction of professionalism and accountability. There is also evidence that the differences of opinion, the dissonance between the team of Mazowiecki, Balcerowicz, Kuczyński and the OKP, were even deeper than Kuczyński portrayed. The following is what I wrote down from my conversation with Geremek, held on his initiative on October 3, 1989:

> [Geremek] proposed to draw up an alternative economic program, [he said] that everyone's gone crazy, even Kuroń is totally wrapped up in the market-privatization role of the government. That this will break

---

*Dear Reader, can you believe this? To a newly elected prime minister of a European country that has just regained its sovereignty comes a self-appointed advisor and tells him whom to pick for the two highest government offices. And he doesn't even get kicked out the door!

down fast. "And then emptiness. Who after Mazowiecki? Ślisz?" The Church is leading to the division of the OKP, separating the peasants from Solidarity. It's already a strong lobby. Wałęsa at the head of the government of National Salvation? In my opinion—W[ałęsa] is running in a blind alley—[according to Geremek] he's frustrated, abandoned, threatened, hence the unwise statements. And maybe there is no other way out. Bugaj ready for criticism, but doesn't want to present a program. A request to me, that maybe together with Brus. I said I was ready to offer critical comments on the programs of Balcerowicz and Beksiak's team, and in further perspective we can work with R[yszard] B[ugaj] on a program when the current team collapses.

The other matter I was summoned for was a proposition of two alternative high posts. I turned down the state posts, but declared readiness to take part in councils (e.g. the National Property Fund) or even NIK (Supreme Audit Office). Motivation: "not the authority type," I wouldn't fit. I see myself writing, teaching, maybe consulting.

I cite these notes because they show that only three weeks after the appointment of the government of T. Mazowiecki the OKP chairman assessed the condition of this cabinet as very weak. It is harder to guess why Geremek would need a program prepared by economists with definitely leftist views. Especially since earlier he had commissioned and received a program brochure from Beksiak's team, whose views were more to the right than those of Balcerowicz.*

A similar entry, showing great reserve toward Mazowiecki's team, can be found in Mieczysław Rakowski's *Dziennik Polityczny* (Political

---

*This was to be our last technical talk about politics. A description of Geremek as one of the architects of the Polish transformation is hard for me. We were too closely associated before 1989 for me to be able to objectively evaluate his later role. Apart from social contacts, we went on work trips together (with numerous discussions) at his summer house in Obory (house of ZLP—Polish Writers' Union), jointly participated in the program committee of TKN (Society for Educational Courses), and worked together in the group of experts advising the strikers in the Gdańsk Shipyard, then in S. The political separation of our paths was not without pain for me. Therefore I prefer to resort to the opinion of

Diary). When Michnik visited him (September 28), Rakowski noted: "Michnik thinks that the government has no concrete program, speaks in a language that is incomprehensible for the ordinary folk standing in queues and if in the next four months it does not do something concrete for the people, it will quickly lose the popularity that no other government has ever had before." And further on: "I told him about the plans to establish a Political Council. And Michnik says, lowering his voice: 'Why should you push yourself into this s—? You want to be held accountable for what the government does? If I were you I would be very careful.'"[18]

Both statements are striking in their distant attitude to the government, naturally concealed before public opinion, awaiting its downfall rather than looking for ways to strengthen it.

More and More Austerity

Balcerowicz became minister of finance and head of the Economic Committee of the Council of Ministers (KERM) as deputy prime minister. Kuczyński writes that Mazowiecki "at first wrinkled his nose" at

---

Geremek's close friend, one of the leading French historians, Jacques Le Goff: "When I talk with Polish friends, I find more convincing the opinions of Prof. Karol Modzelewski than what Prof. Geremek says. I believe that the Balcerowicz Plan was dangerous. It was too brutal. It caused not only injustice and discontent. I think that it was also erroneous economically. . . . A liberal economy and a protective state should not be brutally juxtaposed against each other. Today even such countries as Great Britain are abandoning the doctrine of pure liberalism" (Le Goff, 1994). Nine years later, to the question of what an intellectual should avoid, Le Goff replies: "I don't think, for example, that he could be a politician. Having many important things to say in the battle for political values, he should nevertheless not enter the area of politics. I feel, for example, that my friend Bronisław Geremek, who has played an exceptionally important role in Polish history since 1958 and—one can say honestly—a very positive role, did not come out victorious from this metamorphosis into a man of politics. This 'experiment' was plainly not successful for him" (Le Goff, 2003). On the other hand, it is rather obvious why Secretary of State Madeleine Albright termed Geremek "a diamond of Polish policy."

the other post. He also strongly emphasized the consultative and not the decision-making character of KERM, fearing that it would become a government within a government. Apart from immediate budgetary matters, the first major move was formulating the government position in regard to requesting help from the IMF. The draft was drawn up by Stanisław Gomułka, and Balcerowicz presented it at the end of September in Washington, at the annual session of the IMF. Consequently, the IMF's delegation came to Warsaw in mid-October. But before it appeared, on October 12 the Ministry of Finance published "Założenia i kierunki polityki gospodarczej" (Guidelines and Directions of Economic Policy) as a brochure supplement to the newspaper *Rzeczpospolita*. The basic theses were:

> The Polish economy requires essential systemic changes. Their goal is to build a market system similar to the one existing in the highly developed countries. This has to take place quickly, by means of radical measures, in order to shorten as much as possible the interim period so arduous for the people. This path has been chosen also following the bad experiences of the superficial reforms in the 1990s. . . . No ad hoc measures can change the situation. *Only a bold turn suited to the historical challenge Poland is facing will enable it to come out of the civilizational collapse, to build an order that meets the social expectations."* (emphasis added)

The catalogue of basic systemic changes now comprised:

- Ownership transformations bringing the ownership structure closer to the one existing in the highly developed countries;

- Radical increase of independence of state enterprises;

- Full implementation of the market mechanism, and in particular, freedom in setting prices, with elimination of rationing and compulsory intermediation;

- Creation of conditions for domestic competition through an anti- *[handwritten: Corporate raiding unforeseen?]* monopoly policy and complete freedom to create new enterprises;

- Opening up the economy to the world through the introduction of zloty convertibility;

- Development of a capital market;

- Creation of a labor market.

It turned out that this short text was the only comprehensive public presentation of the program that later would be called the Balcerowicz Plan.

This meant a departure from the Round Table Agreements, but not necessarily interruption of continuity with the intentions and actions of the previous administration. It is worthwhile to focus on this program a little more, since many myths have developed around it. On the one hand, S. activists accentuated the break with the economic policies of the previous authorities, and on the other, many authors pointed out the similarity of the program (or at least this version of it) with the earlier one, presented by the former government to the IMF for negotiation. Here is how Prof. Karol Lutkowski summarized the IMF program:

- Transformation of state enterprises into companies of the State Treasury;

- Sale to private hands or lease of small establishments, administrative liquidation of many material- and energy-consuming enterprises;

- Freezing subsidies to prices, introducing payment for food in hospitals;

- New taxes;

- A uniform exchange rate and system.[19]

Projections included gradually declining inflation (in 1992 it was still 23 percent) and only a 1.2 percent drop of national income generated in 1990 and an insignificant (3 percent in 1990) drop in consumption.[20] To this we can add at least two important proposals. From January 1, 1990, there was to be a complete repeal of official prices and the transformation of State Treasury companies into semi-private companies. Twenty percent of shares were for a "workers' package"; another 20 percent were to remain in Bank Gospodarstwa Krajowego (BGK); and the remaining 60 percent were to be turned over to new investment banks, constituting joint property of state and local government authorities. Both these shares and shares owned by BGK could be traded freely.

This would be commencement on a large scale of processes leading to a market economy and privatization. The idea was that with such ambitious economic transformations, intentionally underestimated indicators of national income and consumption decline would probably have to be adopted. The discrepancy between the planned and actual results of the program would doubtless be great. And so, though this danger was not seen in these indicators, Lutkowski legitimately wrote that "our negotiators without much thought 'bought' the traditional philosophy of the fund with its emphasis on the need for tightening belts, drastic price adjustments, and cuts in social spending."[21]

In general, there is a striking similarity between the concepts of the old and new administration, which simply resulted from the adoption of the general schemes proposed by the IMF. As Piotr Aleksandrowicz wrote: "Each adjustment program drawn up under the aegis of the fund has to essentially contain the same elements and similar solutions."[22] Even this program was initially accepted only in regard to its direction, whereas the IMF continued to report numerous objections, which no doubt meant that the final version would have been even more severe.

Such a process of increasing austerity was to take place in the Balcerowicz Plan. Kuczyński notes that after barely two days of negotiations with the IMF experts (October 27–28), it was still a "very mild version of stabilization. . . . Basically it was not a shock operation concept. In December 1990 the retail prices were to be, according to this version, 572 percent higher than in December 1989, whereas in the final version of the program, that is, in the letter of intent to the IMF, this value was lowered to 95 percent. This shows how much the stabilization program was made more severe in the course of work, because it must have been known that a more radical stifling of inflation required drainage of a much greater quantity of money."[23] May we add that this version included an 8 percent drop in real wages and a 5 percent drop in output?

Kuczyński leaves no doubt that the final implementation of a harsher plan was forced by the IMF: "We were told this clearly many times, publicly and privately, that significant assistance from the West would be possible only after we came to terms with the International Monetary Fund."[24]

Yet the new Polish decision makers agreed to such developments all too easily. Kuczyński stresses that there was a "climate of goodwill" during the negotiations, and the chief of the IMF experts, Michael Bruno (1992), was even surprised by this account, recalling his experience of hard negotiations in other countries. He was visibly astonished that at a certain point the Polish government unanimously chose the harshest variant of those presented by the IMF. Such was the decision of the shock advocates, in their belief that the more radical the program the better it would serve to quickly install the new system.

There was one exception among the Polish negotiators: a high-class budgetary expert who had an excellent understanding of the interrelations of various indicators, Deputy Minister of Finance Wojciech Misiąg. He must have resisted strongly, since one of the IMF's directors (Massimo Russo) was to have asked, irritated, who's the boss here—Misiąg or Balcerowicz? Maybe he was the only one who tried to act in accordance with the suggestion of Prof. Karol Lutkowski and strongly emphasize in talks the "unprecedented character of the changes implemented by Poland," to which the "arch-classical" version of the prescription proposed by the IMF does not fit.

For Lutkowski it was clear that the transformation required a milder program, whereas the leading team steering the economy was doing the opposite. The great change was to justify the particularly harsh and acute character of this prescription.

The numbers in Balcerowicz's plan were sharpened not only in negotiations with the IMF. Kuczyński writes that on December 12, at a meeting of KERM, the rate of indexation for January was still adopted at 0.7–0.8. A couple of days later it was drastically reduced. Let us look at how such a crucial decision for the life of millions of people emerged. Balcerowicz misleadingly stated[25] that he himself arbitrarily decided to lower indexation to 0.3 for January and 0.2 for the following months, risking—as he confessed—"a political storm." However, the facts behind the scenes look different. It was the "invention" of Sachs, Lipton, and Andy Berg, who in a letter to Balcerowicz (December 11, 1989) suggested its drastic reduction. The above-mentioned American trio based their proposal on the following reasoning: "Many people have commented to us that it is 'politically impossible' to give a smaller wage indexation than 0.5 in January. We remain convinced that a tougher policy can be carried out and is likely to be more effective for several straightforward reasons." Shall we pass over these reasons, then? It is enough to cite the glaringly unrealistic numbers projected by them for January 1990. In the table they assume price inflation at 40 percent, wage inflation at 8 percent, and the real wage level compared to January 1989 (?!) at 93 percent. Life itself drastically overturned these estimates, if only because prices rose in that month not by 45 percent, as projected by the government, but by nearly 80 percent. Stanisław Gomułka writes: "Nominal wages did not rise, while prices skyrocketed, so that we had a drop in real wages of about 50 percent in January alone. Later this drop became less acute and over the year this was by about 30 percent."[26]

The drastic fall of wages was noticed by Sachs and Lipton (letter to Balcerowicz and Kawalec, January 31, 1990), but with all their might they opposed wage increases, warning that this was what had led to a "collapse of stabilization programs from Mexico to Argentina." This "Keynesian Rescue" would supposedly lead to several misfortunes all at once, such as a balance-of-payment crisis and unemployment. "Poland suffers from labor shortage, not labor surplus, so there is little chance that an expansion of demand would lead to the absorption of unutilized resources. . . . In fact, a rise in real wages would squeeze enterprises, and probably lead to more, not less, unemployment." If we remember that at the end of 1989 there was already no empty money in the market (it was "eaten up" by inflation combined with slowed-down wage growth), then we can see the entire absurdity of this "innovation" of Sachs-Lipton-Berg-Balcerowicz. In January 1990, industrial output declined by more than 30 percent, which augured a radical reduction of demand of the wage earners.

If the economy were subordinated to the rigors of the commercial code, the decision makers who were responsible for such a dramatic deterioration of living conditions would be held liable for this. But the economy is steered by politicians (even if they do have economics professor titles) who are not bound by these rigors.

There was one other outcome of the growing austerity of the program, effected at the last minute and without any simulation of the consequences. It was a painful defeat of the professional economist Wojciech Misiąg, who had prepared the budget with diametrically different starting values. Following such radical changes, the budget was not recalculated again, as there was no time for this. The magic date of January first was adopted as the irreversible date for implementing the plan. And this was yet another example of the lack of professionalism or a proper attitude to the procedures of a civilized authority.

On December nineteenth [Balcerowicz] turned to the prime minister with the request to express consent, almost right on the spot and without any discussion at a session of the Council of Ministers, to have the letter of intent signed by Baka and Balcerowicz. He delivered a hastily and very carelessly prepared Polish translation of it, and on top of that with dotted places where there were supposed to be numbers because they were still determining something or other at the last minute. There was no supplement added to the letter either with the implementation criteria, in other words the obligations of the Polish authorities to the IMF, the execution of which was to determine whether assistance would be provided. "The reply was firm. There is no way of consenting to the signing of this document until the Council of Ministers becomes acquainted with its full and final version that can be read in Polish."*[27]

Pro Domo Sua

When describing Balcerowicz's group, Kuroń pointed out its similarity to Mazowiecki's group. Both liked to work in a close circle in which they had full trust of the members. This made it possible to survive the "dramatic months," when Balcerowicz was held responsible for all misfortunes. But—continues Kuroń—"being in an ivory tower made Balcerowicz immune to the feedback signals that the economy was sending to its reformers."[28] This apt remark concerned not only signals coming from the economy, but also—in the course of the formation of the program—from economists. These groups, and especially Balcerowicz's group, did not react to the avalanche of warning publications that appeared in autumn 1989, and even to personally delivered reports and analyses.

Let me describe briefly my own experience. Not because I consider the document I delivered to various authority organs to be of special importance, but because I know this case best and I was deeply affected by it.

In mid-December 1989, I belonged to those economists who were deeply worried about the shock therapy that was being prepared. One of the things I did was to deliver personally to the registry offices of the

---

*Władysław Baka (then head of the National Bank of Poland) discloses that at government meetings doubts about the program were raised mainly or solely by the prime minister, Tadeusz Mazowiecki (Baka, 2007: 286, 287). He also writes that during his stay in Warsaw, the president of the World Bank, "turning mainly to . . . the prime minister, strongly accentuated social issues, which came as a big surprise to many. He spoke particularly about the need for social security and measures to protect against excessive unemployment" (295).

prime minister (Mazowiecki), the minister of finance (Balcerowicz), and the head of the OKP (Geremek), a fifteen-page text titled "Uwagi do programu dostowawczego" (Remarks on the Adjustment Program), along with an even more extensive appendix. I sent this to Geremek along with a personal letter. Not without significance was that the addressees were my close friends or colleagues. Together with Prime Minister Mazowiecki, Geremek, and Chief of Cabinet Kuczyński, we had been advisors to the strikers in the Gdańsk Shipyard. The great tension accompanying those negotiations created, or so it seemed at the time, virtually bonds of blood. Maybe it was also significant that it was I who talked Mazowiecki and Geremek into this great adventure. This could have been one of the reasons why Geremek as head of the OKP had proposed to me two ministerial posts to choose from over two months earlier. With Mazowiecki I shared something that could be called a quasi-family bond, and Kuczyński not so long ago used to discuss with me important government candidacies. All of us were associated by the activity in the semi-legal teaching of the "Flying University." Balcerowicz also attended my semi-official seminar, and I took part in his seminar at SGPiS, today the Warsaw School of Economics. At his request, I commented on the typescript of his book on economic systems, mentioned earlier. A copy of the "Remarks" also went to the head of the Central Planning Office, Jerzy Osiatyński—another friend with whom I had worked more than a decade at the institute's unit of edition of the works of Oskar Lange and Michał Kalecki in PAN.

The "Remarks" were written by two well-known economists, Wiktor Herer and Władysław Sadowski, but following joint reflection and discussion were signed by me as well. This was Herer's idea, who felt that my name and acquaintances would make it easier for the analysis to reach the authorities.

Herer and Sadowski were the authors of the just-published book *Zderzenia z barierami rozwoju* (Collision with Growth Barriers; 1989) and many press publications dealing with current issues. The authors of the "Remarks" deliberately omitted directly systemic issues, focusing on the "prerequisites" of the adjustment program of the IMF, and their theses were not formulated arbitrarily but in the form of questions. There is much to indicate that our analysis was totally ignored by everyone, maybe apart from Osiatyński, who I think talked on this subject with Herer. In regard to the direct reactions of the remaining persons, only Geremek thanked me on the stairs of the św. Zbawiciela Church, during the sad occasion of the funeral of a mutual friend.

Did our "Remarks" deserve to be ignored? Here are four issues we raised, in my opinion of key significance:

1. We asked: "Are the harsh and very numerous drainage means proposed by the stabilization program necessary?" We felt otherwise, proving that "the considerable inflationary overhang of money seeking goods and destroying the market" was already eliminated.* In this respect, the situation was essentially different than in the previous crisis of 1981; the cash resources (cash plus savings in banks) were in the ratio to expenditures of the population less than half of those in 1981, and their real value was only one-third.

2. In regard to the drainage planned in the program—sixfold increase of coal prices and electricity respectively, lowering the zloty exchange rate, thirteen-fold increase of depreciation write-offs, increase in rent and interest rate—the authors of the "Remarks" wrote: "simultaneous application of all undertakings implemented within a fortnight or so has to cause a very high and sudden, shocking growth of prices . . . the estimated 46 percent price growth will significantly differ from reality. . . . Therefore we would propose to realistically assess the price growth in 1990 . . . this growth has to be very high." And we know that it turned out to be nearly twice as high.

The "Remarks" were submitted on December 15. Their authors could not know that a few days earlier, the program had been severely tightened in two points: the inflation planned for the entire year 1990

---

*Branko Milanovic (1992), staff member of the World Bank, reaffirmed this, but there was no further discussion.

was lowered from 140 to 95 percent. This was done already after the program and budget had been accepted by the government, in the course of writing the letter of intent to the IMF. We also knew nothing about the new, drastically reduced indexation rate. That is why we were more afraid of wage claims that would destroy the program than wage drops or a violent decline in living standards.

3. We also posed the question whether the planned reduction of budgetary spending would lead to a balancing of the economy. "Is it not that in this matter mistakes are being made by the experts of the International Monetary Fund, who transfer directly to Poland, in a dogmatic way, certain methods applied in poorly developed countries, where private enterprise dominates in the economy?"

4. Another key issue was the problem of the "artificial creation of unemployment." Describing the current situation as a state of suspension (no market, no plan), our analysis pointed out that "profitable enterprises may be very inefficient for the economy, and efficient enterprises for various reasons may be very unprofitable or become unprofitable as a result of the multiplier effect of disturbances in cooperation, caused by negligence in manufacturing certain products." With a badly functioning banking system and mutual debts, the enterprises that should be shut down cannot be pinpointed quickly. Haste can bring great harm: "One of the factors that should keep in check any haste in liquidation actions should be . . . resistance against the creation of unemployment. All things indicate that with a rational policy there will be no unemployment within the next few years. In too many areas there is a shortage of work force that can be hired effectively in the production and non-production sphere. Therefore measures that can create unemployment in an artificial way appear to be unreasonable." We have pointed out the danger of repeating mistakes that were made in 1981 when in the fear of unemployment "the process of massive premature layoffs for retirement was started and massive transfers were made to disability pensions, which brought irreparable losses to the economy."

The "Remarks" aptly anticipated what happened in the years that followed: "For many people, the status of unemployed will turn out to be convenient (free health care, family allowances, benefits) with simultaneous employment . . . in the gray zone. Currently in Poland the possibilities of such work are immense."

And so, the two experts (I was more of a messenger than a co-author) did not even have to refer to the experience of the Chinese or Vietnamese transformations to arrive at the conclusion that growth of employment can be reconciled with the transition to a market-type economy. It sufficed that earlier they analyzed the actual barriers to growth of the Polish economy, at the same time seeing many undeveloped areas (frequent shortage of goods, rickety services).

The "Remarks" ended with the warning "not to program repair of everything at once in a year . . . especially in the face of such difficult and unusually painful matters as implementation of work-free Saturdays in mining and shutting down enterprises that are harmful for the environment. In presenting our analysis, we wanted to caution against aiming toward the immediate creation of systems that are very cohesive and logical inside, but that can be carried out only on paper." The described measures, aiming toward a cohesive system, can create a situation where "we will receive billions of dollars for stabilization and economic growth, but at the same time we will lose billions as a result of the efforts to attain ideal solutions."*

When looking at the "Remarks" years later, and familiar with the way decisions were made, I conclude that the analysis shows our great naïveté. Our effort showed faith in the collective enlightened ruler who hears the signals pouring in from the concerned surroundings. But alas, the authorities—all authorities—tend to shut themselves off from the outside, unless through the pressure of large social groups they are forced to listen and to take up dialogue.

---

*In 1994 Jacek Rostowski was interviewed for Zycie Gospodarcze under the title "Chcieliśmy uniknąć powtórki z 1981 r." (We Wanted to Avoid a Repetition of 1981) (Rostowski, 1994). Paradoxically, from a purely economic point of view, the mistakes known from 1981 were repeated, but on a much greater scale.

The Parliamentary Dash

In late December 1989, the Sejm, in which parties and factions of the old system prevailed, nearly unanimously passed the legislation put forward by the government, allowing for the program to be implemented. For the first package, tabled in early December, the government turned to the Sejm for express examination of sixteen bills, nine by the end of the year.

And so, though the proposition submitted by Lech Wałęsa for endowing the government with extraordinary powers was rejected (even with certain distaste), both the government and parliament acted as in an extraordinary situation. The Sejm appointed the Extraordinary Committee expressly and this inhuman pace was even defended by Aleksander Małachowski, who was otherwise critical of the government's measures. He said: "No normal government or Sejm should consent to such acceleration. But this is not a normal government. It has the great task of leading the country out from collapse and it must be helped in this."[29]

The decisive part of the package came into force on January 1, 1990. The form of presentation of the program and the haste in its ratification made it impossible for public opinion to absorb its significant part, and especially the great leap of the operation. The final version was not and in these circumstances could not have been discussed publicly, in the manner of decisions of great historical significance.

However, even in this lightning-speed debate there were no signs of joy either in the Sejm or among the people, which contradicts the frequent interpretation that the acceptance of the excessively radical program was the result of a euphoric mood that enveloped everybody following the unexpected electoral victory of S. Jacek Moskwa wrote in *Rzeczpospolita*: "The mood is oscillating between confidence in the government of Tadeusz Mazowiecki and the rising anxiety over what the coming weeks will bring. Public discussion may deepen these moods." A parliamentarian of the Democratic Alliance, Tadeusz Bień, cautioned that "the people are all worked up, they don't know what to expect. There is a mood of economic and existential threat." As many as seventy-nine parliamentarians asked questions and expressed doubts. Answers were given, apart from Balcerowicz, by as many as thirteen members of the government. According to the journalist, the parliamentarians expressed apprehensions "whether the government program—as a result of renouncing all state intervention—has not directed its spear against the working people, being geared at acquiring gains for those who are well supplied with capital."*

In light of these facts, one has the impression that parliamentarians, despite the many reservations, preferred to believe that we were entering—as the main program animator assured—an era of "a life of success, instead of pretended success" and voted *en masse* for the presented plan. Many years later, the then-Sejm speaker Aleksander Małachowski would express this in a concise way:

> We were somewhat like sheep led for slaughter and easily gave in to the promises of the politicians, who had the decisive voice in the practical implementation of harmful schemes. I remember how easily, still in the Contract Sejm, we agreed to the shock therapy of Balcerowicz. . . . The only thing we could bring ourselves to do was the statement written by Ryszard Bugaj, setting for the government certain conditions and requirements concerning this therapy. . . . Balcerowicz . . . and his mentor, Professor Sachs, plainly tricked us, parliamentarians without experience.[30]

It was a mere formality to notify the trade unions. And there is much to indicate that the chairman of NSZZ "Solidarity," Lech Wałęsa, had accepted the plan anyway before the final version was ready. Advantage was simply taken of the immense trust that the people had in the first non-communist government. There could be

*The polls also continuously showed respondents were skeptical. Asked whether they thought that as a result of the June election perceptible changes would still take place in Poland in that year, only 36.1 percent had hopes for improvement. Changes for the better were not expected by 33.5 percent, and 15.1 percent feared changes for the worse, over 15 percent had no opinion (Domarańczyk, 1990).

no serious debate, because without a general document presenting a synthesis of the systemic contents of eleven laws and the simultaneously ratified budget, such a discussion was not possible. The parliamentarians acted under the pressure of a race with time, imposed on them by the executive authorities. After many years, Aleksander Małachowski said: "I would not be surprised if the time came for a reckoning of us, deputies of the Contract Sejm, for the reckless consent given for Balcerowicz's shock therapy, being in effect a huge attack on human rights to a minimum subsistence, an attack on the dignity of life of millions of people."[31]

6. The Balcerowicz Plan in Practice

"When in the first half of February Franciszek Kubiczek, at that time head of GUS (Central Statistical Office), announced that in January industrial output had dropped by more than 30 percent, this came as an unbelievable shock and some even said that this man from the *nomenklatura* must be putting us on. He wasn't."[1] Kuczyński attributed this to "a certain numbness to the negative effect of the program."[2] Yet he should have noticed—at least after obtaining the data concerning price rises—that this drop was in proportion to the planned scale of reducing the purchasing power of wage earners.

In 1990 the drop in industrial output turned out to be five times greater than assumed and the trend continued in the year that followed as well, though on a smaller scale. This was alarming, especially since some of the authors of the plan had declared that in 1991 the GDP would rise slightly. For example, Stanisław Gomułka predicted that there would be a 10 to 20 percent rise in national income in 1991–92.[3]

Other existing important indicators differed on the same scale—by 500 to 600 percent—from those that had been predicted. The inflation rate was supposed to fall to a one-digit value at the close of 1990, but this did not happen until the late 1990s. The main cause of the drastic deterioration of living standards was a nearly five times faster price growth than had been assumed, coupled with an unusually drastic wage indexation coefficient. The tax on wage growth (called the *popiwek*) reached 500 percent of the indexation coefficient. Unemployment was to be transitional and limited to 400,000 persons. Meanwhile, in the first year it rose from nearly zero to over one million, in the second year to over two million, in the third year it drew close to three million.* The national income, instead of the predicted 3.5 percent, fell by well over 11 percent in one year, and within two years the drop was more than 18 percent. According to GUS (Central Statistical Office) data, private farmers' incomes fell by more than half, with even worse estimates being given.

And so these were not merely differences within the range of a dozen or even several dozen percent, but counted in multiples. It would be hard not to blame the engineers of this plan for their exceptional bravado fed on lack of knowledge. These discrepancies indeed illustrate the then popular saying that this was "jumping into a swimming pool without checking whether it has water." Grzegorz Kołodko called them "overshooting," but even this term seems too mild. In the past, no other plan of communist Poland's planners had ever been implemented with such grossly missed targets. The first plan in Poland after the Second World War was the Three-Year Plan of Reconstruction and Development, drawn up under the direction of an immigrant from the West, Czesław Bobrowski, and carried out to the highest degree. Bobrowski knew very well that one does not plan everything at once, being familiar with the French saying that if you embrace too much, you get nothing. "One can say that the scarcity of information was cushioned by deliberate restraint in operating with figures related to the decisions."[4] This restraint was what Balcerowicz's team lacked. But even the

---

*Whereas Gomułka and Rostowski predicted 20 percent unemployment, the latter also expressed many optimistic and reassuring opinions. Baka, in turn, reveals that Jeffrey Sachs assessed the social consequences of the prepared shock in an unusually optimistic way. In November 1989 he predicted a wage decline only for the first half of 1990 and by not more than 10 percent, and assessed the scale of unemployment at "less than two hundred thousand persons" (Baka, 2007: 275).

Table 6.1: Projected and Real Growth of GDP and Rate
of Unemployment

	1990	1991	1992	1993	1994	1995	1996	1997	1998	1999	2000
Projected GDP Growth Rate	–15.1	4.7	8.7	7.9	7.5	8.8	6.8	6.8	6.8	6.7	6.7
When Confronted with Real GDP Growth	–11.8	–7.0	2.6	3.8	5.2	7.0	6.1	6.8	4.8	4.1	4.1
Projected Unemployment Rate	25.3	25.4	22.6	20.4	18.1	15.8	15.9	15.9	15.9	16.0	16.0
When Confronted w/ Actually Registered Unemployment Rate	6.5	12.2	14.3	16.4	16.0	14.9	13.2	10.3	10.4	13.1	15.0

Source: *Polish Statistical Yearbook*. Data in first and third row from Gomułka (1990).

bold Six-Year Plan (to a large extent imposed by Stalin) would come out
victorious in a comparison with the Balcerowicz Plan. Both the three-
and the six-year plan were accompanied by profound systemic changes,
yet they produced a wave of growth.

But can this "overshooting" be treated seriously? Were the indicators not underestimated on purpose, so that the impact of the therapy
would be easier to swallow by parliament and public opinion? Since
May 1990 there existed a document, prepared by the Department of
Economic Analyses of the Ministry of Finance, containing a projection that was different from the data included in the government program. Stanisław Gomułka refers to this document in an article[5] titled
"Stabilizacja i wzrost" (Stabilization and Growth). In the table (Table
6.1) "Pierwotne czynniki produkcji i wzrost DN Polski w latach
1990–2000" (*Primary Factors of Production and Growth of Poland's
GDP in the Years 1990–2000*), analysts foresaw percentage values for
their respective years.

The numbers referring to unemployment are overestimated for the
first several years, as they include both open as well as hidden unemployment (estimated at about 10 percent). However, the commentary
of Gomułka, probably one of the authors of this forecast, makes it clear

that for 1990 a more than 25 percent unemployment rate (including hidden unemployment) was foreseen, and the current century was to open with 16 percent, not including hidden unemployment. Gomułka wrote: "If hidden unemployment disappeared completely in the second half of the 1990s, then open unemployment—in the assumed path of growth—will account for 16 percent of the labor resources. In other words, this path is tailored so as not to encounter open unemployment or the barrier of lack of workforce, or to lead to glaringly excessive unemployment."[6] For Gomułka, then, and probably for the planners from the Ministry of Finance, 16 percent unemployment would not be glaringly high. And all this was to take place with a continuously high, at first 8 percent, then nearly 7 percent national income growth rate! Gomułka boldly referred to the example of Margaret Thatcher, but the numbers in this table deserve to be called the ultimate in Thatcherism. Even the Iron Lady would not have dared to plan such dramatically high waste of labor for entire decades.

In terms of systemic changes, from early 1990 several other important measures were taken. Customs barriers were reduced so much that the popular saying was that Poland became the most laissez-faire (free-market) country in the world, just after Hong Kong. Foreign competition produced a two-way effect: stronger firms were forced to restructure while weaker ones collapsed. But there was also increased unemployment with the influx of cheap goods, brought into the country without customs duties or tax burdens, and most often without rent being paid for business premises. The symbolic customs duties and the inefficient tax administration, the unwillingness or inability to exact taxes, as well as the fascination with "foreign" products, created a true El Dorado for a totally unfettered private sector.

Small privatization, that is, the sale (or lease) of state pharmacies, shops, or small manufacturing enterprises, was also carried out very quickly. As a result of both of these changes, within a short time the number of registered private firms rose from over 800,000 to over one and a half million. Bazaar trading and smuggling in particular flourished, destroying the network of cooperative and state shops and most small businesses. Henryk Domański[7] writes that among

[handwritten margin note: Total sacrifice of domestic production]

Table 6.2: Population Incomes in 1989 and 1993

	1989	1993
Total Population Incomes	100.0	100.0
IN THIS:		
Wages	46.2	29.9
Cash Social Transfers	15.7	20.5
Incomes from Work of Individual Farmers	13.5	5.1
Incomes from Economic Activity Outside of Agriculture	7.2	17.2

Source: Bywalec, 1995: 7. Based on: *Statistical Yearbooks*, 1993 and 1994, and Bywalec's own calculations and estimates for the year 1993.

the new entrepreneurs, as many as 38 percent constituted blue-collar workers (unskilled—21 percent, and skilled—17 percent). A middle class of a particularly backward character was emerging. Social psychologist Krystyna Skarżyńska gives a very harsh evaluation of this worker advancement. Writing about the first small owners of firms, she notes: "In many publications at first there appeared opinions that this group is composed of energetic and entrepreneurial individuals and therefore will form the social foundation of market reforms. Meanwhile, it turned out that this was not a pillar, but a curse of Polish capitalism."[8] This is one of the explanations given for the deterioration of working conditions in the new private sector. Since the trade unions, and particularly S., spread an umbrella over such socially sensitive changes, the recession drastically weakened this worker representation.

As a result of the recession and extraordinary expansion of the new private sector, in 1990 to 1993 there occurred "a true revolution in incomes." These are the words of Czesław Bywalec, who presented the altered share of the individual population groups in the general incomes of the population (see Table 6.2).

According to the numbers shown in the Table 6.2, incomes of wage earners fell to a level only several percent above one-quarter of the total income of the population. In 1989 the situation of individual farmers temporarily improved as a result of the liberation of food prices. Now the share of their income fell by more than half. Only the incomes of the "profit earners" grew rapidly—their share rose by two and a half-fold! This was an unprecedented shift in the income (and social) structure in peaceful conditions. A more than one-quarter rise of relative expenditures for social transfers should not create the impression of improvement of the fate of people living off of the state. The increase of rapidly growing expenditures, in fact, included premature retirement benefits, "stretched" disability pensions, and benefits for about three million unemployed persons.

All this was not happening in accordance with the textbook canon of the organic creation of capital: by means of hard work, rising productivity, the Puritan disposition to save, and surplus accumulation. On the contrary, it would be fitting to say that the shock therapy, which was primarily designed to stabilize the economy, became an instrument for the creation of a new, capitalist social structure resembling primitive capital accumulation.*

Shifting income (and property) from the poor to the rich, making about three million workers redundant with small chance of finding work, and concealing the dimensions of lowered employment among disability pensioners and earlier retirees (from 1.5 to 2 million) also meant lower prestige of work, a worse position of the workers, and the deterioration of workplace hygiene and safety. The backbone of the working class was broken, the trade union movement was weakened, and for many years offering work for low wages was sanctioned.

Irrespective of the true intentions of the program architects and implementers, this was not so much a transformational recession, seen as an inevitable cost of great changes, as a transformation through recession, that is, a great social change effected by means of

---

*During this time Leszek Balcerowicz justified the stabilization shock, with its extensive and drastic changes, by explaining that a fire cannot be put out in parts. In his opinion, the economy was in a state as tragic as a house during a fire. Parodying these words, one can say that the massive impoverishment of some and enrichment of others occurred "while putting out the fire."

recession as the tool for creating a polarized society. Władysław Frasyniuk, chairman of the Union of Liberty at the time, said: "In Great Britain the iron Margaret Thatcher for ten years grappled with what we did in half a year. Compared to Mazowiecki, the Iron Lady was but a snail."*9 Paradoxically, he was right, although he probably did not realize the sacrifices such a cocky statement brought. Further transformation consisted more of strengthening the social differences than repairing the effects of "overshooting." Which turned out to be unusually functional in building capitalism of the Anglo-Saxon kind.

A Spoonful of Theory

There is reason to believe that the drastic rise in prices for energy carriers and certain services was as much a matter of chance as were setting the inflation rate and the admissible indexation coefficient. However, the decisions fall into a general pattern, underpinned more or less intentionally by theoretical premises. The basic pattern of undertakings is also very similar in other countries considered to be leaders in reforms. Everywhere there was immense "overshooting," and so there must have been some common source factors.

These common premises can be found in the theoretical concept of the International Monetary Fund. Earlier I mentioned that the government of Poland unanimously chose the most radical version of the stabilization program from among those presented by the negotiating team of the IMF. The first serious criticism of the standard IMF program guidelines came from the Polish emigrant (in 1968) settled in Vienna, Kazimierz Łaski. He was asked for this by his former student,

*The difference between Poland and Great Britain was that it took seven years for the conservative government of John Major to repair the effects of the policies of Thatcher. The incomes of the poorest and transfers for social services were increased, inequalities were tamed a little, and yet the number of poor people remained three times as high as before the Iron Lady took office, rising from four to twelve million! (Her Majesty Treasury, 1999).

member of the government of Tadeusz Mazowiecki and director of the
Central Planning Office, Jerzy Osiatyński.* In early February 1990
Łaski presented his analysis to Osiatyński who sent it out to the most
important decision-makers. The analysis had the modest title:
"Notatka dla p.Min. J. Osiatyńskiego o niebezpieczeństwach związa-
nych z planem stabilizacji gospodarki narodowej" (Memorandum for
Min. Osiatyński on the Dangers Related to the National Economy
Stabilization Plan).[10] In the first part, the analysis contained the effective demand model of Keynes based on the theory of M. Kalecki, and
in the second estimates, based on this model, of the likely effects of
implementation of the economic stabilization plan.

There is no point in going into further detail here over this
analysis, especially since the views of this author are described further
herein, and appeared in real debate more than two years later. The
main message was very clear. Łaski estimated that one of the results of
the program on the demand side would be a 40 percent drop in real
wages. This, in turn, would be one of the main reasons for a decline in
GDP by more than a quarter.

The government's rebuttal was exceptionally harsh.[11] According
to Rostowski, Łaski based his reasoning on an erroneous hypothesis
of Keynes, and his calculations were "worthless." In his analysis he
made mistakes that in the West would be unacceptable "even on a test
in economics during the freshman year." The author of this response
was an economist at University College London, a British national of
Polish origin, at the time acting as one of the advisors of deputy prime
minister Leszek Balcerowicz, and currently a minister in the government of Donald Tusk.† However, it is not hard to see that Rostowski

*The government concept was that this would be an analytical research center
supporting the executive part of the economic team. Osiatyński, expelled in 1968
from the Warsaw School of Economics (formerly SGPiS), had been known earlier mainly for his Polish and English multivolume edition of the Collected
Works of Michał Kalecki (Poland's most eminent economist).

†History likes to play jokes. Currently Rostowski manages Poland's public
finance and in his many public appearances says that thanks to a budgetary
deficit reaching 8 percent of GDP, the global recession has not affected the Polish
economy as harshly.

was expressing the viewpoint of most of the government, in this way indicating that public debate would hamper efforts to implement the program. It seems that this harsh response was directed to both the expert Kazimeirz Łaski and Minister Jerzy Osiatyński, who was indirectly disciplined by the crucial persons in government responsible for economic matters.

In this thorny way began the cooperation of the Vienna Institute for International Economic Studies (WIIW) and the Polish economists, with Kazimierz Łaski soon assuming the role of director. The Vienna Institute drew up many studies that critically, yet always constructively, analyzed the economy of Poland or the region and organized many conferences attended by young and old scholars from Poland. However, there is nothing to suggest that the Polish authorities ever made any use of the institute's studies or activities. And the only occasion for a direct confrontation of the views and ideas of the Viennese center and people of authority among Warsaw's economists was a conference organized by both the Vienna Institute and the Institute of Economics of the Polish Academy of Sciences. The conference was held in Warsaw, in September 1993—during the parliamentary election campaign, which brought to power the coalition headed by the Democratic Left Alliance (SLD).

The debate centered on the path of reforms and systemic changes implemented until now and their implications for the future in Czechoslovakia (then already the Czech Republic and Slovakia), in Hungary and—above all—in Poland. From the very beginning, the debate was both pragmatic and theoretical, reaching the foundations of a typical prescription of the IMF. This prescription was reconstructed by the trio of Kazimierz Łaski, Indian economist Amit Bhaduri, and the director of the WIIW, Friedrich Levcik. In an extensive study titled "Transition from the Command to the Market System: What Went Wrong and What to Do for Now" (1994), they analyzed the assumptions and implementation of the Balcerowicz Plan against the background of similar measures in Czechoslovakia and Hungary. This study is, perhaps, the most theoretically thorough treatise on the subject of stabilization programs of the IMF applied in the three countries regarded as leading in stabilization and systemic reforms. For this reason it deserves special attention.

The role of a supplementary paper defending the Polish "shock" was played by the translation of the English article by Stanisław Gomułka, "Polish Economic Reform in 1990–91. Principles, Policies and Outcomes" (1994), and a shorter text by the same author, "Stabilization Policy in Poland 1990–93: Questions and Answers" (1994), taking up a direct polemic with the "Viennese" authors. They agreed that the transition from a command economy to an economy whose growth is limited by the demand barrier calls for a certain reduction of demand. But at the same time, they said that this reduction should concern that part that constitutes an inflationary money overhang. And when such an excess of money does not exist, regulation of demand would have to take place in a systemic way, that is, by giving enterprises autonomy, but simultaneously imposing on them a strict budgetary constraint. Apart from the extent of the necessary reduction of demand, they also expressed different views and did not agree over the following issues:

- the policy instruments by means of which this reduction should be done, in the short run;

- the effects of this reduction on the stimulation of supply (in the long and short run), as well as on the need to apply additional instruments;

- the political and social consequences of the rising costs of systemic transformation.

They also pointed out that the stabilization programs recommended by the IMF in the post-socialist countries were very similar to those it applied in Third World countries. And although the former have the "additional goal" of transforming centrally planned economies into market economies, "usually these programs are not adjusted to the specific nature of the given country, or customized to it, nor do they take into account the main structural factors or the conditions at the moment of the commencement of transformations. This uniformity of the IMF's programs makes it possible to identify their underlying theoretical model and the resultant policy recommendations."[12] The authors found the basis for reconstructing such a model in the old treatise of Jacques Polak, "Monetary Analysis of Incomes Formation and Payments Problem,"[13] in which the situation of foreign trade and banks is examined.

The Viennese trio noticed that Poland succeeded in creating a buyer's market, that following the initial period of growth the inflation rate began to fall and the trade balance improved. However, especially with regard to the second and third factor, the results turned out to be much more modest than had been assumed. The social costs of a deep and prolonged recession still needed to be explained. According to the authors, the collapse was the result of an essential mistake lying in the theoretical model: consistent ignoring of domestic demand as a barrier to growth. Contemporary economies dominated by oligopolies react to a change in demand with changes in the output volume, and not in prices, which in the majority are markup prices and not a result of the play of supply and demand in a free market. Ignoring this fact in the period of creating the stabilization program, and especially the inability to explain the reasons for the unpredicted depth of the recession, were considered by the authors to be the main theoretical weaknesses of the stabilization programs imposed by the IMF. "This conceptual defect of conventional stabilization policy, resulting from not taking into account the full impact of reduced global demand, must be removed in order to better plan the fiscal and monetary policies for the interim period."[14] In their opinion, "The removal of excessive demand does not have to signify a drop in real consumption if it in fact is solely limited to this excess."[15]

In addition, in the discussion it was revealed that it is not excessive demand but an artificially evoked growth of production costs that pumps up inflation. Thus inflation was related mainly to costs, not demand. The sharp rise in the prices of services that were set by the government, such as rent, heating, electricity, and transport, more so than other prices, combined with the excessively high interest rate and the price increase of imported components as a result of zloty devaluation, make a developing economy "extremely vulnerable to the new type of cost inflation."[16] The authors warned against the danger of "launching the spiral of a recession decline of output and productivity due to continued lowering of the extent of utilization of production capacity."[17]

Efforts to balance the budget during recession by cutting expenditures in response to the diminishing state income were regarded by the Viennese trio as a serious mistake, leading to deeper recession. In Poland, "attempts to reduce budgetary deficit by cutting state spending ended in 1991 and 1992 with an increase of this deficit."[18] They also pointed out that liberalization of foreign trade and the pace of integration with the global economy should be gradual. This could be beneficial for economies with a developed market and competition, whereas for economies departing from the command-distributive system it may be seriously damaging. The situation is similar to privatization, which should be spread out in time. And where there is extended coexistence with the public sector, state enterprises should be restructured before they are privatized. For these reasons, "during the transition from a command to a market economy the state has to support enterprises financially for a longer time so as to enable them to take part in free competition at all."[19]

An Objection

Defense of the strategy of the implementation of the Balcerowicz Plan was taken up by Stanisław Gomułka,[20] advisor and co-author of it. He outlined his reasoning in the two above-mentioned texts, where he dwelt on several selected issues. Regarding the dependence of the recession on the stabilization program, he argued that the depth of recession was determined not by the program itself but by the systemic changes. Referring to the concept of "transformational recession" popularized by Janos Kornai, he said that in Poland it was

evoked mainly by inadequate liberalization and systemically fundamental structural changes. This would explain the occurrence of
recession in all post-socialist countries, regardless of the advancement
and type of applied stabilization program. In his reasoning, transformational recession is an inevitable cost of creating a new economic
system and not a stabilization undertaking. He considered the charge
that there was a wide discrepancy between the assumptions of the stabilization program and its execution misplaced, given that, as early as
August 1989, he himself was in favor of a Thatcher-style shock operation, openly speaking of the high social costs. The same view was
shared by a "significant portion of the Balcerowicz group." He said
that the budgetary deficit, in Polish conditions of its financing almost
solely with bank credit, given the fast money circulation and the small
savings of the people, is much more inflation-generating than in a
normal market economy.

In the discussion that followed, Dariusz Rosati recalled that there
had in fact been no exhaustive public debate over the Balcerowicz
Plan, as it was formed in a climate of "remarkable secrecy and an
atmosphere of 'conspiracy' that surrounded the preparation of the
program."[21] Jan Mujżel questioned the uncompromising statement of
Gomułka that "nowhere has it been possible to enter a path of effective systemic transformation, avoiding recession," referring to the
examples of China and Vietnam, which for many years now have been
on the path of capitalist changes, while simultaneously boasting an
unprecedented high growth rate.

It is a pity that no one noticed a European country that has also
achieved similarly good results—Slovenia. Kazimierz Łaski recalled
the notoriously overlooked hypothesis of Michał Kalecki that a "budgetary deficit finances itself." This is so when there is unused production capacity and quantitative adjustment of output, as well as with full
utilization of the production facilities, and thus also with price (inflationary) adjustment. In both cases savings grow.

It was strange that among the discussion participants there were
none—besides Rosati—of the economic politicians who were, in the
autumn of that year, in the government. I have in mind the successive

ministers of finance, economic deputy prime ministers, and ministers of economy: Marek Borowski, Grzegorz Kołodko, Marek Belka, Jerzy Hausner, and Wiesław Kaczmarek. This could not have been accidental, but merely showed that the establishment had closed itself off from the outside. There was also nothing to indicate that the economists associated with the outgoing government (Gomułka, Fornalczyk, Osiatyński) were inclined to reflect on this issue and act accordingly to alter the economic policy. And so there would be continued reinforcement of the policy of low wages, maintenance of high unemployment, and the accompanying poverty.

In stressing the transformational (systemic) character of the recession, defenders of the official policy line did not notice that they were placing themselves in positions that were even harder to defend. Next to the existing ailments—the collapse of output and reduction of people's incomes—there developed a system that came to be known for its massive and continuous unemployment, for many years the highest in Central Europe, and later the highest in the European Union; one of the greatest income disparities; and the dismantling of the protective state. To this can be added the breakdown of the bargaining power of the workers. Particularly in Poland, the shock operation signified consent for the implementation of the worst form of capitalism. This was truly a great but wasted opportunity.

7. The Alternative after the Shock

Defenders of the Balcerowicz Plan cite two kinds of arguments. The first denies the existence of alternative programs; the other admits they exist but denies them realism. Let us begin with the first kind.

Here is the version of the Polish TINA*: "Successive right-wing and left-wing governments have continued this policy [of the Democratic Union/Union of Liberty, DU/UL] not because secret informers from the old intelligence service were within their ranks, but because there was no other realistic policy of change."[1] The authors believe that the program of the DU/UL group "was in a way a natural plan of transformation of a post-communist country, with social and international legitimization."[2] "Is there—they ask rhetorically—anyone, any other groups or other people that would better guide Poland through this labyrinth of the first years after 1989? No one can validate this now and so it is easy to constantly criticize the Union Party circles, while the alternative programs created *ex post* can politically lure those who reject the Third Republic."†[3] This reasoning has

*Abbreviation for the famous saying of Margaret Thatcher, popular in Great Britain: "There Is No Alternative."
†"The Third Republic" is a popular term for Poland after 1989. The Kaczyński twins (in the intermezzo 2005–7) fought for a change of policy under the slogan of "the Fourth Republic."

been expressed even more bluntly by former president Aleksander Kwaśniewski. To the question "Could it have been better and at a smaller price?" he replied: "I think so, but today everyone is wiser. And earlier no one was."[4] The persistence of such thinking is so strong that some more attention is due here.

There were indeed those who were wiser earlier, and quite a few at that. First of all, the matter of "social legitimization" is not as evident as the journalists of *Polityka* would have it. On the basis of research of CBOS (Public Opinion Research Center) from 2005 and later, a CASE (Center for Social and Economic Research) report states that "in society there is a predominance of a feeling of being the losers of transformation. . . . What is particularly disturbing is that a negative attitude to transformation and egalitarian attitudes are popular also among Poles who are well off."[5]

Moreover, to regard the Polish path of change as "a normal plan" is to say it makes no difference that in a given country (such as Hungary or the Czech Republic) there is unemployment of only several percentage points, and in another, for years, double-digit unemployment rates, even as high as 20 percent. To call this normal is to accept the range and depth of poverty, particularly among children. Or to interpret the biggest emigration in peaceful times, especially of young people, by now numbering more than two million, as merely a sign of the success of Poland's entry in the European Union.

In presenting other proposals for systemic changes, one must of course remember that there were no operational programs ready for implementation, as these come into being only within the structures of an administration that has access to the essential information resources.

The Swedish Connection

The great popularity of the Swedish model in Poland was translated into practical implications already in early 1989. An attempt was made to examine what could be applied in Poland from this model. At the turn of January, a study group of nine economists was sent by the

Consultative Economic Council (advisory body to the government) to Stockholm. The result was an extensive report, over seventy pages long, describing in great detail the possibilities of Poland making use of the experiences of this country. And although this material gives the impression that it was written on the spot, we do not know whether and to whom it was delivered during the Round Table negotiations, or even if it was circulating earlier in the form of a typescript. There is also no information on why the report was made public as late as June 1989, and then only in the form of photocopies.

Referring to the then fashionable slogan that it is worth reaching for solutions "proven in the world," the authors pointed out the diversity of such solutions:

Whereas the basic market mechanisms function in the developed industrial countries in the same way or similarly, the proportions of national income division or the principles of economic policies can be fundamentally different. From this point of view, the Swedish economic model is worthy of special attention. The Swedish economy operates in conditions of strict efficiency rules imposed by the international market. Thus there is no room in it for paternalism toward permanently inefficient enterprises or sectors. Yet even immense restructuring programs, such as shutting down practically the entire shipbuilding industry (until recently considered to be one of the most modern in the world) take place in peaceful conditions, despite the continuous strength of the trade unions. The secret of success lies in what the Swedes call an active employment policy. Instead of allocating money for unemployment benefits, job possibilities are first sought for potential candidates for unemployment status. Among the workers of the shut down shipyards, no one was left to his own devices.... Economic radicalism coexists in Sweden alongside social solidarity, while the philosophy of resolving conflict situations is a contradiction of Thatcherism. In England the elimination of inefficient enterprises usually entails increased unemployment and what follows, strikes and social tension. In Sweden such an operation is carried out relatively without conflict.[6]

The authors point out that the shipyard industry was liquidated by the Social Democrats, whereas the Conservatives who had governed before had subsidized this industry.

The Swedish principle of "equal pay for equal work," irrespective of the condition of the firm in the market of a given branch, was seen by the authors of the report as an interesting mechanism of automatic restructuring of the economy, where weak firms are eliminated and other firms are motivated toward innovation. They also confronted the Swedish and Polish reality concerning such issues as the attitude of the basic social forces to structural changes in industry, understanding the priorities during structural changes, the mechanisms governing them and their financial aspects, the management of enterprises and the organizational structure that steers industry, the agricultural policy, the cooperative movement, and so forth. The report is amazingly mature for such a brief, five-day visit to Stockholm, which is partly explained by the substantial help provided by emigrants from Poland there.

In a way, the general message addressed to the Polish authorities anticipates the provisions of the later constitution of Poland: "One can see a considerable similarity between the values underlying the economic and social policy in Sweden and those we are implementing or trying to implement in Poland: full employment, wages determined by work input, social security. All the more reason to examine the Swedish experiences, some of which may be directly applicable to the process of economic reform and current policies."[7]

Attaching particular importance to the industrial policy, and especially to the restructuring of the old sectors, the authors prepared special annexes devoted to consensual restructuring of two sectors: the steel and shipbuilding industries.* It can be said that they maintained

---

*The report also tells us that a study on the general principles of the Swedish industrial policy was available for reading at the KRG (Consultative Economic Council) headquarters. And Danuta Gotz-Kozierkiewicz (1989) published an article on the Swedish tax system. How odd that the participants of the Swedish visit, who subsequently took part in the Round Table negotiations (Prof. J. Mujżel and M. Święcicki), did not even once refer to the Swedish experience.

reasonable proportions between the description of the principles of the Swedish economy and the urgent pragmatic issues resulting from the model's premises.

Sweden furnished one other good example: the elementary canons of Keynesian economics were preserved in its economic policy, which was no doubt connected to the fact that Swedish economists had co-created it. Here the "entrance" of monetarism and Reagan's free-market rhetoric was very limited. This was expressed in the response to the crisis of the Swedish economy experienced in 1991–94. At the peak moment of the crisis, unemployment reached 13 percent. And what was the reaction of the authorities? In 1993 they employed a budgetary deficit that was sky-high for a developed country. The difference between the share of state income in the GDP (60 percent), and expenditures (73 percent), that is, the deficit of the public finance sector, accounted for 13 percent of GDP. In addition, in saving the currency and the liquidity of banks, Sweden showed an ability to reach out for drastic instruments. Home-grown neoclassicists and neo-Keynesians usually clamor that such thoughtlessness is paid for in the long run. But Sweden (and also Finland) demonstrated an unusual ability to combine the process of overcoming the crisis with a modernization leap. Several years later it ranked first in the world in the knowledge-based economy. Potentially, the experience of Sweden was aimed against a shock operation of the kind functioning in Poland—the Balcerowicz Plan.

Alternative Options of Brus-Łaski and Kornai

There were also interesting concepts of a more theoretical nature. In 1989 two books appeared, as if in response to an urgent public need. These books were different but had a similar message. One was the work of the Hungarian economist Janos Kornai, *The Road to a Free Economy* ([1989, 1990], 1991), and the other, *From Marx to the Market* ([1989], 1992), was written by two Polish economists, Włodzimierz Brus from Oxford and Kazimierz Łaski from Vienna, both emigrants after the March anti-Semitic *dintojra* of 1968. Brus was well known in the world for his several-decades-long effort to effectuate the reform of socialist economies. His autobiography is titled *The Bane of Reforming the Socialist Economic System.*[8] Łaski, his disciple and friend, was less known until their book. From that moment on, he was "stigmatized" by the new "bane" of improving the transition paths to a private economy. One could say that Łaski in a way took over what his master had been working on, the latter repeating in private conversations that "I've given enough advice in my time."

Brus and Kornai were the most outstanding of the economist-reformers of the Soviet bloc living in those times, first as advocates of really existing socialism, even in the Stalinist years, then increasingly of its critics. Initially believing that real socialism could be made rational, in the late 1980s, no longer with any such hope, they sought an alternative. But this is where the similarities end.

Kornai—molded in a country in which socialism had been "executed by gunfire" on the streets of Budapest in 1956—bid farewell to the party, and with one exception (sitting on the board of the central bank), he made real socialism the subject of an objective analysis, avoiding giving any prescriptions. Meanwhile, from 1953 Brus persistently fought for reforms, took part in various party and state groupings (he was deputy chairman of the Economic Council of the Council of Ministers and one of the chief authors of its famous program documents). He left the party late, in 1967, and in world literature is known as the author of the model of a "planned economy with a built-in market mechanism."

In the matter of the form of the future system and the path leading to it, Kornai and Brus differed significantly. In 1989 the former abandoned the scholarly approach in favor of a prescriptive, at times scurrilous, battle for a concrete form of capitalist economy. In his book the reader will find dozens of recommendations and as many caveats. In a way it resembles more a catechism than an analytical work. He strongly manifested his attachment to a "free economy," that is, a capitalist free-market economy, and in theory showed a clear penchant for monetarism ("Inflation is created by governments"), while denying any socialist leanings (even "The market socialism idea has misfired. . . . Never again!").

Brus and Łaski, on the other hand, spoke up in favor of a mixed economy with a predominance of private ownership. Whereas they rejected socialism (also in its market form) as an alternative to capitalism, they nonetheless did not renounce socialist values. On the contrary, they seriously considered economic policy tools that encourage full employment and the mitigation of cyclic economic swings and income disparities.

Yet despite these differences, in the face of the fundamental choices that had to be made by the two countries—Hungary and Poland, and then by other post-communist countries—there was something important that these two books shared. Although Kornai begins with ownership issues while the Polish economists end their reflections with them, in both books property is regarded as the basic pillar of the new order. The key matter is the prospect, accentuated by all three authors, of a rational creation of the new social order and recognition that the main issue is an ownership transformation that will be the basis of an efficient economy. In both cases this is an evolutionary development. Kornai not only submits relevant propositions, but severely reprimands the "cavalry brigade" of the Hungarian radicals, rejecting the idea of giving away public property and opposing thoughtlessness in underestimating the price of state firms for sale.

The following is the general picture of transformation according to Kornai:

> In [my] opinion we will have to reckon for the next two decades with the *dual* economy that emerged in Hungary over the past ten to twenty years, and with its two constituent parts: the state and the private sectors. . . . The share of the state sector can be decreased only gradually, and we should not entertain vain hopes. There is no miracle cure that will transform it into a sphere of genuine entrepreneurship. Like it or not, the state sector will retain many negative features. Therefore we should strive to minimize these negative features through strict financial discipline and appropriate parliamentary

supervision, and try to prevent the state sector from siphoning off excessive resources to the detriment of the private sector. The operating conditions of the private sector must be liberalized in a consistent manner, and its bureaucratic constraints dismantled. Appropriate fiscal and monetary instruments are needed to promote the private sector's fast and energetic development.[9]

The Polish economists wrote in a similar way, yet not entirely:

One has to keep in mind that the subject of our discussion here is not the choice between abstract alternatives in empty space, but the direction of evolution of "real socialism." The process unfolds from a position in which state enterprise dominates, and this fact of life cannot be changed overnight. Thus a mixed economy where various forms of state enterprise would gradually be made to compete on an *equal footing* with private firms and cooperatives seems the only realistic prospect for MS [market socialism] in the near future. This means that the question of whether state enterprise can be fitted into a genuine market framework, including the capital market, and if so to do it with minimal losses, remains highly relevant. . . . In other words, MS may not require renunciation of public ownership, but certainly requires renunciation of any sort of ownership doctrinarism. The economic system becomes open-ended.[10]

The declaration of the Polish authors requires two explanations. First, market socialism was understood by Brus and Łaski as "marketization" of the economy, forced out by circumstances, in conditions of long-term predominance of state enterprises. Second, they were in favor of an "unbiased test" of efficiency "on equal footing." Here there was less pessimism than in the case of Kornai regarding the efficiency of state firms. Such an approach was suggested to the authors from the British experience, among others. Referring to the opinion of "certain observers," who placed the blame for poor results not on public ownership as such, but on an inappropriate policy of the government, they wrote: "Somewhat ironically it might be said that the latter point

found a paradoxical corroboration in the improvement in performance of public companies in Britain when in the jump to privatization
the Thatcher Conservative government hardened the budget constraint to use again Kornai's term, and forced nationalized industries
to become respectively profitable."[11]

Kornai proposed a different sectoral policy. He openly recommended discrimination against the state sector, highly privileged in
the past. A noteworthy idea of his is the twenty-year-long prospect of
a dual economy, in a country a fraction of the size of Poland and, more
important, more advanced than Poland (except in agriculture) in commercialization and privatization following the 1968 reform. In addition, Kornai clearly preferred the emergence of enterprises of private
individuals, and only those that become rich and powerful could associate in companies. Such a strategy was to favor the organic path of
creating a healthy middle class by the method of accumulation of savings. The general message of Kornai was that systemic transformation
may and should be the result of "good work," which presupposes the
absence of haste.*

Kornai assumed a cautious position with regard to foreign capital.
He mentioned the benefits stemming from it, but at the same time
pointed out that it should be admitted only to a certain extent, when
this agrees with the national interest. He even wondered whether the
boundaries of its admissibility should not be laid down in advance.

The ultra-radical elation of the Polish authorities and their self-iso-
lation are evident in neither the original Hungarian version (1989) nor
the English version (1990), nor did the Polish version (1991) of
Kornai's book raise any great interest. The book of the two Polish

*This message was what made Fundacja Polska Praca decide to translate
Kornai's book into Polish as quickly as possible. We only underestimated the
simple fact that its publication under a leftist organization would become an
obstacle to its acceptance in the bookstore network. It is interesting that Kornai
strongly acknowledges his intellectual debt to Marx. In his Japanese lecture he
said: "People sometimes ask me whether I am a Marxist. My answer is a clear
negative. [But] if forced to name those who have influenced me most, I mention
the names of Schumpeter, Keynes and Hayek, but first on the list comes the
name of Karl Marx."

authors shared a similar fate. Successive English editions (1989, 1990), as well as the Polish translation (1991) and Brus's visit to Warsaw and Kraków in late summer 1989, were completely ignored by the establishment, including the leading media. Today, only for study purposes, one can play around with these ideas, wondering how the Polish variant of capitalism could have developed if the authorities had behaved in a rational way, taking up reform measures after seriously studying, absorbing, and interpreting the contents of both of these books. All this could have been done within a few weeks.

Allow me to add one more thing. Although Balcerowicz's team so eagerly referred to the works of Hayek, in matters considered here it was not they, but Brus, Łaski, and Kornai who were in agreement with the Austrian economist. Here is what Hayek warned politicians against in connection with the transition from a war economy to a market economy:

> However much one may wish a speedy return to a free economy, this cannot mean the removal at one stroke of most of the wartime restrictions. Nothing could discredit the system of free enterprise more than the acute . . . dislocation and instability such an attempt would produce. The problem is at what kind of system we should aim in the process of demobilization, not whether the wartime system should be transformed into more permanent arrangements by a carefully thought-out policy of gradual relaxation of controls, which may have to extend over several years.[12]

And in a more pronounced fashion: "The one thing modern democracy will not bear without cracking is the necessity of a substantial lowering of the standards of living in peacetime or even prolonged stationariness of its economic conditions."[13]

The reformers could thus resort to both an analytical description of practical experience (the Swedish model) and theoretical analysis. They could also reach out for works that outlined a more reasonable path for carrying out reforms.

A False Dilemma

Another kind of argumentation against alternative programs referred to Poland's real position as debtor, or the reasoning of trade union activists as being contradictory to building a social-oriented economic order. Added to this was the social imagination of intellectuals who created a no-alternative world. The following is a small, though very symptomatic sample of the latter.

Several years ago, a poll showed that as many as 81 percent of CBOS (Center for Research of Public Opinion) respondents wanted a "protective state that would intervene in the market and limit the earnings of the highest earners." This fact was interpreted by the sociologist and director of CBOS, Mirosława Grabowska, as a threat to an efficient economy. It was seen as an effect of the fact that "among Poles the habits of the former People's Republic still prevail—we want to have more equality and security, but unfortunately do not realize that this is not possible. The hopes associated with transformation were immense—it seemed to us that we would be working as in socialism and earning as in the United States."[14]

To me, these words of one of the leading Polish sociologists are evidence of a glaring lack of knowledge. The same can be said about the journalist who is incapable of delving deeper into the subject and of referring to the experiences of many countries where the impossible has not only turned out to be realistic, but is even combined with purely economic success. Many countries have to this day a developed system of social security, progressive taxes, and social transfers, and they intensely intervene in the market and in setting the wage level. It is sad to see that the research of Polish sociologists and statisticians is often based on the mistaken belief in the impossibility of reconciling greater income and wage equality with efficiency. Yet this is possible, and even leads to high-ranking positions among knowledge-based economies (in the first years of this century, the countries that ranked highest were, respectively, Finland, Sweden and Denmark). This false dilemma often radically lowers the value of research that does not confirm this contradiction.

The Predetermined Fate of the Debtor?

The claim of absence of an alternative would be unjustified in the case of the productive economic sociologist Juliusz Gardawski. His (and his co-authors') book, *Working Poles and the Crisis of Fordism*,[15] is the crowning achievement of research of more than twenty years. It would be a great loss if economists, sociologists, and politicians did not absorb and assimilate this work.

Unlike Grabowska, Gardawski is aware of the existence of alternative propositions, in particular of the West German and Scandinavian models. In the early 1990s, in the books published by the F. Ebert Foundation, Gardawski focused on examining the aspects that made the Polish workers consent to the implementation of a market economy, on the condition that it would be people-friendly, ensure full employment, and would not create glaring inequalities. However, when he dwells on the most general, systemic matters, he is unable (unwilling?) to go beyond the schemes disseminated by our ruling establishment. In this outstanding work, I find theses that, most oddly, comply with these schemes, but contradict the facts the author pointed out in earlier works.

Gardawski formulates his new viewpoint as a polemic with my view on the subject of shock therapy, ironically summed up with the conclusion that Prime Minister Tadeusz Mazowiecki made a "Columbus mistake" when he wanted to go to Bonn for a model (looking for his Ludwig Erhard), but his confidants bought him a ticket to Washington (the Washington Consensus) and Chicago (headquarters of Milton Friedman's school) instead. According to Gardawski, this was not a matter of a mistake, but an expression of a sad necessity. He writes: "Poland's international creditors and global financial institutions were ready to help only if this assistance would not be wasted. From their point of view, this could only be guaranteed by a decision to adopt the Washington consensus."[16]

This is a surprising but very open admission that the form of transformation was determined by Poland's dependence on foreign capital (international creditors). Gardawski in realistic words describes the social and political consequences of this (in my opinion false) "necessity." He continues:

> In practice, this [the debtor's fate] limited the possibility of negotiating the transition with the unions, also reducing the influence of workers' self-management bodies in enterprises. In the first state of the transition, the country embarked on the path of a liberal, open-market economy, following a model of English-speaking countries rather than Germany or Scandinavia. Paradoxically, it was politicians from the Solidarity movement who were responsible for the direction in which the transformation proceeded. . . .[As a result] from January 1990, worker self-management was gradually eliminated . . . trade unions weakened, as did the position of the working class. . . . It was the beginning of the ideological deproletarianization of the working class [and its] fragmentation. Employees lost the sense of group solidarity, the ability to take collective action, and the class struggle instinct strong in 1980–81.[17]

Yes. This was a false necessity that was, unfortunately, implemented. And it was not the idea of necessity, but its hasty implementation, and particularly foreign capital taking over (about 75 percent) the banking system and wholesale trade that highly restricted Polish sovereignty. It seems that Gardawski realized this quite quickly.

To return to this necessity, it is a matter of great satisfaction that in his newest book on social dialogue in Poland, Gardawski[18] demonstrates his openness to the arguments and the documents with a readiness to radically change his views. He now writes: "Kowalik extremely aptly . . . wrote . . . that 'Mazowiecki made a "Columbus mistake"—he was looking for a model in Bonn, but given the model from Chicago and Washington instead. . . . The choice of trajectory . . . in the light of information gathered by T. Kowalik, turned out to be the sovereign choice of the Polish reformatory elite. . . . Endowed with the trust of the people, the reforming elite could impose any model [of capitalism] whatsoever."*[19]

*Gardawski dropped this view before the book was published in Polish.

With the Help of the "Other America"

Of greater importance to me is Gardawski's statement on Poland's dependence on its creditors and how this was crucial in determining the ensuing system. It is worth remembering that the IMF, which the authorities were counting on for a bailout, has an obsession with budgetary matters, deficits, inflation, or balancing public finance. Listed among the ten "commandments" of the consensus was privatization, but without specification of its form or pace. Privatization was more a subject of interest for the World Bank. But there were no known pressures on their part for a specific form of privatization or, in general, the form of Polish capitalism.

The Polish authorities did not try to compensate for the unfavorable position of debtor by launching the pioneering character of Poland's undertaken changes, or the power of the myth of Solidarity, still popular in the West. This is what Karol Lutkowski[20] had been requesting. According to him, the IMF should have treated Poland in a milder and different way than usual. However, the leaders governing the economy, deaf to such suggestions, appeared to proceed in the opposite direction. The great changes were to justify the particularly acute and painful character of the prescription. The S. elites who made the key decisions did not make them either in conditions of a threat to self-government, or any open imposition by the West of specific forms of a market economy. They did not *have to* so much as *wanted to* take a "shortcut" to reach the Anglo-Saxon model, and there was plenty of evidence for this. The following are a few examples.

One of the consultants of the IMF, Michael Bruno, was quite surprised that—unlike in the case of the thorny negotiations with Third World countries—in Poland the fund's propositions were so readily accepted. To his astonishment, the government unanimously chose the harshest variant of those put forward by the IMF experts. This was so despite the fact that these propositions had their negotiating logic and the IMF probably treated such a variant primarily as an element of bargaining. Moreover, this expert, then governor of the Israeli central bank and author of a successful reform, sent a message to

Leszek Balcerowicz at the crucial moment of formation of the latter's plan (December 3, 1989), which was radically different from this variant. The following are the most revealing points. After saying that "there may be no need to devalue" and supporting his suggestions with some observations, he enumerates the following ingredients of the policy package:

- Don't devalue or announce only a small devaluation;

- Abolish restrictions on exports and imports for exports;

- Intermediately introduce alternative means of real savings;

- Completely abolish subsidies on coal and the tax on coal exports;

- The most important implication of all: there will be a smaller correction needed in the initial price level jump and the required wage compensation. A minimum threshold guarantee of real wage can be ascertained by combination of an up-front income of the nominal wage (85 percent, say, of the expected price jump in the first month), a wage freeze for three months, and a precommitted new COLA agreement (no compensation below 1 percent monthly inflation, say, and 85 percent above it)—all these numbers are, of course, given only for illustrative purposes;

- Most important caveat: all of this is relevant only if the fundamentals in terms of the real budget balance and credit ceilings are well in place.[21]

He also informed Balcerowicz that other experts of the IMF, Stanley Fischer and Jacob Frenkel, "entirely support the argument and its consequences."

It is rather obvious that this radically differs from the version accepted at that moment. We do not know the reaction of Balcerowicz. But we do know that the subsequent changes in this version went in the entirely opposite direction—tightening the plan even more. As said above, the coefficient of wage indexation reduced from 0.7–0.8 to 0.3 and 0.2.

There are several other factors indicating that even among the propositions of the American experts, the authorities chose only what fitted their more radical free-market preferences. Earlier I commented on the successive plans for Poland prepared by the influential American financier George Soros. It is true that he financed the visit of the shock operation promoters Sachs, his assistant David Lipton, and Stanisław Gomułka. But even he submitted propositions more or less different from the standard programs of the fund and from the advocates of the market "leap" mentioned here. I pointed out his proposal of trying for a three-year moratorium on debt, a low interest rate, and financial assistance for Poland from the West.

In addition, in the matter of privatization, Soros's propositions were rather restrained, leaving a broad range of ownership transformations within the state sector. With regard to state-owned enterprises, he postulated corporatization based on profit and distribution of their shares among an adequate number of state-owned financial institutions, such as pension funds, investment banks, and foreign debt-servicing funds, so as to make it possible to create a stock and bonds exchange. This resembled more the cross-shareholding in the style of the Japanese *keiretsu* than the classical British privatization. He saw the need for incentives for foreign capital, but felt that the government should specify the admissible percentage of foreign ownership.

There is also much to indicate that the proposals of Soros were designed to be more or less competitive with the IMF prescriptions.

When looking at his five successive plans of reforms and stabilization of the Polish economy, a distinct evolution can be seen. In the first plan (March 1989), Soros does not even mention the IMF. In the next two (May and June), he writes of assistance from the IMF in preparing a stabilization program, combining this even with the Big Bang. And in the last two (July and August), in the part titled "Monetary Stabilization," a surprising statement appears: "This would be arranged with the assistance of the IMF, but it would resemble the German currency reform of 1948 rather than a typical IMF program."[22]

A couple of months later, Soros's interview appeared under the meaningful title, "Musi wybrać społeczeństwo" (The Choice Must Belong to Society). If to this we add Soros's restraints in the matter of privatization, we obtain an extended prospect of rather gradual, publicly negotiated changes, that is, a concept contradicting that of the government, and especially the 1989 ideas of Lech Wałęsa, who wanted to grant to the government extraordinary powers that would embrace, in one sweep, restructuring of the economy, ownership changes, demonopolization, the tax system, the accounting system, the operation of banks, and changes in the structure of the state, including in local governments.

Naturally, nothing is known more about how Soros understood a "typical IMF program" and particularly its opposite—the 1948 price-monetary reform of Ludwig Erhard. Possibly he had in mind only currency exchange. But it is important that Soros's proposals could create for Polish authorities a certain space for negotiations with the IMF and the World Bank.

Such space could also be broadened by certain astonishing proposals of Jeffrey Sachs. The September 5, 1989 program of Sachs and Lipton, never published or translated into Polish, in an original way announced the second phase after curbing inflation, which shows Sachs's opposition to what people began calling the Washington Consensus.

> My model for the future [that is, after curbing inflation] would be Sweden, in which national negotiations go on between the employers' confederation and the trade unions. In order to set a basic wage agreement, room must be found for wage increases. The target inflation for the coming year is set, and then expected productivity growth is calculated. The appropriate wage is then set to have real wages grow at the same rate as productivity. Note that wage growth is based on future expected inflation, not the past inflation rate (as in a rigid indexation rule). The trick to implementing such a style of wage set-

ting in the future would be to create an "employer" structure that is somewhat independent of the state.[23]

Naturally, Sachs did not realize that there was a glaring contradiction between the prospect of the Swedish system of negotiation and his proposals of the big jump to the market, which meant that a considerable portion of incomes would be shifted from the poor to the rich, that there would suddenly be high unemployment and poverty. A society of primitive capital accumulation was formed. This must have given rise to mistrust of the people in the authorities and in the emerging new social order. And because the main trade union at the time spread out a protective umbrella over this "jump," it cut off the branch on which it was sitting. Several years later, Jacek Kuroń (1994), with this in mind, would write that the administration and the government had destroyed the social movement S.

From the purely political point of view, a direct imitation of the Social Democratic Swedish model in 1989 was very difficult, to some politicians bordering on the impossible. It was much easier, in my opinion, to combine the S. movement with the renewed liberal thinking coming from across the ocean, which would be the perfect synthesis of the "argument of force" (the S. movement) with the "force of argument" (social liberals). Contrary to the general belief, not only the neoliberal prescriptions of the Hayek-Friedman and Reaganite type came from America. These were not only the enthusiasts of an unlimited market, but also emissaries of social-liberal thought.

The latter arrivals from across the ocean were mentioned briefly just recently by Leszek Balcerowicz and unfortunately only in an abbreviated form: "I remember," he said, "how various Americans were coming who had not managed to implement their ideas in the U.S. and proposed them to us. My answer was: try them out on yourself first. . . . To me it was obvious that since Poland had become free, it would be most idiotic to carry out some third path."[*24] And

---

*A severe critic of the Balcerowicz Plan at the time, Karol Modzelewski, said recently: "At that time I felt that there may be a political and economic alternative.

although the capers of the counter-reformation of Ronald Reagan and George W. Bush, with their disagreeable social effects, were being verified, those arrivals from America could have told Balcerowicz that they had tried out their concepts with good results. Such a successful attempt had been Roosevelt's New Deal and the "American miracle" during the governments of John F. Kennedy and Lyndon B. Johnson.

Balcerowicz touched here on an important aspect of the history of the beginnings of the Polish transformation. In deciding on the fastest possible "jump" into the free market, Poland lost, perhaps, a chance to follow the path of Japan. Let us recall the beginnings of one of the most interesting systemic innovations of the second half of the last century—the emergence of the new socioeconomic order of this first "Asian tiger," which infected first South Korea and Taiwan, then somewhat later several other countries of the region. The founder of Sony, Akio Morita (1996), describes the beginnings of the Japanese system. It all began when the American intellectuals imposed on Japan the ideas of a social-liberal labor code. This happened with the support of the chief of the U.S. occupational forces, General MacArthur, who was said to have applied Roosevelt's New Deal to Japan. When these ideas were crossed with the culture and inventiveness of the

---

Today I feel that there wasn't any." He believed that gradual transition to a market economy was feasible in China, which was made possible by the dictatorship. "In our case there was a dictatorship that collapsed, so we had to come out of the old economic system quickly, otherwise we would be smashed by rubble" (Graczyk, 2007). For many reasons I do not share this view. First of all, it is not true that in China "the path to evolutionary transformation led through Tiananmen Square"; the beginning of the evolution goes back to 1978. Second, in Poland the stabilizing factor was (could have been) S., in the economy the self-management movement, and above all the Round Table Agreements. Third, also in Europe there is a post-socialist country that has saved the economy from a shock operation. In this country, even more than in Poland, the framework of liberal democracy was created not only after the fall of the "dictatorship," but also after the fall of statehood. This is Slovenia (Mrak et al., 2004). A questionable explanation is that underestimation of costs resulted from lack of models—"When you tread a path that has never been trodden, this is inevitable." Indeed, it is inevitable, but what is questionable is the scope of the underestimation. If it amounts to several hundred percent, it seriously undermines the professional credibility of the plan's authors.

Japanese people, there emerged an interesting socioeconomic system. In a similar way, though this time with the participation of the British and the French, the market economy model in the Federal Republic of Germany was formed. It turns out that in the Poland of the times of great systemic choices, the American liberal "welfarists" also pressed their views. In vain, they tried to reach the main craftsman of Poland's shock therapy.

In light of the enunciations of Balcerowicz, one should take a different look at the socialist study adventure of Joseph Stiglitz. In spring 1990 and the early 1990s (1993, 1994), he published three studies devoted to criticism of market socialism. They open with two lectures delivered at the University of Stockholm, as part of the Wicksell series, available only in copied form. In all of them Stiglitz attempted to answer why the hitherto existing concepts of market socialism had failed. However, this was not a simple rejection of socialist ideas in general, but an indication of where errors lay in both the concept of market socialism, itself, and in the more fundamental assumptions of the neoclassical theory on which this concept was based.

The "War on Top" as an Opportunity

It took Mazowiecki twenty years to finally see the association between the character of transformation and its beginning, and in this way to quite fundamentally undermine the path that Poland embarked on in 1989. And although he still says that the painful shock operation was necessary, he expresses a view that says a lot. The following is a summary of the conference on the "Polish Year 1989" at the University of Warsaw: "It hurt a lot, but it had to. Had I known that unemployment would grow to 19 percent, I would have thought twice over the decisions on economic transformation."[25] According to an account of a *Gazeta Wyborcza* journalist, these words were spoken by the former prime minister who was deeply concerned by the drama of his then lack of knowledge. Let us think what this "had I known" meant and let us read these words as a regret that followed a lost opportunity.

First, I shall point out that Mazowiecki could have gained knowledge about the projected high unemployment; it was "within reach." It only depended on the circulation of information available to the prime minister, on whether his closest co-workers delivered the relevant documents and publications to him. And, of course, also on whether the prime minister sought such information, whether he "wanted to know." As we know, in the ministry of finance at that time, a (desirable, not warning) scenario was drawn up on the development of the Polish economy until 2000, and it envisioned unemployment on this scale. In 2000, eleven years after 1989, it was to reach 16 percent, with a very high annual GDP growth rate at that, between 6 and 8 percent.[26]

And now let us see what happens if we let our imaginations loose, but within the limits of what was realistic. It is late spring—beginning of summer, 1990. The economy is still deep in recession, but inflation has definitely slowed down and shop shelves are now stocked with merchandise. And we have an unexpectedly high surplus in the budget and in foreign trade. In these conditions Lech Wałęsa's "march to Belweder" (location of the presidential office at that time) begins. His ammunition is an attack on the government of Tadeusz Mazowiecki, and on the destructive effects of the Balcerowicz Plan.

This could have been a strong incentive for the prime minister to "surge forward." Let us assume that Mazowiecki is agitated when he learns about the plans of the Ministry of Finance, which is projecting a high unemployment rate for a whole decade. He categorically demands an alternative from his advisors. He emphasizes that you cannot continue defending the status quo, being deaf to scholars, forgetting the Round Table Agreements, the electoral program of the Solidarity opposition, and the admonitions of John Paul II. And the experts prepare for him an alternative program for the time after the six-month shock operation announced earlier by the authorities. Not wanting to fall into disfavor with the IMF and World Bank experts, or Poland's right-wing groups, to appease them but also to place them in a difficult position, the prime minister resorts to the above-mentioned ideas of the Americans, and to the Swedish experience, but expressing it in the language of Jeffrey Sachs. He makes use of George

Soros's opinion on the Erhard reform. He invites Stiglitz to draw up an outline of a more egalitarian privatization program. He announces that the new program would be negotiated with both great trade union centers, in this way making it easier for them to get over the recession's shock.

The most difficult obstacle could be Balcerowicz's resistance. In the best scenario, talks with him would end with a shift in government. And if he resigned from both positions, he would surely remain loyal to the administration, not risking destabilization of the economy. Perhaps he would be replaced by Witold Trzeciakowski or Jerzy Osiatyński, who would be given a chance to cautiously correct the Balcerowicz Plan. To note, Osiatyński commissioned an analysis from Kazimierz Łaski, knowing, of course, that it would not be favorable for a shock operation, whereas Trzeciakowski was the only candidate for minister in Mazowiecki's government who openly referred to the Swedish model. As was noted in the press, he said during a hearing before the Sejm committee, that his dream was "a market economy in the Swedish version, that is, a capitalist system of production, but socialist system of distribution. . . . He would not strive for privatization at all costs—preferring indirect paths, pointing out the efficiency of empowered state enterprises in e.g. Italy."[27]

Such measures would have significantly weakened Wałęsa's assaults. While the "war on top" was probably unavoidable, it would have been waged over programs. Even if Wałęsa had "captured Belweder," Mazowiecki would have had no reason to dissolve the government. The "Polish Kutuzov"—as the prime minister was called in advance—would have come out the victor from the siege. Which would have benefited the country.

PART TWO

Elitist Ownership Transformations

If the tendency of legislation had been to favor the diffusion, instead of the concentration of wealth—to encourage the subdivision of the large masses, instead of striving to keep them together; the principle of individual property would have been found to have no necessary connexion with the physical and social evils which almost all Socialist writers assume to be inseparable from it.

—J. S. MILL, *The Principles*, 1:268

Poland is again in the initial primary stage, when ownership titles must be distributed among the participants of the social game. . . . Truly everyone is taking part in the war for power, property and wealth, though the opportunities were not equal at the start and this inequality lets itself be known time and again—in the sense of injustice on the one hand and arrogance on the other.

—JACEK KURCZEWSKI
Gazeta Wyborcza, January 27–28, 1995

8. Ownership: From Taboo Topic to the Round Table Agreements

Economists say that ownership forms make up one of the main pillars (next to the market) and, in certain arrangements, the main pillar of every economic system. The foremost feature of a capitalist economy is considered to be "private ownership of, and private enterprise with the means of production."[1] On this score, there is no difference between the American neoclassical economist cited here and the Marxist Oskar Lange. And yet ownership issues as a subject of research still remain in the shadows of the market and are not a favorite economic topic. This is easier to understand in the case of countries with a stabilized capitalist economy, where economists, as a rule preoccupied with short- and medium-term problems, can afford to accept the ownership structure as given. But to disregard these matters in countries undergoing great systemic changes or to downplay them as mere strategic or even technical issues of privatization can be disquieting.

Particularly in Poland, interest in this especially conflict-generating and so to speak "class-generating" domain is much smaller than, for example, in allocation and market issues. It would also be futile for us to look for a more profound acceptance of the newer schemes and trends in this area. Whereas in the 1980s the property rights theory "journeyed" to us in a quite popular and superficial version, afterward it was virtually no longer taken up. The theoretical-empirical research of the school of Elinor Ostrom (1994) on common-pool resources is not known in Poland. Nor is the abundant literature on the pros and cons of a cooperative enterprise. In the first years of the accelerated systemic changes, somewhat better treatment was given to American theories concerning employee companies (ESOPs), and this thanks to the enthusiastic advocates of this form of ownership, the emigrant Krzysztof Ludwiniak (1989), and the author of many brochures, Jan Koziar from Wrocław. But this interest, too, became a thing of the past, even though Polish employee-owned or employee-managed companies brought a big surprise: they proved to be more efficient than it would follow from the prevalent theoretical views.[2]

Overcoming the Political Taboo

Poland was a unique country within the Soviet bloc: a significant private sector had survived and (except in agriculture) had even rapidly expanded. Therefore, it is surprising that ownership transformations, and especially privatization of state firms, remained a taboo topic for many years. You could freely talk about implementing the market system in the economy, but not about ownership transformations. An open debate on this subject was started almost twenty-five years after the appearance of the program postulates for introducing a free-market system, discussed broadly in the model debate of 1956–58. The taboo survived in the official and semi-official line of thought on reforms until the mid-1980s. To recall, the Solidarity program ratified in October 1981 did not go beyond self-management market socialism. The first program thesis of the union was: "We demand the introduction of self-management reform at all management levels, a new socioeconomic order that will associate the plan, self-management and the market."[3]

The ownership transformation postulate was absent even in the annexes to this program. The boldest proposal was presented then by Stefan Kurowski who wanted to "shift a certain portion of production and service activity between the state sector and the non-agricultural private sector."[4] However, he had in mind only investing in production and services "in the hands of private thesaurized [accumulated] foreign exchange resources."

In the 1980s it seemed that self-management market socialism was not weakened but strengthened, and this belief persisted until the close of the decade. The trend came to an end with the publication by Colloquia Communia of the book *Zachodni spór o socjalizm rynkowy* (Western Dispute over Market Socialism), a selection of texts with an introduction by T. Kowalik (Warsaw 1990), and the analytical forecast of development by W. Brus and K. Łaski, *Od Marksa do rynku* (From Marx to Market).*[5] Such was the mood of a large portion of economic writings of those years.

With the introduction of martial law in 1981, the very possibility of effectively reforming real socialism was questioned more and more often. Most critics still took it for granted that the ossified system would continue (in stagnation) for a long time to come. Such an assumption was shared by the group of economists and sociologists associated with S. who drew up *Raport: Polska 5 lat po sierpniu* (report: Poland 5 Years after August).[6] In the postulative part, the Report limited itself to marketization as the only prospect of thorough reform of the economy[7] and of management methods. In the section titled "Stosunek do własności" (Regarding Ownership), it is stated that "reprivatization"† is not a realistic alternative for our economy. However, by gradually socializing state property, by various methods we can create the prospect of involving great masses of the working people in overcoming the crisis.[8]

---

*In the Anglo-Saxon countries a stimulating debate on market socialism was continued until the mid-1990s (Roemer, 1994; Stiglitz, 1994; Roosevelt and Belkin, 1994).

†In Poland the notion of reprivatization was used for a long time to mean privatization. The two were differentiated only after 1989, when the matter of restitution of legally or illegally nationalized property appeared on the agenda. The word privatization came into use only in the early 1980s, as it did in the United States (Savas, 1992, 10).

Only a few foresaw the collapse of real socialism, something that created the prospect of changing the whole system. Probably most vividly, although still not without semantic limitations, this thought was expressed by Stefan Kurowski. Having summed up the pitiful results of the three reform attempts in Poland, he wrote: "And so there will be no fourth attempt at reform. There will be a change of the system. The central planning system must perish, so that no stone is left unturned. In its place another system will be built. . . . This system is market capitalism—a pluralist economy of many entities, in other words a society managing its affairs."[9] This was nonetheless an underground publication, referring to a possible mobilization of social forces capable of effecting systemic changes.

Later, in 1984, a conference was organized by the Institute of Economic Development of SGPiS (now the Warsaw School of Economics) under the title "Systemy własności a proces gospodarowania" (Ownership Systems and the Management Process), which proved to be crucial for the way of thinking of the economic circles about ownership issues. What was important here was not so much the still vague reform plans, as placing the problem of ownership at the center of theoretical and reform-related considerations. The conference was dominated by the topic of transformations of state ownership within the sphere of non-private ownership (social ownership, self-management, autonomy of firms, and the like). However, the privatization taboo was now being undermined in an increasingly bold way, which was most distinctly expressed, though still in Aesopian language, by Adam Lipowski:

"The Polish economy was in a state of stagnation, experiencing a relative reversal. In this situation it would be expedient to treat ownership relations in a pragmatic way, which of course does not predetermine anything. The point would 'only' be not to treat them as a taboo excluded from scholastic consideration. But on the other hand, we know that this sphere is treated in non-economic categories, with regard to which such considerations as the danger of degradation of the economy are perhaps of secondary importance. Yet is such an approach viable in the long run?"[10]

Proposals also appeared for actions toward differentiating owner-ship forms. This, in turn, initiated the process of the creation of plans for ownership transformations that included privatization, maybe still not yet on equal ground with, but alongside the postulate of marketization. The material of Kraków's Congress of Polish Economists of 1987 reveals the highly conservative leanings of these circles at the time, especially visible in what was eventually published in the bimonthly *Ekonomista*. However, certain progress could also be seen in thinking about entrepreneurship in association with ownership. The postulate of Wacław Wilczyński of consistent implementation of reform based on the famous three S's (self-reliance, self-management, and self-financing) was accompanied by the proposal of entrusting state prop-erty to the employees, including even the possibility of employees buying stock in their firms.[11] This, however, did not mean going beyond the framework of a certain form of market socialism. The fol-lowing is a typical declaration for those times: "The creation of a demand barrier is necessary not only with regard to consumers, but also in the area of production. . . . The key role in creating the condi-tions for the operation of the new system must be played with a dif-ferent approach to commodity-monetary categories. The shift of emphasis in market relations, in pricing practice, acknowledgment of the key role of profit, of economic surplus as an efficiency criterion are postulates that require a profound change in mentality."[12]

In the same year (1987), ownership changes also appeared in a document coming from a government organ. The "Tezy w sprawie II etapu reformy gospodarczej" (Theses Concerning the Second Stage of Economic Reform), published in April by the Committee for Economic Reform, spoke of pluralism and the necessity of equal treatment of various ownership forms. A possibility was also included for the transformation of state-owned enterprises into State Treasury companies that would be supervised by commercial banks under the principle of capital shares. In the years 1987–88, the first proposals were also submitted concerning the enfranchisement of employees. In non-governmental circles, employee companies were becoming very popular.

In 1987, Lesław Paga and Michał Zieliński had been among the first to formulate the postulate of the radical privatization of state enterprises. In early spring 1989 the conference organized by the Economic Section of the Catholic University of Lublin showed its preference for privatization in the very title: "Drogi i bariery prywatyzacji gospodarki polskiej" (Paths and Barriers to Privatization of the Polish Economy). The similarly named final document expressed the need for a radical change of the ownership system.[*] But the theoretical groundwork was still missing.

In Polish literature, probably the most theoretically sophisticated work on ownership is the book of Piotr Jasiński (1994),[†] who for years has resided in Oxford. Apart from this, Polish achievements in this area have been but an imitative reflection of just one trend of Western economics, mainly the American trend. Among translations, the work of E. S. Savas (1992), a specialist in housing and urban planning and a high-ranking official in the government of Ronald Reagan, can be distinguished. In the transforming countries, the work has been treated at times almost as a privatization handbook.

The reasons for the scarcity of ownership threads in economic literature can be sought in the following circumstances. First of all, economists less often than, say, sociologists generally take up social issues, and especially conflict-generating ones (maybe apart from public finance matters, especially concerning taxes). Second, problems of the market, allocation, and coordination tend to attract economists like a refined mathematical toolbox. They are a focal point of the standard education of young economists, not only in Poland. Charles Lindblom pointed this out in these dramatic words:

Dearth of orthodox econ. on ownership

---

[*]See *Res Publica* 7/1989. Cited after Maciej Bałtowski (1998), where the reader will find more details.
[†]The book can be regarded as a popularization of a more extensive and more theoretical work (Welfens and Jasiński, 1994) and Jasiński's unpublished doctoral dissertation, defended at the University of Oxford (see also Jasiński, Szablewski, Yarrow, 1995).

In many young minds efforts to master market system concepts prevail over intellectual development. In assimilating the market system ideals, young people for the first time try to grasp the puzzle of social organization, the possibilities of an order created in an unintentional way, the potential precision of unplanned allocation of resources, the idea of general equilibrium and the possibility of tracing the endless causal chain. . . . However, this illumination, like a strong beam of light, lightens up some while leaving other phenomena or processes in the shadows. And so they are overlooked or perceived only at random. The knowledge acquired in the course of study—derived from reading material, lectures, contacts with fellow students—fails in confrontation with life itself, since nearly everybody has the same views. . . . Economists may thus pay—and pay too much—for learned knowledge with impoverishment of their ability to understand the real world, a nearly genetically coded one-sidedness of attitude (cultishness and inbreeding) and abstraction of perception. I went through this process myself, in the beginning completely swept away by it. Later I tried to see both the market mechanism and matters remaining in the shadows. However, the impact of my early college years was so captivating that I never managed to free myself from it entirely.[13] →

Third, throughout the past decades we have witnessed a real invasion (not only in economics) of theories of decision making, theories of individual and public choice, or game theories, which fit snugly into the logic of the neoclassical theory of general equilibrium. The wealth of the market model creates the impression of an equally great wealth of research problems. However, there is much to indicate that ownership issues are potentially just as abundant as market issues, albeit greatly neglected these days. And though it is true that over the last decade neoclassical economics has turned more toward studies of institutions, this mainly concerns those created by the market or constraining the market.

Fourth, the specific situation of the transforming countries encouraged disregard for ownership problems. Many of these countries were plagued by high inflation and budgetary imbalance. This imposed

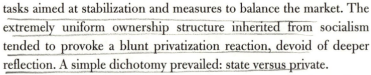

Post-socialist transition & dichotomous thinking

tasks aimed at stabilization and measures to balance the market. The extremely uniform ownership structure inherited from socialism tended to provoke a blunt privatization reaction, devoid of deeper reflection. A simple dichotomy prevailed: state versus private.

This situation existed not only in the countries of real socialism. Criticizing the well-known theorem (pitfall) of Garrett Hardin, who proposed privatization as the only remedy for the "tragedy of the commons," Elinor Ostrom wrote: "Limiting institutional prescriptions to either 'the market' or 'the state' means that the social-scientific 'medicine cabinet' contains only two nostrums."[14]

In nearly all the countries of real socialism, the process of privatization proved to be resistant to any concepts for lightning-speed measures and effects. It became clear that the formal and legal changes must be accompanied by evolutionary social transformations. This follows from the close association of organizational and legal changes with institutional changes. On the social scale, the institution of ownership is linked with the internalization of types of conduct relevant for a given form of ownership. This concerns behavior of the ownership title holders, as well as the employees entering with proprietors into a contract of employment.* To a lesser extent this also concerns suppliers and recipients. However, whereas awareness of the evolutionary character of ownership changes is by now adequately widespread, research on the process of institutionalization of the new system of ownership, and especially of the dependent social structure, is still in its infancy.

Ownership Theories

THE THEORY OF PROPERTY RIGHTS emerged in the United States at the turn of the 1960s. Irrespective of the highly charged ideology accompanying it, the theory contributed to a better understanding of contemporary mixed economies and to greater precision

---

*More about this in Kowalik, 2011.

of terminology. Thanks to this theory, the economic notion of owner-ship as a bundle of rights acquired greater wealth than plain legal own-ership titles; it also made possible more detailed research on the dis-tribution of property rights among various entities.

Yet all theorists of this concept associate it with the view (often accepted silently) that the most efficient is a free-market economy based on full, that is, exclusive and transferable, private ownership. The principal message of James Buchanan for policymakers of the post-socialist countries was: "Above all an individual has to have full ownership rights of the means of production that generate economic values, regardless of whether this concerns human or real capital. Only private ownership creates the right incentives. The basic argu-ment for private ownership has been known since the days of Aristotle. The human individual will care for production resources and their proper use only when there is a correlation between effort and the anticipated reward."[15] Similar premises were resorted to by the Nobel Prize–winner Gary Becker (1995). Thrilled with the Czech voucher system, which he described as a brilliant idea, Becker strongly encouraged politicians of countries undergoing transformation to carry out the fastest possible privatization.

All property rights theorists ignored the concept of functional ownership, very similar on the theoretical level, but implying opposite normative conclusions. It had been advocated several decades earlier by the British sociologist Richard H. Tawney (1921) and the Swedish law theorist Östen Undén. In more recent times, its proponent was the Swedish economist Gunnar Adler-Karlsson (1968). The concept is interesting in that it was created with full awareness of its social and structure-generating implications.

THE SOCIAL SIGNIFICANCE OF PROPERTY OWNERSHIP. In economic writings property ownership is treated as the main, some-times nearly the only, precondition for improving efficiency. This is to be ensured by privatization, because the driving force of entrepreneur-ship is to be an interest of the actual owner in the results of property use. However, there is little interest in the question of how a given ownership form affects incentives of those individuals who are deprived of property. To put it in a more general way, the equally important and extensive social functions of ownership transformations are overlooked, above all, as a factor of the new social stratification. And yet ownership co-defines and at times even determines many areas of public life. I shall refer here to the opinions of two outstanding American economists and political scientists: Robert Dahl and Charles Lindblom.*

Dahl considered ownership relations and an unequal division of control functions over property in society to be the biggest threat to liberty and equality. He emphasized that ownership lies behind great differences in income, status, skills, information, control of the mass media, and access to political leaders. He demonstrated that from the ownership structure one can even predict the life chances of the unborn.[16] He applied great effort to theoretically and practically justify employee participation in management, which he called economic democracy. An equally abundant thread concerns corporate ownership, represented by the pioneering book of the American authors Adolf A. Berle and Gardiner C. Means (1932), on separating management from ownership, the no-less-known book by James Burnham, *The Managerial Revolution* (1941), and similar output by Joseph Schumpeter. This trend of thinking also includes the refined studies on the principal-agent theory (Eugene Fama, Michael Jensen, William Meckling) and the "information economics" of Joseph Stiglitz. Particular attention is due to the hypothesis of Ivan Szelenyi and co-authors, derived from this trend, that a managerial capitalism was emerging in the countries of Central Europe, that is, "capitalism without capitalists."

*These two authors are eminent representatives of American liberal thought. Dahl, a political scientist with a sound economic background, and Lindblom, an economist who also became a political scientist, began their scholarly careers with the well-known book *Politics, Economics and Welfare* (1953), which for a long time was regarded as a kind of handbook serving socio-technical improvement of a capitalist economy through the implementation of fragmentary reforms. However, two decades later, both, though each already under his own name only, abandoned this optimistic stand in favor of a criticisms of the American (or Anglo-Saxon) type of capitalism.

Similar ideas were expounded by Lindblom: "Because public functions in the market system rest in the hands of business, it follows that jobs, prices, production, growth, the standard of living, and the economic security of everyone all rest in their hands. Consequently government officials cannot be indifferent to how well business performs its functions."[17]

In the light of these arguments, a realistic description of the emerging socioeconomic order, that is, the comprehensive transformation process, has to take into account research on the ownership structure and relationships. Though it is true that historical experience and theoretical research have proven that an economy totally subordinated to state bureaucracy is inefficient, drawing hasty conclusions from this that state enterprises are inefficient in principle in other circumstances as well would be a mistake. Evidence can be found in the many efficiently operating state-owned enterprises.

Quite often one hears, and rightly so, that state enterprises are more exposed to the moral hazard of (at times corrupt) influences of politicians and the state bureaucracy. Many theorists, however, question the general hypothesis that state enterprises are inefficient in principle. "It cannot be expected that one form of ownership will be superior to the other in all industries and in all countries," aptly wrote George Yarrow,[18] an ownership theorist and privatization researcher in Great Britain.

The same thought is expressed even more emphatically by other British economists:

"The question of public enterprise efficiency cannot be divorced from politics. Such efficiency depends on the attitude of the state toward issues like competition and budgetary policy, which in turn depends, above all, on the ability of the state to insulate itself against conservative pressures. . . . Where the state can insulate itself adequately, public enterprise may be every bit as efficient as private enterprise. It may even offer certain additional social and economic advantages. On the other hand, it may well happen that following privatization, there will be continued pressure on the part of the bureaucrats."[19]

Similar views were expressed by Stiglitz (1994). He even pointed out that corporate governance of a state firm can at times be more efficient and cheaper than in a private firm with dispersed ownership. However, these were reactions, more or less theoretically underpinned, to strictly private or exclusively state ownership.

The 1980s brought heightened interest in various group ownership forms. There has already been mention of the research of Elinor Ostrom.[20] This scholar, together with her team, focused their research on such specific areas as water reservoirs or fisheries. It is, however, difficult to say to what extent this research throws a new light on group ownership forms in other areas of economic activity. This would concern all forms of ownership that are somewhere between state ownership and purely private ownership, or between individual owners and joint stock companies.

Probably the oldest of these group forms is the cooperative, with its origins dating back to Robert Owen. At the beginning of the twentieth century, in Poland the concept of Edward Abramowski, called the Cooperative Republic, was popular. A form similar to cooperatives was the Israeli kibbutz, popular in the 1950s to 1970s. A related form to the cooperative was employee self-management, beginning with the English guild socialism of the 1920s, through various theoretical generalizations of the Yugoslav experience, up to the program of the "Self-Governing Republic," accepted in 1981 by the Solidarity Trade Union at its first congress.

More refined theories were also formulated within this trend. For example, following the appearance of the well-known article by Benjamin Ward, "The Firm in Illyria" (1958), dozens of authors carried on a dispute on the advantages and disadvantages of a self-managing cooperative or similar enterprise.* In the United States many writings appeared on Employee Stock Ownership Plans (ESOP). In Europe there was even more lively discussion, especially in the 1980s

---

*The following took part in it, inter alia: Evsey Domar, Joan Robinson, Jaroslav Vanek, Benjamin Ward, Branko Horvat, James Meade, Mario Nuti, Laura d'Andrea Tyson, David Levine, and Milica Uvalic.

and early 1990s, about the different forms of employee self-management or the participation of employees in decision making. Here particular mention should be made of the theoretical treatises of the 1986 Nobel Prize holder from Cambridge, James Meade (a collection of his treatises was published in 1993). The two volumes of studies and sketches issued by the two British theorists D. C. Jones and J. Svejnar under the title *Advances in the Economic Analysis of Participation and Labour-Managed Firms* (1985, 1987) offer a good idea of the ambitions and vastness of interests of this trend. Next to these, interesting practical experiences include the famous, innovative, and thriving cooperative Mondragon in the Basque Country, present also in Poland, evoking great theoretical interest among sociologists and economists.

At the interface of these two trends, so to speak, there appeared concepts searching for a liberal alternative to the Anglo-Saxon version of capitalism. The 1985 book by R. Dahl, *A Preface to Economic Democracy*, contains a critique of the hierarchic, undemocratic ownership structure of capitalism and the reasoning behind the postulate of far-reaching employee participation in management.*

All of the ownership concepts referred to, of which most cannot be classified as only state or only private, form the basis for normative (postulative) considerations on the ideal or target system (for example, of the "Self-Governing Republic"), or for reform of existing systems. In various countries and to various extents, they already have their designata. Irrespective of their practical significance as target concepts, they can be seen as thought constructions that facilitate analysis of reality and create the analytical framework for it. They are usually situated within even more general systemic concepts. The best-known ones are the socialist visions, utopias.† However, it was not only socialists or communists, but

---

*Social justice, that is, "support for a fairly just and stable society—truly democratic not only in the political, but also in the social-economic sphere," was also sought by Zbigniew Brzeziński (1999), otherwise a rather conservative liberal.
†Probably the most outstanding critic of socialism of this kind in the 1940s and 1950s was Abraham Bergson, and in the 1990s Joseph Stiglitz. The former criticized it within the framework of neoclassical theory, the latter criticized certain foundations of this theory.

liberals as well that have had their utopias. In political economy one such utopia has been the concept of perfect competition. Presented as a theoretical generalization, it is often treated as a normative concept, an unattainable target goal that should be pursued. In the 1930s and 1940s, theoretical welfare economics, intended as normative, came into being, serving as the basis for many programs of economic policy. Some created on its basis systemic visions of a more efficient, yet also just economy. These include Oskar Lange's concept of market socialism, which to this day provokes discussion. But welfare economics has served best as an instrument for criticizing existing systems: capitalism, various versions of socialism, and communism.

Turning to Privatization and Mixed Forms

In actually existing ownership relations throughout the world, there has been a general reversal from public ownership in favor of private ownership, but two other directions of change have been just as important. The first is a steady expansion of the sector of nongovernmental organizations not operating for profit. In various Western countries, they employ from several to over 12 percent or so of the workforce.[21] They, of course, have property at their disposal, though probably this is less than their share in employment. These organizations cannot be easily classified, but one thing is certain: their property is neither "purely" private nor state-owned.

Another development has been the extensive intermingling of various forms of ownership within the same enterprise. State firms can resign from a large portion of direct activity, turning it over to private hands in the form of a lease, franchising, and so on. Even a state or municipal hospital can downsize its staff and outsource some of its services to private physicians and nurses, clinics, or dentists. Often partial privatization is carried out through the sale of a portion of shares or stakes, with the state leaving for itself only the controlling stake.

This is characteristic not only for economies moving toward a capitalist market system. Similar processes occur both in highly developed economies and those in transition to a capitalist market system. Among the countries of real socialism, processes of diversification of state ownership occurred earliest and most visibly in Hungary. In the early 1980s, Janos Kornai presented a table titled "Combinations of public ownership and private entrepreneurial activities," where he enumerated leasing (also through public auction), rental, teams working in a state firm and paying for the use of space and other means of production, but also contributing their own means and a certain rent fee, as well as workers illegally using equipment of state firms.[22]

Both of the developments referred to above lead to ownership that is described as "neither private nor state,"[23] that is, social or private-state, or, depending on the proportion, state-private.

Ownership Transformations at the Round Table

During the Round Table negotiations of 1989, a marked difference of opinion occurred concerning the future ownership structure, dividing the democratic opposition and the ruling party. It is interesting that not only the general concept of the new order, but also several other important provisions managed to gain the acceptance of both parties to these talks.

First of all, there was acceptance of the cardinal demand for a "constitutional guarantee of the durability of a pluralist ownership structure" and agreement to eliminate the existing founding bodies and to establish an institution representing the State Treasury, namely the National Property Fund. It was to be vested with the power to administer state property, which would include the sale of state assets under statutorily defined principles. And so privatization was not treated as something marginal, since already in 1989 postulates were put forward to reduce the then huge budgetary deficit with resources derived mainly "from the sale and lease of components of state assets: apartments, land, shops, production facilities and ownership stakes (shares and the like)."[24]

There was a dispute over the fact that the government party was avoiding concrete commitments in ownership transformations, whereas the Solidarity Party postulated the declaration of concrete ownership forms: employee and joint-stock companies, leases concluded as a result of competitive bidding, and renewed cooperative forms. In a broader view of the property rights theory, many settlements and one-sidedly submitted postulates in other sectors of social and economic policy indirectly concerned ownership transformations, and especially the process of de-statization of the economy. It was even agreed that by 1991 (which is exactly when this happened), the Stock Exchange would be established, which naturally assumed the existence of a significant number of private firms. In terms of a program, a whole "new economic order" was on the agenda, although implemented by the evolutionary method. The same principles were repeated, though in a more general way, by Solidarity in the pre-electoral declaration in May 1989.

The rapid growth of the private sector, as well as the privatization of state firms, at least at the speed of the years preceding the creation of the National Investment Funds, acquired adequate political support at the time. Thus the view of Piotr Jasiński[25] that privatization was not present in the Round Table Agreements is not true.* The official settlements deny this. However, there was no consent for any strong privileges for these newly emerging enterprises. The principle of equal rights for various ownership forms was adhered to. When designing the radical reform, it was not clearly settled what shape this "new economic order" would assume. Nothing was planned that would stand in contradiction to, shall we say, the Austrian or Scandinavian models. And it could not have been in any other way, as the new system was to be formed in close cooperation with the trade unions.

*Cezary Józefiak shows memory loss when he writes that at the Round Table "discussion on the ownership structure did not come about. Ownership was mainly discussed on other occasions. For example, when we demanded reduction of the budgetary deficit, we advised that more apartments, shops, small factories should be privatized" (Gajdziński, 1999, 160).

And yet, in September 1989, an entirely different path and different program were chosen. A leap to a private market economy was proclaimed, supposedly based on tried-out schemes, and therefore free of the risk of costly experimentation. But it turned out to be a great experiment because of the chosen method, bearing no comparison with the postwar leap into a centrally planned economy, which, after all, had been accompanied by quite rapid growth.

The proclamation in late summer 1989 of a speedy transition to private economy and the free market signified an unexpected victory of the theories and ideologies of the school (doctrine) of property rights and the free market concept of J. Buchanan, M. Friedman, and F. A. Hayek. This had a significant impact on the perception of ownership itself and on the course of privatization.

The first bill on privatization, prepared by Krzysztof Lis, which aimed almost solely at capital privatization, transforming state firms into joint-stock companies, was received with criticism (of probably the majority) of the Economic Council—the government's advisory body—headed by Witold Trzeciakowski. Its deputy chairman, Jan Mujżel, felt that the biggest shortcoming of the government program was the withdrawal from the principle of pluralism of ownership transformations (accepted, after all, in the Round Table Agreements). He referred to the recent list published in *Fortune* of 500 enterprises with the highest gains, saying: "We have on it among world giants 80 state firms, where in efficiency as a rule they rank higher than the places on the list corresponding to sales volume. Meanwhile, the authors of the privatization program indiscriminately declare that a state enterprise is in principle inefficient."[26] He also warned against a crusade opposing employee self-management and shareholding. "Opening the road to such conflict is a great political burden on the whole concept and an immense, purely pragmatic weakness of the program. The self-management milieu should and can be a powerful ally in ownership transformations."[27]

May I add that the bill contradicted not only the aims of the employee self-management movement, still strong in Poland at the time, but also the whole intellectual and legislative structure fought for and won mainly by S. It was a blow to the employee councils existing in nearly all state enterprises. Consequently, a sharp conflict of the authorities with this movement ensued.

Let me recall the most important events. The participants of the employee self-management movement began preparing various concepts of non-state, but not purely private, ownership forms. These encountered the opposition of the authorities, which at the beginning were in favor of a dogmatically understood privatization of state firms in the form of joint-stock companies (or, less willingly, limited liability companies). The most consistent advocate of this form was the government plenipotentiary for ownership transformations, Krzysztof Lis. In his letter to the British embassy, he emphatically objected to the plan for employee companies that had been prepared with the participation of British experts. He protested against the financing of these experts by the British know-how fund, maintaining that employee companies were contradictory to government policy. Employee companies were also opposed by L. Balcerowicz, who said that they were an expression of leanings toward cooperative socialism, whereas the target goal should be a private market economy.

The conflict with the self-management movement protracted the negotiations on the bill on privatization. A dozen or more successive bills were drawn up, and after thirteen or so iterations, the Act on Privatization of State-Owned Enterprises was prepared, to be passed by the Sejm on July 13, 1990.

The main controversy in parliament took place within the otherwise liberal Civic Parliamentary Club. A small group of left-wingers (derisively called a "cooperative") demanded greater participation rights for workers, reduction of the rights of the state organ responsible for privatization (in the beginning this was to be an agency, not a ministry), and the observance of the principle of pluralism and equality of ownership forms. This principle was already expressed in the very name of the law (on ownership transformations and not on privatization).

In the end, not much was gained. The postulate of pluralism was taken into account in the name of the ministry—Ministry for Ownership Transformations—but not in the name of the privatization law. The only significant gain of the "cooperative" was the introduction in the law, although in a very general and abbreviated form, of provisions allowing state firms to be turned over to employee companies in the form of leasing. Certain rebates in the leasing installments, however, were accompanied by a very high—for the recession conditions of the time—barrier of attaining 20 percent of the firm's value as the initial capital contribution of the new company. This encouraged, if not downright forced, employees impoverished by the recession to mobilize funds illegally or on the borderline of legality, or—worse yet—artificially reducing the firm's value. The authorities also created criteria, later tightened, concerning the size of firms that could be turned over to employee companies.

Many economists and politicians realized that the debate over the Act on Privatization was of fundamental significance for the shape of the emerging system. This, however, was a surrogate battle, compensating for the deficiencies of the public discourse over the earlier stabilization program, which the authorities did not want to have.

9. Open and Hidden Privatization Strategies

In economic literature, the following privatization objectives are enumerated (not in order of importance):

1. Improvement of efficiency of enterprises and/or the entire economy.
2. Expansion of the range of competition through the constraint of monopolies.
3. Limitation of intervention of the government and administration in the activity of enterprises (their depolitization).
4. Concentration of private capital as a source of accumulation and growth.
5. Reduction of government subsidies to state firms, that is, elimination or reduction of soft budget constraints.
6. Increase of state budget income to finance other reforms; for example, of the pension system.
7. Creation of a favorable framework for foreign investment.
8. Facilitation of EU integration.
9. Reduction of foreign debt.
10. Creation of a middle class as the basis of democracy.

11. Weaken trade unions and pressures to raise wages in the public sector.
12. Gain support of the employees for the privatization of their firm.
13. Gain purely political-electoral advantages of local politicians.
14. Creation of conditions for intended benefits from personal arrangements (clientelism) or even encouraging corruption.
15. Dispersion of ownership (for example, aiming toward property-owning democracy) in the form of stocks or employee companies.

The above list clearly shows that the ruling groups or claimants to power are in no hurry to reveal their true intentions. To a no lesser extent, this concerns the forms and paths of privatization, which depend not only on the political and economic "imagination" of the people in power but also on their interests. For example, opening the path to non-private and at the same time non-state forms of ownership may be hindered by the belief in the decisive significance of the principle of exclusivity and transferability of property rights. More often, though, earthly considerations are decisive. But obviously no politician is going to reveal that he has in view an opportunity to obtain bribes or access to lucrative stakes or even purely political (electoral) interests. Similarly, weakening the influence of trade unions is more openly discussed by people close to the authorities than by the authorities themselves. This is especially so when the ruling parties are doomed to the support of large trade unions.

The decisions of politicians are largely dependent on their doctrinal beliefs. If they are convinced that private firms absolutely surpass state firms in efficiency, they will press for fast privatization, without showing much regard for the short-term costs. This is also true in the case of faith in the power of the capital market as a mechanism of verifying the efficiency of individual firms.

For analyzing the mutual interdependence of the system and privatization, it may be particularly significant to refer to the distinction of two types of privatization, as introduced by Bruno Dallago (1998). The first denotes methods of ownership transformations that favor spillover of the whole system in the direction of improved efficiency, even when they themselves do not become a good example. The other mainly consists of an improvement of the internal capacity of a firm for adaptation, imitation, and innovation. Ownership transformations leading to greater microeconomic entrepreneurship are "contagious" for the whole system, but only indirectly. They encourage other enterprises, managers, employees, and state institutions to changes in a similar direction. Such an approach is closely linked to what has been called corporate governance, but not only that. The advantage is that it directs attention to effective forms of ownership transformation in close association with management. In effect, this is a departure from the traditional division: state or private and the related mad dash to privatization, never mind in what form, so long as it limits state participation as quickly as possible.

The Pace of Privatization

Many domestic and foreign academic economists advocated rapid privatization in the decisive period of transformation.* Voices calling for restraint were much more scarce.† Such "fast track" advocates as Rafał Krawczyk, Janusz Lewandowski, Jan Szomburg, Irena Grosfeld, and above all Jeffrey Sachs and David Lipton, postulated one form or another of giveaways. The first was in favor of turning over enterprises to employee self-management, but with the clear intention of later following this up with a fast concentration of stocks. The remaining three recommended mass privatization first in the form of vouchers, then in the form of "participation certificates" of National Investment Funds.

*The most important names include Gary Becker, James Buchanan, Marek Dąbrowski, Irena Grosfeld, Rafał Krawczyk, Janusz Lewandowski, Jan Macieja, Jan Szomburg, Jeffrey Sachs, Jan Winiecki, and Stanisław Wellisz. A typical slogan of the "impatient" group can be the words of Michał Zieliński in the title: "Prywatyzujmy, prywatyzujmy, prywatyzujmy" (Privatize, Privatize, Privatize) (Zieliński, 1992). Many times I declared that there is no method of organization that would ensure even minimal efficiency to state enterprises.
†They were expressed most clearly by Joseph Berliner, Ryszard Bugaj, Włodzimierz Brus, Janos Kornai, Kazimierz Łaski, and Zdzisław Sadowski.

The first non-communist government succumbed to the illusion that it was possible to rapidly shift from a dominant state sector to a private sector. The belief shared by many economists, that privatization was a question of just a few years, continued to prevail. But this was not so with Krzysztof Lis, appointed Government Plenipotentiary for Ownership Transformations, who favored the case-by-case method of privatization, in the preferred form of joint-stock companies. This is something that cannot be done quickly. It was only a few years later, when fast privatization had become a fact, that it became clear that haste was bringing more harm than good. Yet even recently, it sometimes happens that esteemed economists accuse the Mazowiecki-Balcerowicz team of having overlooked the opportunity for rapid privatization, thereby "wasting the historical chance of radical, irreversible economic changes in the early 1990s, in conditions of extraordinary trust of the people in state authority."[1] This daring suggestion would be hard to defend as being responsible. Nevertheless, the parties of the right-wing opposition have often attacked the authorities for carrying out privatization too slowly.

In this context, the views of two American economists are interesting. Joseph Berliner, a well-known researcher of the Soviet economy, expressed the following opinion before a committee of the American Congress: "The fact that it would be better to have had private enterprises rather than state enterprises in the first place is not an argument for rapid privatization, or for slow privatization, or even for any privatization at all. It all depends on what funny things might happen on the way to the forum."[2] He also warned that the social and economic benefits from privatization in Russia or in other countries with similar economies may turn out to be much smaller than anticipated. In his opinion, the main faults of the Soviet system did not lie in the form of ownership but in the absence of realistic prices, which made it impossible for firms to make rational decisions; in the absence of free entry, especially for small firms; in planning in physical units; in foreign trade monopoly; in separation of R&D institutes from industry; in the centralist form of management; and in the bureaucratized system of investment allocation.

Without denying that privatization of large enterprises can improve efficiency, Berliner cautioned against haste, which would encourage incompetence and the transfer of property into the wrong hands. Hasty privatization cannot be carried out well, and so it is more of a hindrance than a factor facilitating the transformation process.[3] He compared Russia with China, the latter having set its stakes on far-reaching marketization of the economy, without rushing with the privatization of large and medium-sized enterprises.

These two large countries were compared in a nearly identical way by Joseph Stiglitz, who especially emphasized the conditions contributing to corruption in cases of fast privatization.[*] In his opinion, "some evidence suggests that much of the gains from privatization occur before privatization as a result of the process of putting in place effective individual and organizational incentives."[†4]

There are two other arguments for slower privatization. The first is that the experience of the initial phase of transformation has shown that a large state sector can be reconciled with the market and growth of economy if the market is open to foreign competition and if state firms enjoy broad autonomy. The second is that the autonomy of firms must be accompanied by the belief that they cannot count on significant financial assistance from the state coffers. In this respect, Poland's experience in the first years of systemic transformation has been telling. The market was thrown wide open to external competition and the economy underwent radical marketization, while the public sector remained predominant. This did not hold back the economy from entering the path of relatively fast growth for several years.

---

[*]Similar warnings were addressed to the socialist countries by the outstanding expert in financial markets, Oskar Lange's student, Hyman Minski (1992). Instead of privatization, he recommended public holding companies, as an interim stage, pending the establishment of a real market.

[†]This can be seen in the well-known fact that British Steel Corporation became one of the most efficient firms of this sector in the world just when it was being prepared for privatization. In the late 1990s even the World Bank was no longer demanding fast privatization, nor did it place emphasis on its key significance (Nellis, 1999).

The above throws an interesting light on the polemic, little known in Poland, between Stanisław Gomułka and Janos Kornai. Earlier, the Polish economist had questioned Kornai's hypothesis that the most important and immanent feature of really existing socialism was widespread shortages.[5] He returned to this issue after the first years of transformation, pointing out that liberalization of prices nearly at once eliminated most shortages.[6]

Maybe the hypothesis of the Hungarian could be formulated in a more cautious way: over a longer time span, private ownership "feels" better in predominantly market surroundings than in bureaucratic-centralist surroundings. The market, in turn, as coordinator, favors the transformation of property rights in the direction of their privatization. There are, of course, periods when it is necessary to intensely mobilize unused resources, in which case bureaucratic coordination is tempting, with the dominance of state ownership. This ensures high efficiency of the extensive type, with great capacity to rapidly mobilize unused forces and means. For a certain time this can produce a high rate of growth. But it is hard to prevent the high barrier to further reforms that may be created by social groups formed in the context of such a structure. This is evidenced by many experiences of the countries of real socialism, where imperious interest groups have blocked the transition to intensive methods of economic growth. In addition, they pose a threat to liberty.

The second argument for slower privatization is more of a political nature. If there are no prospects for a strategic investor, privatization may bring benefits only in the distant future. The proliferation of inefficient private entities would simply lead to a further erosion of faith in (any kind of) market economy. In deciding on privatization, both the economic and social costs of this process must be taken into account, as well as the possible gains in the foreseeable future.

Ever since the mid-1990s the privatization of individual firms in Poland has been mostly determined by two factors: a desire to weaken the bargaining power of the trade unions and efforts to increase state budgetary income in order to hold in check the budgetary deficit and public debt. From the moment of the implementation of the pension reform (1999), funds were needed to co-finance it. And with the accession to the European Union, new funds were needed not only for payment of the membership fee, but also to support projects co-financed by EU structural funds.

When faced with these tasks, postulates to restructure enterprises before their privatization are doomed to oblivion. Only after many years of unsuccessful attempts to reform mining have the authorities come to understand that restructuring entails considerable costs.

The Pact on State Enterprise in Jacek Kuroń's Version

The Pact on State Enterprise covered many problems, and it is not easy to categorize it. Its most important feature was the proposal for rapid privatization, but with the cooperation of employees. This concept of Minister of Labor and Social Affairs Jacek Kuroń was drawn up and disseminated by two of his deputies: Michał Boni and Andrzej Bączkowski. It was said to have germinated during the government of Tadeusz Mazowiecki (1989–90), and a similar scheme had been worked on during the government of Jan Krzysztof Bielecki (1991), to become crystallized during the government of Hanna Suchocka (1992–93). It would be the first pact, soon followed by others, for example, on reconstruction of agriculture and rural areas.[7]

> The essence of the Pact on State Enterprise is the proposal that the workers and administration staff of enterprises take part in deciding on their fate, on their transformation and reform. Therefore we are proposing a whole new set of laws and amendments to old ones, for the purpose of changing the conditions of operation of state firms. In talks with the trade unions we would like to establish the conditions in which an enterprise should operate and undergo transformation. Within three months workers could resolve how their firm would change.[8]

These words opened the elaborate propositions of the government, which included a list of possible transformation forms, facilitations for employee leasing, a declaration on changes in regulations on collective agreements and health and safety at the workplace. From summer 1992 to March of the following year, negotiations were under way with the trade unions and employers, leading to changes in the content matter of the individual drafts. The political parties also carried on disputes, and differences of opinion surfaced within the coalition of the government of Hanna Suchocka. When the agreements were already signed with the major trade unions and the first bills had been tabled to the Sejm, Suchocka's government fell. The victorious new coalition (SLD-PSL) did not take up the main propositions of the pact, with one exception: it established, in the spirit of Kuroń's concept, the Trilateral Commission, which is active to this day, though in a rickety and at times vestigial form. In the words of David Ost (2010), it is an example of "illusory corporatism."

I consider two guiding ideas of the pact to be the most important. Kuroń (and thanks to his efforts, the otherwise quite conservative government) understood that further reforms should not be carried out above society, but with its participation. Several years later he wrote about this in dramatic words:

> Today's parties resemble more a line waiting for fruit preserves than people gathered around a vision for Poland. . . . The state has been captured [by parties], which means there are various kinds of corruption and if people who want to do something are admitted to the top, then this is to deprave them. . . . Unexpectedly, it turns out that they have obtained some very lucrative posts—they become presidents of companies, members of supervisory boards, plenipotentiaries or advisors without in fact any significant qualifications. Also because of this most people . . . have a decidedly skeptical attitude to any reforms. These are not their reforms. These are reforms of the authorities and in the eyes of a large portion of society they serve only the authorities. I realized all of this very late. But when I noticed this mechanism . . . I pushed through the Pact on the State Enterprise. . . . I wanted to finally put an end to bureaucratic privatization.[9]

The reverse side of this coin was much worse, not to say astonishingly naïve. To recall, Kuroń (the government) imagined that these strategic decisions would be taken within three months! Even after this period was extended, following negotiations, to six months, and taking into account that the whole operation was to encompass as many as 6,000 to 6,500 enterprises, the whole idea bordered on sheer fantasy. The line of thinking: bad officials, good workers, and managing staff contrasted with the then visible unethical conduct (of not only the managing staff) that was so common during this unprecedented deep collapse. Oversight of the privatization process became a necessity.

Remembering Kuroń's acceptance of the "jump" into the market in the way proposed by Jeffrey Sachs, the pact could be evaluated as follows: with no prospects for a privatization leap to be performed by the government and administration, let us try to do this together with the people. In other words, Kuroń still did not relinquish the philosophy of jumping into the new system "at one go." He did not understand that the bigger the concentration of changes within a short time, the greater the corruption. It is sad to write this, because at the end of 1993 he returned to his leftist views, and in 1994 he presented a very fundamental critique of the effected transformation.[10]

10. Ownership Transformations in Practice

In the second half of the 1980s, there was an eruption of uncontrolled privatization of the economy from below. Just before the collapse of the previous system, the legal framework was furnished for this process. The main path of privatization of the national economy was at first expansion of the old private sector (growth of existing firms), but even more of a new private sector, emerging and operating outside the state sector. According to economists,[1] the pace of growth of this sector was determined by five factors:

1. Legal ease in the establishment of private firms;
2. Existence of many niches, especially in trade and services, neglected or even banned in the previous system;
3. Taxes and insurance fund payments were a fraction of those in state entities;
4. Extreme liberalization of foreign trade;
5. Immense surpluses of the state production apparatus, part of which had been transferred at a very low cost to private firms, often in corrupt ways. (The well-known *nomenklatura* companies were created in this way.)

These and other facilitations for the private sector are overlooked by Jan Winiecki. And so he can endlessly carry on that "the most successful were those which thanks to liberalization/deregulation with one sweep of the pen were left to be resolved by spontaneous market processes. Unleashed human initiative not without 'friction' and by trial and error quickly generated an efficient mechanism of stimulation and selection that led to the expansion, faster than anywhere else, of a private sector created from the ground (privatization 'from below')."[2] For Winiecki, the spectacular expansion of the private sector from below is confirmation of "Hayek's theory of spontaneous order, formed as a result of decentralized decisions of producers and consumers." In his opinion, this theory has the advantage of being generally applicable and has played a special role in the post-socialist countries, corrupt and unusually slow in making ownership changes.

In this general movement, the players of the *nomenklatura* offshoot of privatization consisted of managers of state firms of various rank, government and party functionaries associated with them, along with their families. The process, commonly called "enfranchisement of the *nomenklatura*," deserves attention because it was then that the phenomenon of corruptive privatization, or arranged clientelistic privatization, developed. This led me to formulate the warning, as early as 1988, against "the threat of Panamization of the Polish economy."[3]

The state sector shortly became a cash machine, which was made easier by the authorities through relevant legal regulations. In October 1987, the Act on State-Owned Enterprises of 1981 was amended. A provision was included allowing for the establishment of state companies not only with other legal entities, but also with private individuals. In this spirit, an appropriate implementing regulation of the Council of Ministers was drawn up, thereby allowing for the creation of private companies on the basis of assets of state enterprises. This was done during the government of Zbigniew Messner. The subsequent government of Mieczysław Rakowski went even further. The Act on Financial Management of State-Owned Enterprises of 31 January 1989 stipulated that "property components of state assets may be transferred to legal entities or private individuals to be used … for the purpose of conducting economic activity."[4] And the Act on Certain Conditions of Consolidation of the National Economy (called a special law) allowed for the transfer of part of state assets to private companies in lease. These laws sanctioned the plunder of the state sector earlier begun by its own managers. The state sector was highly taxed to maintain the entire state infrastructure and doomed to hopeless competition with the nearly tax-free private firms that were also paying infinitesimal customs duties.

Under these circumstances, the number of private owners of firms doubled within just a few years. In the decided majority, these were persons outside the *nomenklatura*, which brought financial (to a lesser extent social) advancement for hundreds of thousands, and together with families, well over a million people. Interestingly enough, among the new entrepreneurs, a large portion consisted of unskilled and skilled workers, comprising two-thirds of this group, and only one-quarter came from the intelligentsia and white-collar employees.[5] Such owners could not become carriers of social progress. On the contrary, they along with the workers hired by them imitated nineteenth-century work relations. Breaking elementary rules of the labor code concerning safety at the workplace or the statutory obligation of concluding written contracts became quite commonplace in these firms. What is worse, the reports of the National Labour Inspectorate (PIP) were invariably alarming for many years: *Prawo pracy coraz częściej łamane. W pracy bardziej niebezpiecznie* (The labor law broken more and more often. More dangerous at workplace).[6] According to this source, in 1995 alone, the number of accidents on the job rose by 20 percent compared to the year before; the number of penal sentences rose by 12 percent. In as many as 70 percent of the inspected firms, it was discovered that "regulations on wages were broken; among other things there was payment of wages lower than the minimum wage."[7] The number of accidents and offenses was increasing faster than the number of firms. PIP reports of subsequent years were similar.

Beginning with the 2000 recession, there have been recurring delays in the payment of wages. The daily *Gazeta Wyborcza* (2004) wrote: "Two-thirds of the inspected firms are behind in payment for work—according to information of the National Labour Inspectorate. The situation is improving, but slowly. It is still catastrophic, we are a disgraceful exception in Europe—the trade unions complain." The deputy minister of economy and labor cited by *Gazeta* expressed the view that "in Poland a 'culture of not paying employees' has developed." And a bulletin of a government institution referred to the words of John Paul II, who called this pathology "a sin that cries to heaven for vengeance."[8]

Repeated infringement of the labor law in the private sector stood out in a negative way against other legal systems in the civilized world. This tendency was gaining in strength and even at the outset of transformation sociologists warned that such "untamed" developments may become the most serious obstacle to reasonable transformation.[9]

The costs of the hasty and uncontrolled emergence of private firms do not exhaust the whole issue. Taking all this into consideration, it would be hard to perceive the rapid expansion of the private sector of small enterprises in Poland as a sign of social progress. The "firms"— in the beginning spreading out their wares on camp beds in street and bazaar stalls—did not produce many true business individuals, not to mention the illusory hope that a middle class would ever be formed as the social basis of democracy and contemporary capitalism. The expanded assortment of goods in the consumer market and the advancement of some of the workers to the position of proprietor do not offset the obvious deterioration of working conditions and the dehumanization of social relations at the workplace. Often this is ordinary primitive nineteenth-century exploitation, not without its effect on the culture of statutorily regulated privatization of the state sector.

The situation began changing, people of business remembered they had a social responsibility, and employees partly regained the capacity to claim their rights only following entry in the European Union, and especially after the resultant mass emigration. The leading mass media, usually serving business circles, this time also changed their tone.

Privatization
of the State Sector

The trend of enfranchisement of the *nomenklatura* and the expansion of the old and new private sector remained in the background of interest of the government authorities, who focused their attention on statutorily regulated ownership transformations of the state sector. Shortly after the enactment of the provisions of the Act on Privatization, it turned out that the so-called British path of classical privatization was unusually time-, labor-, and fund-consuming. The concept of mass privatization of Janusz Lewandowski and Jan Szomburg (1990), both from Gdańsk, would serve to speed up the process significantly. Employee ownership was now also tolerated, as it turned out to be the most often chosen form of ownership transformation. However, all the privatization forms put together allowed for a much slower pace than planned. The declaration of the government of T. Mazowiecki to privatize half of the state sector within three years turned out to be totally unrealistic.

In general, it can be said that—as in the case of the program of stabilization and liberalization—the ultimate result of the privatization measures turned out to be different from the program initially put forward by the authorities. In reality, ownership transformations proceeded at a much slower pace and along tracks quite distant from those initially recommended. This concerned not only the exaggerated optimism relating to the technical efficiency of the government apparatus, but also the influx of foreign capital.

The decisive role in modifying the initial program was played by a confrontation of the government plans with the interests, efforts, and apprehensions of different social groups. The authorities aimed at speedy privatization, in accordance with their own ideas, which awakened strong opposition among various social groups. Many compromises had to be settled on, and above all consent for privatization had to be "bought." In this respect, Janusz Lewandowski with Jan Szomburg (1990) and Rafał Krawczyk (1990) were right when they warned that conventional privatization methods would turn out to be slow and generate social conflict. Against this background, concepts of civic and employee enfranchisement emerged.*

Lewandowski and Szomburg proposed a kind of voucher privatization, whereas Krawczyk advocated self-management enfranchisement of employees. But all three treated this as the beginning of and acquiescence for concentration of purely capitalist ownership. The actual course of ownership changes conformed to their proposals in general, although on a much more modest scale and by way of a chaotic, conflict-generating, enforced strategy that was not thought out.

Below we shall take a look mainly at the experiences of employee companies and the National Investment Funds. Both forms are similar, though not identical to the proposals of enfranchisement of the two Gdańsk authors and Krawczyk.

Before that, however, let me cite several basic figures that characterize the stage of privatization achieved by then. According to data of the Central Statistical Office (GUS) (2006), in the years 1990 to 2005, of the 8,453 state enterprises existing in 1990, privatization was carried out in 7,263. Of these, 1,584 firms were subjected to commercialization and transformed into single-entity companies of the State Treasury. Of these in turn, 512 were transferred to the National Investment Funds and 349 were privatized in an indirect way (by the capital method). Some of them—more than 10 percent—underwent liquidation or declared bankruptcy. Direct privatization encompassed 2,132 and 1,825 were liquidated for economic reasons. Among state farms (PGR), 1,654 were turned over for privatization or leased into the hands of the (state) Agricultural Property Agency, which until then had taken over more than three-quarters of the land. The pace of privatization declined with the passing of time. The least privatization was carried out during the government of the SLD-PSL coalition, then during the rule of Jarosław and Lech Kaczyński.

*I set aside here the association of the pace and form of privatization with the shock therapy, although it is obvious that the crisis-provoked drastic decline of wages and savings made privatization harder, not easier, giving rise to general uncertainty and mistrust, discouraging external investors, and unfavorably affecting sale prices.

In terms of employment, the scope of ownership transformations was still small. All privatized firms and those included in the privatization plan were employing only 783,000 persons at the close of 2005, of which the highest number (227,000) were in the State Treasury companies. Firms privatized by the capital method had 221,000 employees, of which 145,000 were in companies with domestic capital and about 77,000 in companies with foreign capital participation. Even fewer (100,000) were employed by firms remaining in the National Investment Funds program. Well over a thousand companies defined as employee companies (usually becoming by then managerial-employee companies) employed only 138,000 persons (mainly in the processing industry and housing construction). The most advanced privatization occurred in banks and the insurance sector as well as in retail trade (mostly via foreign capital).

In general, privatization still encompassed not many of the nine million hired laborers and even less if we take away companies of the State Treasury (over half a million persons alone). Of course, the scope of privatization of state assets is much greater, especially of privatized and private enterprises in the economy, than the ratios of employees. The authors of the CASE report[10] aptly write that "detailed analyses indicate that a large portion of enterprises are 'stuck' in the initial phases of transformation and enterprises privatized in fact and till the end account for less than 60 percent."

National Investment Funds

Janusz Lewandowski and Jan Szomburg wrote about the mass participation of citizens in property ownership, which created an entirely illusory impression that this denoted a new form of socialization, more effective than state ownership. The program, it was said at the time, would consist of "handing over property" into the hands of all adult citizens, "democratization of ownership," and creation of "people's" or "democratic" capitalism. The most recent models were supplied by the prime minister of Great Britain, Margaret Thatcher, who under this slogan carried out privatization of firms nationalized after the war and of housing. A similar concept of privatization was declared and in a modest portion implemented during the same time by the government of Chile under the dictatorship of General Augusto Pinochet.

In truth, the initiators of this program had clear objectives outlined from the beginning, but only some members of the new power elite admitted this openly. The idea was to consist of mass privatization that would indirectly lead to the rapid concentration of property in private hands. A great role in propagating the concept of mass privatization, and maybe even more in awakening unrealistic expectations, was played by Lech Wałęsa. During the presidential campaign of 1990 ("A hundred million for everyone") and also later, he promised citizens a considerable share in the national assets (a loan of ten thousand dollars under unusually favorable terms). It is hard to say what he was aiming at, apart from electoral victory.

Conservative liberals (especially Lewandowski and Szomburg) were looking for a way to have speedy privatization that would at the same time be acceptable for the people. In the beginning, they proposed a model similar to the voucher scheme, which was widely propagated, thereby becoming popular in many post-socialist countries. In a dozen or so of these countries, particularly in the Czech Republic and in Russia, similar schemes were projected. In Poland, however, its scope was narrowed down and changes were made that brought a new program into being, the National Investment Funds (NIF), although for a certain time it continued to be presented as the mass privatization program (PPP), and the continuity of the course was represented by Janusz Lewandowski as minister of ownership transformations. The change occurred in mid-1991, and its circumstances say a lot about the character of the entire privatization process in Poland. Namely, that it was borrowed from abroad.

Jacek Tittenbrun, who devoted nearly the entire fourth volume of his extensive work to the NIF program, says that in the first half of 1991 a group of experts appointed by the Ministry for Ownership Transformations and headed by Jerzy Thieme began working on mass privatization. The team included, inter alia, A. Cordet from the

World Bank and J. Ledóchowski from Bank S. G. Warburg & Co. Ltd. The experts of this bank worked until the end of 1993 for this group under the contract of Warburg with the Ministry for Ownership Transformations (MOT), as the main advisor to the ministry, in the implementation of the NIF program. The contract was financed by the special British Know-How Fund and "as a result of the strong pressure of the advisors from Warburg, a significant modification of the original concept was made."[11] Several years later, Lewandowski explained this change: "The art of managing funds was not known in Poland, when in 1991 the mass privatization plan came into being. Therefore I insisted that there be an occasion to import others' skills, which were to be harnessed to work for Polish participants of mass privatization."[12]

I think that this statement better fits reality than the following opinion of Tittenbrun: "It is said that as a result of the strong pressure of the advisors of Warburg, a significant modification was made in the original concept. . . . A guarantee that this importation be in fact carried out was also attended to by the Western side; the World Bank and the European Bank for Reconstruction and Development conditioned allocation of preferential loans to the planned investment funds on the conclusion by them of agreements on management with Western managing firms."[13] It seems to me that Tittenbrun certainly accentuates "strong pressure" too much. As we remember, Balcerowicz's team enthusiastically chose the harshest stabilization program variant of all those presented by the IMF. Successive governments readily accepted the high influx of foreign capital and Janusz Lewandowski took a decisive stand in the privatization process. Taking all this into account, I tend to see an obliging ease with which the minister and those surrounding him accepted the advice of Western experts.

The very composition of the team, in which foreigners or Polish emigrants prevailed in number and in terms of preparation, betrayed a pro-Western (or, more precisely, pro-Anglo-Saxon) stance of the MOT and its chief. And Lewandowski's predecessor, Minister Waldemar Kuczyński, wrote with a certain pride that in his ministry one could hear the English language just as often as Polish.

There was another strong argument in favor of accepting the concept of investment funds. To recall, the Warsaw Stock Exchange had just made its debut, having been established at a moment when it was already clear that the Anglo-Saxon prescription for privatization of state firms, launched by Krzysztof Lis, did not pass the test. It turned out that privatization, and particularly transformation of state firms into joint-stock companies, was much more time-consuming than initially assumed. Advocates of the Anglo-Saxon model were keen on strengthening the stock exchange on the occasion of the mass privatization program and to weaken the already strong trend among managers and employees to transform enterprises into employee companies.

Naturally, the reservations mentioned here do not negate the opinion of Tittenbrun that "the shape of the whole program was highly influenced by the interests of a specific cofraternity represented by the British advisors."[14] This was so, at least with entrusting management of the funds to foreign firms, which became particularly apparent when the amount of their compensation was being determined.*

The NIF program proceeded slowly and with difficulty, which partly resulted from the complicated substance at hand, but the main cause was aptly perceived by Tittenbrun in the specific character of the Polish social conditions. He writes:

*One more remark about Tittenbrun's work, which I value highly and refer to readily. I think, however, that at times the author unnecessarily makes the task easier for possible critics. I appreciate the title: *Z deszczu pod rynnę* (Out of the Frying Pan Into the Fire). The subtitle informs us well about the book's content matter: *Meandry polskiej prywatyzacji* (Meanders of Polish Privatization). But between the title and subtitle, the author or editor needlessly included the sentence: "Privatization of Polish economy is one great scam." The book shows dozens of examples of the struggle of workers against the "accelerators" or tricksters, which very often had a very beneficial effect on the privatization process. It is difficult to compare Balcerowicz's shock operation with privatization, but in my belief, both the way in which the concept was formed, the extent and depth of the social effects, and the degree of professionalism in the preparation and implementation of ownership transformations make the notion of "great scam" more fitting for Balcerowicz's plan than for the privatization concept of Lewandowski, Kaczmarek, and Wąsacz.

The main reason for the obstacles and delays in the implementation of the PPP lies, as in the case of other privatization paths, in the logic of interests. One of the features distinguishing Poland from other countries of the former socialist bloc was the much higher degree of articulation of classes, which were not only aware of their own interests, but were also able to exact them effectively. The autonomy of enterprises, the large role of the trade unions, the sense of strength of the working class supported by a rich tradition of class struggle—these factors did not exist in such intensity and in such a combination in the neighboring countries and that is why those countries outpaced us in the implementation of mass privatization.[15]

The program went through a long legislative track, reaching the Sejm for deliberation only toward the end of the government of Hanna Suchocka. After being rejected by the Sejm on March 18, 1993, and following the inclusion of significant changes, it was passed on April 30 of the same year, under the reading: Act on National Investment Funds and Their Privatization. The most important provisions were: employees of the firms included in the program, under certain terms (also retirees of these firms), and in certain cases of close cooperation also farmers and fishermen, received 15 percent of the shares for free, with a deferred sale option. The State Treasury kept 25 percent of the shares. The funds that were to manage the enterprises within the program received 60 percent of the shares. Each fund received leading stakes, amounting to 33 percent of the shares of their "own" firms, usually called portfolio companies, and 1.95 percent of the shares in firms belonging to the remaining funds. The funds were obligated to restructure the enterprises subordinated to them in preparation for their privatization. In the ultimate version of the program, a change was made: the firms joining the funds would have greater benefits on this account. First, they were exempted from the guillotine tax on excessive wage growth (the famous "*popiwek*" tax). Another change increased the powers of the workers and the directors, which in effect hampered and prolonged the completion of the list of firms to be included in the program. The directors and worker councils were given the option of reporting within forty-five days a binding objection to a proposal of the MOT on accession to the funds (until then the MOT had been making arbitrary decisions).

In the end, fifteen funds were created, among which 512 portfolio firms were divided up randomly. The management companies and members of the supervisory boards of the Funds were chosen by a selection committee appointed by the MOT and headed by Professor Cezary Józefiak, which took nearly nine months. The selection itself gave rise to much emotion and uncertainty, and what was going on behind the scenes of the decisions along with all other documents of this committee was treated as a confidential matter by a regulation of the prime minister.[16] It took even more time to establish the list of over five hundred portfolio companies. This was because many workers and directors of enterprises that had been doing well took advantage of the right to object. In the end, the program entered into force only toward the end of 1995.

The universal character of the program meant that every citizen who had reached the age of eighteen, having paid PLN 20 in administrative costs, received a "participation certificate" with the right of immediate sale. This certificate was later converted to one share in each of the fifteen funds. Following the adjudication of the Constitutional Tribunal, the right to the certificates was also granted to persons not registered anywhere as residents (the homeless). Altogether, nearly 26,000,000 citizens participated in the program, almost 96 percent of all those eligible.

Such was the formal and legal side of the NIF program. Before I assess the operation of the funds, it is worthwhile to at least hypothetically answer the question why, despite the attractive terms (15 percent of free shares and exemption from the *popiwek* tax), many enterprises decisively rejected the proposal of acceding to the NIF program. This was accompanied by a very low, not to say negative, evaluation of the NIFs in public opinion polls. For example, according to research of CBOS, in November 1993 only 14 percent of respondents felt that the implementation of this program would be advantageous for them, and 22 percent felt it would be damaging.[17] The effects of implementing the NIF program on the whole economy were evaluated no better by the respondents.

I think that the following factors were instrumental. In the mentality of the workers the prevalent belief, for years repeated by the authorities, was that ultimately the workplaces are public property and thus their property as well. Therefore, the closest thing to the implementation of their thus far vague and hazy rights was the transformation of their firms into employee companies, which at that time was the most frequently employed form of de-statization of state firms. The myth of the "Self-Governing Republic," formulated by the first S. Congress (1981), was merely expressed in different wording but drawn from the egalitarian doctrine of real socialism. Hence the frequent complaints of pundits and the journalists, economists and sociologists in their service. Włodzimierz Pańkow often spoke of the dilemma that the non-communist authorities were then facing: how to reconcile the liberal objectives of the government with the social-democratic attitude (or views) of the social base.

But there were also other circumstances at work, and it is hard to say which were the most decisive. Naturally, for firms that had already carried out restructuring and now had an eye on or were already negotiating terms with a chosen domestic or foreign investor, the funds were not very attractive. For a large number of firms, it was also important not to let in an unsafe "inspector." During the deep recession, in many enterprises a certain community of common interests was formed, operating on the verge of the law or breaking it. Such a community did not wish to bring in an external comptroller. But even firms free of such associations perceived the funds as a form of constraint to their recently gained autonomy. This was especially so when the authorities were seen through the prism of the profound recession of their own making and of a magnitude unprecedented in peaceful times, which greatly undermined trust in the government. The effects of the recession continued to be visible in rising (until 1993) unemployment, afterward for a long time remaining at the level of three million people. The economic breakdown was such a brutal experience that many directors turned a blind eye to any employment overgrowth. And the workers sensed well that when a stranger appears, there will be layoffs, which shortly turned out to be true.

But if citizens had such a negative opinion of the NIF program, then why did they take part in it so massively? The answer appears to be simple enough. First, not without significance was the belief that "the enterprises are ours," which was in a way reaffirmed by the "participation certificates" (only later did it turn out that this occurred in a perverse way). And second, the massive sale of these certificates at a lower and lower price seems to confirm the opinion of Jacek Mojkowski that "most people collected the certificates thinking: since they're giving something, take it. You would have to be stupid not to make a profit by changing PLN 20 into one hundred."[18]

When a comparison is made of the initial declarations of mass privatization as a form of dissemination of property among citizens, promotion of a property-owning approach among citizens and democratization of developing capitalism in Poland, as set against the actual dimensions of the NIF program (about 5 percent of the assets under the State Treasury), it can be said that "the mountain brought forth a mouse." A mouse that had engaged great legislative and organizational efforts, high financial costs, and for many years held the attention of millions of people.

Another factor that pushed the program to the sidelines was the long-lasting bear run on the stock market. It had the most intense effect on the NIFs. During 1998 alone, the index of stock prices dropped by as much as 47 percent! The price of the coupons grandly called participation certificates fell even more. And if they did denote participation, then this was more in a game resembling the state lottery than in actual enfranchisement. At first, attempts were made to buy the certificates at a price not much higher than the administrative fee. It is astonishing that the record was probably broken by the state bank PKO BP, whose headquarters "established the maximum price of redemption at PLN 32," while its local branches tried to redeem them at PLN 25 (Kraków and Olsztyn), PLN 28 (Wrocław). Later, the prices rose to PLN 100, and in places even to PLN 200. In the last phase of their exchange, the retail market price (accessible for holders of one or several certificates) was only twice as high as the initial fee. If one takes into account the high inflation of those days, then a citizen who did not sell his certificate in the early phase of the still high prices received from the state as a gift the equivalent of at most a few dollars. This was less than one thousandth of what Wałęsa had pledged. And without having a large number of certificates, due to the cost of the operation and the necessary time, he could not become, even symbolically, a stock exchange shareholder of the fifteen funds.

[handwritten margin note: NIF about return on shares to public]

It can safely be said that the Mass Privatization Program (PPP), so loudly propagated in the beginning as an act of social justice, ended in a complete fiasco and was also a great manipulation. Henryka Bochniarz and Andrzej Wiśniewski (1999) are skirting the issue when they say, "No one ever said that a single citizen can obtain any significant sum for the participation certificates (or for shares of funds obtained for them or for dividends)." Yet here is one of many examples: according to a journalist of *Gazeta Wyborcza*, Prime Minister Hanna Suchocka had said that "mass privatization will give everyone a fragment of the national assets and will enable people to directly feel the benefits of reforms."[19] The actual architect of the program, Minister for Ownership Transformations J. Lewandowski, made it clear many times that the purpose of the Mass Privatization Program was to "disseminate ownership."[20] But what happened had little to do with general ownership. The critics of such privatization are right when they say that citizens have been misled by the popular slogan, which inevitably intensified their mistrust in other reform measures of the government.

Sometimes the NIF program was praised as allegedly better than the Czech voucher privatization scheme. Undoubtedly, this small country decided on a much broader program. However, to say nothing of the scale of the undertaking, in the structure of the Polish program the degree of risk borne by the initial (usually temporary) holders of the certificates was certainly smaller than in the Czech program. As we know, the differences in the real value of the Czech vouchers could be in the range of 1 to 1,000.[21] Whereas the price of the Polish "participation certificates," and then shares, depended mainly on the economic cycles in wholesale trading and in access to it. And the stock market prices were all that time much higher than at the exchange desks (that is, for petty holders). Still lower prices were paid for certificates purchased from employees by managers of the privatized firms, or persons set up by them. The local differences in prices with individual sellers were not of much significance. Possibly, the Polish program also created fewer opportunities for corruption. But this is where the differences end. The processes of concentration of ownership were similar in the Czech Republic and in Poland, far from the earlier declared ideals of a property-owning democracy. This conformed to the expectations of the Gdańsk and Czech conservative liberals, who in both cases were aiming at rapid concentration of rather symbolic ownership titles handed out to citizens.* However, the Polish program facilitated much more the parasitic entrance of foreign capital.

The Further Fate of the NIFs

A harsh light on the illusory character of the "enfranchisement of citizens" is cast by an interesting study by CASE (Center for Social and Economic Research),[22] devoted to what has been called secondary privatization. It provides excellent insight into the evolution of the ownership structure within the NIFs themselves and in the portfolio companies and shows in whose interest this distribution of ownership took place.

The general financial performance of the portfolio companies and detailed polling research indicates that the main aim of the managers of the NIFs was to have financial operations that quickly brought maximum gains. Yet the superiority of the NIF program over voucher privatization, as emphatically declared by the authorities, was that one of the principal tasks of the funds was to restructure the portfolio compa-

---

*Another aspect is that the long bear run was an unexpected factor that marginalized the significance of the NIF program both for the authors of the program and for the citizens anticipating mass participation in the country's assets.

nies within the program. Minister for Ownership Transformations Wiesław Kaczmarek placed emphasis on this, saying: "We have established with Deputy Prime Minister [Marek] Borowski that the main purpose of the program is to be the restructuring of industry. The firms must have faith in this."[23] Shortly after this, Borowski was no longer deputy prime minister, but Kaczmarek had a chance to force this out from the funds, which were still state-owned, meaning they were subordinated to him. The question is, why did he not do anything to make them fulfill the statutory obligation? The absence of such action weighs on the entire SLD-PSL central-left coalition for leading to the economic disarray of the companies entrusted to the funds.

When the list of firms chosen for the NIF program was still being established, these firms showed economic performance similar to that of other groups of enterprises undergoing privatization.[24] So what advantages did the firms have from entering the NIFs? Daniel A. Korona (2002) says that in 1994 only one-third of the companies still showed losses. But from then on, the companies began declining despite several years of good overall economic performance. The CASE team offers an interesting explanation. Barbara Błaszczyk writes: "In 1995 [the year of the actual start of the funds] the gross profitability of the NIF companies fell rapidly and the whole group became deficit-bearing. Later their performance continued to worsen (with the exception of 1997). In 1999 the NIF group had the worst performance of all the analyzed groups. The net profitability began falling. . . . Much better results were achieved by other groups of privatized enterprises, and even State Treasury companies."[25]

Without exaggeration, it can be said that the program declaration that prior to privatization the funds would improve the efficiency of the firms subordinated to them, found its perverse fulfillment: the funds broke the records of ineptitude. The most important reason for this is not hard to find. The managers of the portfolio firms legitimately (in accordance with the program) were expecting aid from the funds and felt they were relieved from taking up independent initiatives, or were waiting in uncertainty for decisions on the sale of their enterprises to be made by others.

A more complicated picture emerges in the case of companies that for various reasons left the NIFs and were subjected to "secondary privatization," meaning they were purchased from the funds by domestic or foreign corporations, by individual investors, or by the employees. Altogether, 278 portfolio companies found new investors by December 2000, of which twenty-seven were ultimately listed on the stock exchange. In addition, seventy-eight companies were subjected to liquidation or bankruptcy procedures and fifty-seven firms were sold to foreign investors. The sales dynamics, which the authors of the study considered to be the most credible indicator, were negative for the entire group in 1995–99, similar to the results of sales of firms still belonging to the NIFs. The best results were achieved by enterprises that were sold to domestic and foreign corporations the earliest (when the best of them were being sold). The worst situation was in firms purchased by individual investors and by the employees.

Now, let us take a look at the ownership changes from the point of view of the initial shareholders. After the participation certificates were converted into shares, the State Treasury retained only shares corresponding to the unredeemed participation certificates (there were not many of these) and shares apportioned for paying the firms managing the funds. In 2001 the State Treasury had 13.4 percent of such shares. Within a few years, the proportion of small owners and individual investors declined from 85 percent to 41 percent of the shares in favor of institutional shareholders and large investors. The proportion of foreign investors became significant (26 percent, twice as much as domestic investors). The rapid concentration of shares in the hands of institutional, domestic, and, above all, foreign investors can be seen in the fact that in October 1998 Credit Suisse First Boston already had over 5 percent of the votes in thirteen funds, PZU in eleven, Merrill Lynch in four, and PKO SA in three.

Taking note of these and other facts, H. Bochniarz and A. Wiśniewski claimed that in 1999 "foreign shareholders mainly belonging to hedge funds . . . have attained a dominant position among the shareholders of the NIFs. They are able to form groups of shareholders altogether holding 20–30 percent of the capital and (in cooperation with for example PZU) to obtain 50 percent of the votes at the general meetings of shareholders, to elect supervisory boards and in consequence to assume full control of the funds."[26] According to them, the predominance of foreign high-risk capital would have grave consequences in the future. They named cases of acquisition by shareholders of NIF shares with very great discounts (from one-third to one-half), warning:

> The repercussions can be very serious. After selling several of the best companies from each NIF one can already have a profit satisfying a large shareholder, and the remaining weaker companies can be sold off at any price whatsoever, without properly safeguarding the interests of the companies themselves and their employees. The governing bodies of the funds or their managing firms may therefore be forced to conduct liquidation measures and to sell off assets of the funds at any price. Unsold assets (unsellable companies in poor economic condition) may thus become a big problem for the State Treasury.[27]

The matter was exacerbated by the fact that "domestic investors enter alliances or provide capital support for foreign investors."*

The system and level of remuneration of the firms managing the funds merits special attention. In accordance with the law, the remuneration for the management firms was to consist of two parts: an

---

*In the light of these observations, assurances by the authors that the process "essentially" conforms to the program assumptions, and only with the passing years "as usual various unforeseen circumstances came up," are not very convincing. Not only do the facts described here contradict this opinion, but also the recommendations for the State Treasury made by the authors of the article, full of concern for the future of the NIFs, and especially the postulate for a "different strategy than until now" of the state. May I add that H. Bochniarz was Minister of Industry and is now president of NICOM Consulting Ltd., which carried out the first selection of enterprises apportioned for the Mass Privatization Program. In a sense, then, she was a co-author of the program.

annual lump sum and percentage compensation for financial performance each year (altogether 1.5 percent of the value of NIF shares). The
lump-sum rates were established at the level of PLN one million from
the beginning, but efforts to attain the best possible financial performance were mainly aimed at increasing the mobile part of the remuneration. One problem that arose was when the management of several
funds was assumed by a single firm. There was a well-known case of a
certain management group that covered as many as six funds and was
excluded from only two of these following the intervention of the
Ministry of Treasury.[28]

The available information on the exorbitantly high levels of remuneration of the managing firms is shocking and probably nowhere else
in the world can we find anything like it. As B. Błaszczyk and others
write: "At the close of 2000, the costs of the management services
exceeded the enormous amount of PLN 756 million, which was equal
to 42.4 percent of the total capitalization of the funds . . . the costs of
one of them accounted for 91.3 percent. Unlike the rest, the only fund
in which costs were maintained below 15 percent was the fund that
did not avail itself of the management services of a foreign firm."[29] This
was the Eugeniusz Kwiatkowski, or ninth NIF.* The authors logically
concluded that the costs of managing the funds might soon absorb the
whole value of the managed assets, and consequently force the authorities to end the entire program before the planned time limit of 2005.
Unfortunately, we do not know to what extent the practice of hoisting
up remuneration spread out and affected the appetites of the directors
of the NIF portfolio firms.

An analysis of these unprecedented doings did not arouse any
indignation on the part of the authors of the study. On the contrary, the

---

*This fund fared so well that in 1997 an attempt was made at a hostile takeover. Its
shares were silently bought out, so as to lead to favorable decisions at the general
meeting of shareholders. However, the fund's president managed to thwart these
plans. (see Tittenbrun, 4:63). In the end the fund was purchased in 2006 by
Grażyna and Roman Karkosik "in order to transfer to it shares and holdings of their
own companies" (Tittenbrun, 4:181), as the NIFs continued to enjoy the privilege
of being exempted from income tax on gains from capital investments in the NIFs.

conclusion arrived at by the head of the research team deserves to be immortalized:

> On observing this performance, one wonders whether the one-sided negative assessment of the operations of the funds is grounded. The relatively fast privatization of the portfolio companies (from the moment that the systemic obstacles were removed) and the new ownership structure being forged in these companies, giving hope for improvement in the future, can speak in favor of the funds.[30]

The belief that apart from the NIF program privatization could not have been carried out relatively quickly at a much lower cost and with better economic results appears to be unfounded. For example, privatization in the form of employee companies could have been an alternative to the NIFs, with better prospects for completing all the tasks imposed on the funds. The final results seem to justify the view that even in an essentially employee (and not civic) privatization there would have been more diffusion of ownership among citizens than with the offered participation certificates. As for the opinion of B. Błaszczyk and her team, it seems to stem from the conviction that there is no price too high for the privatization of state firms.

Summing up, the NIF program, and especially its implementation bordering on scandal, with the introduction of investment funds and bringing in foreign firms to manage them, which in the words of Janusz Lewandowski was supposed to be an instructive experience for the young financial market, turned out to be a bitter lesson on what not to do.* The editor of the Paris Polish monthly review *Kultura*, Jerzy Giedroyc, once accused the Polish elites that after winning elections they behave like invaders, plundering the land they have just conquered. In this case, foreign capital acted as the conquerer.

---

* Notably, Janusz Lewandowski is now serving as EU Commissioner for the Budget.

Employee Companies

Two typical paths of ownership transformation had essentially different outcomes: whereas the NIFs turned out to be a failure bordering on scandal, employee companies achieved success, even if limited.

Many theorists disqualify employee companies for their lower motivation to invest, as opposed to purely private firms. The reasons given are diverse: the specific character of the incentives in a firm with group ownership, the shortsightedness of the workers interested primarily in fast income, and, in cooperatives with indivisible capital, the imperfections of their property rights. Although this accusation is repeated often, so far it has not found any substantiation in empirical research. One of the first studies and the first on this scale was published by Estrin and Jones (1998), who examined ten years of operation of 270 French manufacturing cooperatives. The study did not show any connection between investment volume and ownership form, or any difference between the efficiency of cooperatives and private firms. But it clearly showed the dependence of the investment rate on access to the financial market. The authors drew the conclusion that in the future what should be monitored is not the inclination to invest but the relations between firms with group ownership and the financial market. In Poland, an additional factor in need of analysis would be the dominating role of foreign capital in the banking sector, which may be particularly hostile to this form of ownership.

The reports of GUS from the late 1990s did in fact show a lower (gross and especially net) profitability of employee companies than the average profitability of the whole group of firms subjected to ownership transformations. However, they maintained high financial liquidity (of the first degree), the highest aside from foreign firms, and also first place among firms bringing profits. An economic problem is indeed their relatively low investment rate. There is unfortunately no research on whether after the leasing installments have been paid and property rights have been fully acquired, that is, after obtaining access to bank credits, at least the majority of them turned out to be no worse in developmental capacity than the rest of the private sector.

Enterprises established as employee companies are at any rate a part of our economy and its history. Therefore, it is worthwhile to reflect on what this experience has brought, and especially what an employee company's place is in the new social order. From this perspective, the most important factors determining this place are the internal transformations of these companies, which clearly took place because of an unfavorable environment. High state officials often treated the companies as a transitional form on the way to "real" privatization, and the actions of the former Ministry for Ownership Transformations and its successor—the Ministry of Treasury—showed at least an unfavorable attitude of the authorities toward employee companies. On January 17, 1991, the minister of ownership transformations sent a letter to the founding bodies responsible for direct privatization, recommending the initiators of such companies to invite external strategic investors to participate in them.[31] This letter was clearly dictated by a desire to speed up the processes of property concentration in these companies. One of the most active directors of the MOT even conducted a campaign against imitating the American ESOPs.* In his opinion, "The ideological approach to privatization was rejected five years ago by the Sejm, which did not agree to the doctrinal, collectivistic concept of ESOPs as supposedly the only right panaceum."[32] Disabling Polish employee companies from applying that experience, as allegedly ideological-doctrinal-collectivistic, created an atmosphere of aversion to the employee participatory character of the companies. The same official argued that employee companies are either "managerial" from the start, or quickly transform into such.†[33] The entire government administration did a lot to deprive employee companies of their essence.

*ESOP: Employee Stock Ownership Plans. In the early 1990s the companies were employing over ten million workers.
†The concept of using employee shareholding as a path leading to normal joint-stock companies was presented earliest by Rafał Krawczyk. From the beginning, he treated employee companies as an instrument of conflict-free transition to a joint-stock system, and not as an end in itself (Krawczyk, 1990, 152).

All this is especially odd in that only in the first years of systemic changes could the neoliberals fear that this form of transformation—the most frequent at the time—would dominate in the Polish economy, or at least in the state sector existing until then. For a long time now, it can be seen that their share in the economy, particularly in employment, has been very modest, and even smaller in the ownership of fixed assets. And when during the first few years they demonstrated a relatively high, at times even the highest, rate of return and profitability, and later fared quite well, the nervous anticipation of the time when they would finally cease to be "employee" firms can only be explained by ideological prejudice or group interests. Employee companies should have and do have the option of transforming into "normal companies." Some of them would take advantage of such a possibility in any conditions. But they should not be treated as a transitional anomaly or fettered by the nonsensical charge of collectivism, which is used in Poland almost as a synonym for Soviet communism.

When reflecting on the evolution of employee companies and their great initial popularity, one must remember that their social base was the employee self-management movement, which at the beginning of transformation had its own association, newspaper, institute, and even resorted to foreign experts. In the years 1989 to 1991, the activists of this movement quickly adjusted to the new conditions and when the transition to a private market economy was announced they were able to put forward many initiatives and concepts. However, they were operating in a particularly unfavorable atmosphere. For example, cooperative entities were administratively eliminated, instead of being subjected to de-statization measures.

State Farms: The Social Outcasts

The dramatic fate of the State Farms (PGR—Państwowe Gospodarstwo Rolne) and their employees brings to mind the key theses of this book. The general shock stabilization-systemic operation was unnecessary and essentially dictated by political considerations. It had no economic substantiation. This was also the case with the shock operation eliminating state farms, prepared in 1991 by the government of Jan Krzysztof Bielecki and carried out by subsequent cabinets.

Augustyn Woś was certainly right when he wrote: "Restructuring of agriculture can be effectively undertaken only in conditions of overall good economy . . . and even economic boom. No European country has taken up this task in conditions of a general slump in the economy. Today we are far from the state of prosperity that existed in Western Europe in the two postwar decades, when the main restructuring tasks were being carried out."[34] I shall add that despite the economic boom, Western Europe modernized agriculture with a very high customs safety shield, targeted mostly at imports of American grain, and with immense financial and logistic involvement of the state. The circumstance that the restructuring of Polish agriculture coincided with systemic change and privatization of the public sector does not negate the validity of the view expressed by Woś (and many other specialists), but underscores it instead.

In Poland the program of agricultural restructuring was imposed on the wave of economic crisis and in a way taking advantage of this, which most painfully affected the state farms, their employees, and families. This concerned almost half a million employees, who in turn were supporting about two million people. Autumn 1991 witnessed the peak of the economic breakdown, of dimensions unprecedented since the Second World War. It was then that the government of Jan Krzysztof Bielecki, with Leszek Balcerowicz as deputy prime minister and minister of finance, put through parliament the Act on the Management of Agricultural Real Estate of the State Treasury, for the purpose of implementing ownership transformations in agriculture (dated October 19, 1991). By this act, the Agricultural Property Agency of the State Treasury (AWRSP) was established, to speedily take over assets from liquidated state farms (and from the State Land Fund, which I am not dealing with here).

The act entered into force on January 1, 1992, just when Jan Olszewski became head of the government with his populist program.

If he had wanted to be loyal to his views, he would have halted the implementation of this law—the intellectual creation of Balcerowicz and Bielecki, probably the two most fervent enthusiasts of privatization at any price. This was the worst possible moment to treat a large social group to yet another shock operation. But above all, this showed that the authorities, holding steadfast to their own concept of systemic changes, turned a blind eye to their own experiences. People were now feeling the effects of the drastic misalignment between the assumptions of the Balcerowicz Plan and its execution, with differences in the basic indicators reaching several hundred percent. Yet despite these results, one more unrealistic program was applied with the same sort of proselytizing zeal.

This was a particularly harsh affront for agricultural economists. In Poland, among so-called sectoral economics, agricultural economics represented the highest standard not only in the country, but also in the entire Soviet bloc. Mass collectivization of agriculture had not been carried out in Poland, and so private ownership dominated in the rural areas, which were potentially the most mature for acceptance of market principles. For a long time among agricultural specialists there had also existed the tradition of family farms. Meanwhile, the elimination of state farms in this form was carried out not only without but also against the opinion of the most eminent agricultural specialists.

To fully understand the conditions in which the successive shock therapy was carried out, one must remember how agricultural specialists had characterized agriculture and the situation of the rural population at the outset of transformation, given in my own abbreviated form here:

- Agricultural production shrank in 1990–91 on a scale similar to the decline in GDP;
- Following a radical reduction of customs duties, transforming the Polish economy into one of the most laissez-faire economies in the world, Polish farmers were forced to compete with the highly subsidized imports from the European Union (I myself could even buy Dutch potatoes in the local store!). Only later, in 1994, were

temporary equalizing payments introduced, followed by an import tax—also temporary;

- As a result of the opening of the price scissors, within two years of the "shock therapy" (1990–91), the price of a product unit generated by farmers was lowered by 63 percent;
- In the years 1990–91, the real income from work in individual farms declined by 40.3 percent, much more than wages, which dropped to the level of 65.9 percent;
- The tax and social transfer policies were unfavorable for the farmers;
- The consequences of the Balcerowicz-Bielecki shock operation transformed rural areas into a "repository of the unemployed," most of whom were deprived of the right to social benefits in subsequent years;
- The breakdown in the whole economy shrank the extent of the two-trade status of many small farmers, that is, deprived them of employment outside agriculture. This meant loss of work for about 700,000 peasant laborers;
- The hugely indebted food processing industry experienced an economic breakdown.[35]

All these developments and processes created unfavorable conditions for the state sector in agriculture.

The act referred to above imposed on the Agricultural Property Agency of the State Treasury, established in early 1992, the following tasks:

- The creation and conditions encouraging rational utilization of the production capacity of State Treasury (ST) resources;
- Restructuring and privatization of ST property being used for farming purposes;
- Trading in real estate and other components of agricultural property of the ST;
- Administration of resources of agricultural property of the ST creation of farms;

- Safeguarding assets of the ST;
- Supporting private farms on land of the ST;
- Creation of jobs in connection with restructuring of the state agricultural economy.

Here I have to point out that as in the case of the NIFs the agency turned out to be incapable of meeting so many obligations. And even though an extensive apparatus was created with over a dozen regional offices, it in fact did not go beyond administering, leasing, and privatizing property turned over to it, and did hardly anything to "create new jobs." Indirectly this was recognized when at the close of 1993, by the strength of a successive law, another organ was established, the Agency for Restructuring and Modernization of Agriculture (ARMA), which has not had many successes on record either.

In numbers, the main achievements of the AWRSP were as follows:

In the years 1992 to 2005 it took over more than 4.72 million hectares of land, 3.76 million hectares from state farms and 0.6 million hectares from the State Land Fund; of this it managed to sell 1.586 million hectares of land. Various public institutions (for example, the Polish Academy of Sciences) received over 300,000 hectares free of charge. The main part of the property (over 2.7 million hectares) was leased out. Over 330,000 hectares were entrusted against payment to private individuals or legal entities for temporary administration of separated farms. Toward the end of this period, about one million hectares were still "waiting to be developed."* In 2002, the AWRSP ended its operations, turning over agricultural resources still controlled by the state to a new organ—the Agricultural Property Agency (ANR).

It would be hard to call the agricultural restructuring program a success even in privatization categories. The form of lease prevailed and a large portion of land awaited development. True, the changing conditions suggested that by maintaining leaseholds pending EU

*These are the most important data, rounded off, from Table 6 (602) of the 2006 Statistical Yearbook (704–5).

entry, and especially with the signs of a global food crisis, there were chances to obtain increasingly higher prices for land. But no significant success was reached either in the attempt to improve the structure of individual family farms. It could not have been otherwise, as agriculture was in a state of collapse, and the authorities continued in their belief that "the market knows better" and the state is but a necessary evil.

The resources of state-owned land and real estate became a tasty morsel for all kinds of capers, a breeding ground for corruption and clientelism, the territory of the most extreme inequalities that in today's Europe are by now hard to find. On the one side were the great landholdings with thousands of hectares of land whose owners or leaseholders are known only from hearsay or from press accounts, and on the other the former employees of the state farms, now forming ghettos of unemployed people, "to be scrapped," whose children, often undernourished or even hungry, inherit the status of their parents.

This is the social group that the crisis has hit in the most ruthless and most painful way. It is too easy to claim that their fate follows from being accustomed to the protective role of the state and their own passivity. In a situation of mass unemployment, reaching 70 percent in some areas, it is difficult to break away for even enterprising individuals. The post-PGR unemployment, the high unemployment among peasant laborers, and the blocking of the outflow of young people from rural areas have made the countryside a repository for a disproportionately large portion of unemployed people, especially the long-term unemployed. A derivative is the wide range of indigence, or even extreme poverty.

In his four-volume work, Jacek Tittenbrun (2007) devotes three chapters to the post-PGR reality of privatization: "Największa prywatyzacja" (The Greatest Privatization), "Z czworaków na kuroniówkę" (From PGR Housing to Social Aid), and "Nowi farmerzy" (The New Farmers). He points out the significant difference between the conditions and methods of privatization in state-owned enterprises in industry and services and the privatization of the state farms. In cities, an authentic struggle of the workers took place over the forms, conditions, and pace of privatization. The people were aware of their rights, organized, and well oriented in the situation of the country and the company. There were many manifestations of "class" struggle—as Tittenbrun rightly calls it—between capital and labor. Often this had a positive effect on the form and pace of owner-ship changes. This was missing in the state farms, where authentic trade unions were not firmly entrenched and employee self-management was not active. The state farms did not have their representation in parliament either. The social effects of these differences had to be lamentable.

Unfortunately, only one policymaker, Michał Wojtczak—a former businessman and an influential deputy minister in Balcerowicz's team—has shown any feelings of remorse. Following a stroke, having spent several years in hospitals and after creating a highly impressive center for people with disabilities, when asked by a reporter whether he had been a scoundrel, he said:

> Twenty years ago, in Mazowiecki's government, I was responsible for restructuring agriculture and I know that because of me several dozen or even several hundred thousand people from the old state farms were left stranded and practically without any means of subsistence. I cannot forget this, because whenever I happen to be on grounds for-merly belonging to the state farms I see what this has led to. . . . I used to belong to a six-member government team for economic reform of the country. . . . I could have fought against it, yet I practically agreed to Balcerowicz's concept. . . . Intuition told me we were doing the wrong thing. I could have tried to convince Balcerowicz, and if I failed I could step out of government. This would have been the right thing to do. [36]

11. More on Enfranchisement and Foreign Capital

From the time of the first pledges made by Lech Wałęsa, mainly involving giveaways of state property, the concept of enfranchisement resurfaced in public debate many times. Let me recall the main theses of Wałęsa's program. In the beginning, in the course of the presidential campaign, this was to be an ordinary giveaway. Then in 1991, the program took on the shape of a highly preferential loan equivalent of $10,000, granted in the form of coupons and repaid over twenty years. The loan was to be interest-free for the first ten years, then bear a 10 percent interest rate. The repayment collateral was to be the assets of the borrower. The coupons could be used to obtain shares of privatized state enterprises, municipal and cooperative apartments and other municipal property, and even products of enterprises. The program was discredited by the president's advisors as being ignorant. Consequently, the government rejected it as a utopian undertaking.

No better treatment was given to the idea of granting a PLN 300 million loan to each adult Pole, as proposed by the "Network" of Workplace Committees of S.* This plan was set against the National Investment Fund program in the last phase of work on the appropriate bill. The "Network" plan also provided for the purchase of apartments, stores, stocks, and the like. Loan preferences would be even more favorable than in Wałęsa's program: the proposal was for repayment over thirty years, with a one percent interest rate, and included the option of debt forgiveness in accordance with the length of employment.[1]

Other concepts did not directly refer to Wałęsa's proposals, but on certain points were a continuation of them. In the circles of the S. trade union, enfranchisement of citizens was a popular subject for many years. A relevant blueprint was approved at the Sixth Congress of NSZZ "Solidarity" in June 1995. It was backed by President Wałęsa, and in five questions/desiderata addressed to the Senate he effectively requested, like S., that a nationwide referendum be held on this matter. The referendum took place in February 1996, but due to inadequate turnout was deemed invalid.

The idea of general enfranchisement assumed the form of a parliamentary bill directly after the Solidarity Election Action (AWS) Party took office in 1997.[2] However, the government of Jerzy Buzek backed away from this idea, submitting its own bill, in which it wanted to combine the enfranchisement idea with compensation for the absence of indexation of wages and pensions, which had been ordered by the Constitutional Tribunal and passed by the Sejm. The bill also included cofinancing of the capital pension reform being implemented just then. On the part of the AWS Party, this was an attempt to deliver on one of the most important pre-election pledges.

The author of the most radical plan for enfranchisement was Adam Bielan, a professor of the Catholic University of Lublin. He obtained the most support from the Regional Enfranchisement Societies, associ-

---

*The "Network" gathered a representative group of Solidarity members from large enterprises throughout the country. Others who took an active part in the periodical meetings included specialists in law, economics, and sociology.

ated with part of the AWS and cooperating with the Catholic and nationalistic Radio Maryja. The authors declared a desire to level out the injustice resulting from the fact that employees of privatized state firms were given the right to a free 15 percent of the stock of their enterprises (according to the first Act on Privatization of 1990, this right was to 20 percent of the stocks purchased at a price equal to half of their market value). This time citizens would be "enfranchised" who until now had not enjoyed this right in the form of free stock.

The plan provided for two kinds of enfranchisement: direct and indirect. The former would be for tenants of cooperative apartments, perpetual lessees of land, and of recreational land plots who would become their rightful owners for free. The rest were to receive bonds equivalent in value to the average annual wage. These could be exchanged for stocks and shares in companies, for real estate of the Agricultural Property Agency, or for stocks in pension funds.

A competitive scheme of twenty-one parliamentarians was less radical. The participants would obtain the right to a stake in the value of apartments, larger or smaller land plots, up to the value of a participation certificate, which was also equivalent to the average annual wage. The difference of a higher purchase value (for example, in the price of an apartment) would have to be paid from their own savings. The National Enfranchisement Funds (the idea of Treasury Minister Emil Wąsacz) would be the implementing entity of indirect enfranchisement. Their assets would consist of stocks and shares of the State Treasury in already privatized firms, as well as in firms slated for privatization. Citizens not taking part in direct privatization would receive bearer investment certificates, admitted to trading in the future, and after a certain time exchanged for participation certificates of a similar nature as the certificates known from the NIF program. A government program was also announced. All these programs failed to be enacted. When a trimmed-down version of A. Bielan's scheme was passed by parliament, President Aleksander Kwaśniewski effectively vetoed the bill.

The protracted dispute over enfranchisement makes one wonder whether a better solution would have been to keep a portion of the assets in state hands and subject them to public scrutiny. This could be considered as a kind of enfranchisement with actual socialization of state ownership. In areas that to a lesser extent depend on the varying tastes of consumers and foreign competition, this could be a fair and efficient enough form.

A part of the dispute related to enfranchisement revolved around the Act on the Office of the State Attorney. The more than one-year-long dispute over the form of this office flared up in 1998 to the extent that it threatened to break up the coalition. The bone of contention was whether the Office of the State Attorney would be (as its predecessor from the first postwar years) only a legal and opinion-giving representative of the State Treasury or an office independently overseeing the privatization policy of the State Treasury, and thereby a superior body. The initiators of the enfranchisement program obviously wanted to halt privatization in the forms existing until that time, so as to retain as much as possible of the property for use under their transformation program. The Act on the Office of the State Attorney, based on this assumption and passed by parliament, was vetoed effectively this time as well by the president.

The Never-Ending Dispute
over Reprivatization

Every once in a while the government that happens to be in office seems to return to the subject of property restitution and retribution. It might be worthwhile to describe in brief the fate of the bill that seems to be more mature and legislatively more advanced than earlier ones. Such a bill on reprivatization was tabled to the Sejm in 1999 by the government of the AWS-UW (Solidarity Election Action and Union of Liberty) coalition.

According to this version, former owners were to receive (in kind or in the form of bonds) half of the value of their former property. The scheme was widely criticized for being too far-reaching, however, mainly due to three features.

First, it negated the legality of the decrees on agricultural reform and state ownership of forests because they did not provide for compensation, which was thought to contravene the constitution in effect at that time. This was something new, as earlier schemes, with perhaps one exception, focused on repairing damages that had occurred from infringement of the binding law during the execution of decrees on agricultural reform. Until then it was thought that decisions complying with the law currently in force were not subject to redress.

Second, compensation claims were provided for by the January 3, 1946, Act on Nationalization. Compensation paid out in the form of securities was abandoned then, even though such a provision was included in the act referred to.

Third, the group of eligible people included Polish nationals (and their successors) who had been deprived of property, beginning with the moment of the outbreak of the war in 1939. This meant that not only claims of citizens residing until 1945 in the eastern borderlands (of the "Zabużanie" people) were acknowledged, but also all those first expropriated by the German occupiers, with their property subsequently being taken over after the war by the Polish authorities, who deemed it as deserted.

According to the opinions of jurists, the arguments supporting the bill were feeble. The decree on agricultural reform was regarded as unconstitutional, as in postwar Poland the Constitution of 1921 (the so-called March Constitution) was supposedly in force, which allowed for "taking away of property only against compensation." The only grounds for such a claim was the declaration of the Polish Committee of National Liberation (PKWN), questioning the validity of the April 1935 Constitution and of the London government-in-exile. Later, a similar standpoint could be found in the so-called Little Constitution (of February 19, 1947): "The Sejm, pursuant to the basic assumptions of the March Constitution of 17 March 1921, resolves as follows . . ." but for many constitutionalists this was a "metalegal" formula or an "interpretation rule" and not the binding law.

Opponents of the bill pointed out that its authors one-sidedly referred to prewar constitutional settlements. They overlooked the practice of Poland's authorities between the wars, which did not "compensate for the damages" of participants of the 1863–64 January Uprising who had been expropriated by tsarist Russia. The principle of limitation (the expiration time of both confiscations was nearly identical) and the current social interest turned out to be more important in the Second Republic of Poland than respect, measured by money, for combatants distinguished in the struggle for Poland's independence. The prevailing view was that the effects of great historical turmoil cannot be simply reversed; the material losses of past generations would have to be paid for by generations to come.

By treating agricultural reform and nationalization of industry as "communist" pillage, it was also forgotten that the former prime minister of the London government and, on his return to Poland, a deputy prime minister of the Provisional Government of National Unity, Stanisław Mikołajczyk, felt the absence of compensation in the decree on agricultural reform worthy of imitation. Naively believing that the "communists" would implement the provisions of the decree, he obstinately fought in the Sejm against the principle of compensation proposed in the nationalizing act, demanding that the owners of factories be treated exactly like the land proprietors in the agricultural reform. The matter of compensation was treated in a discretionary manner in many countries. To recall, some parties within the Polish government-in-exile also demanded a radical agricultural reform, resembling the one implemented.

The case was similar to the nationalization of key branches of industry in other countries. A telling example is the Japanese agricultural reform carried out on the order of the American occupying authorities, in which compensation was rather symbolic. Big family fortunes (*zaibatsu*) were transformed into modern corporations (*keiretsu*) in a similar way. And so, neither agricultural reform, nor nationalization of industry, can be attributed solely to "communists," as is notoriously done in Poland by the noisy Association of Former Proprietors.

In the discussion, it was also pointed out that the government could follow in the footsteps of the "Hungarian precedent," setting the threshold of compensations at a very low level and limiting the range of eligible persons. The Hungarians handled quite unceremoniously the historical overhaul of property rights. They did not return property in kind and there are known cases where former owners repurchased from the state "their own" former property. The compensations were symbolic. But this did not hinder the influx of foreign capital, relatively (per capita) the highest among the post-socialist countries. The Hungarians thus proved that restitution of property from more than half a century ago was of marginal significance for foreign capital. If, however, they destabilized the state budget with excessive reprivatization expenditures, they would have scared off foreign investors and lenders. It would have been easier for the government of Poland to explain a low level of compensations by referring to the immeasurably greater obligations ensuing from the shift of state frontiers, independently of the Polish authorities.

In addition, the danger of privileging one small social group was pointed out, as this could strengthen the belief in further shifting costs of systemic changes onto the poorer part of society and reawaken vindication claims. In ethical terms it would be difficult to explain that the decisions of the government (not elected by anyone) are to be paid for half a century later by the entire population. With the passing of time, with the murdering and dying off of a significant portion of the initial owners, there is not much strength to the argument that the beneficiaries of reprivatization would be people who had accumulated wealth through their own efforts (of work and skills). The authors of the program assessed the costs of reprivatization at PLN 95 billion (over 15 percent of GDP). This was an immense sum, and there was reason to believe that in practice the costs of the operation would turn out to be even higher. There would be expenses for persons residing in Poland, as well as a large group living abroad.

In only a few cases, and in a small portion at that, could reprivatization mean a return of workplaces, and even less often could it lead to a greater number of true entrepreneurs. The assets apportioned for reprivatization would be a burden for the state budget (that is, ultimately for the taxpayers) in the form of lost revenues from the possible sale of these assets.

Acknowledging rights to property restitution and compensation to all those who had property first seized by the occupying German forces, then by the state, with the simultaneous questioning of the decree on agricultural reform and nationalization of industry would entail grave consequences. In 1939, on territory then belonging to Poland were numerous properties owned by Polish nationals of Jewish or German origin, who (usually their descendants) were now residing abroad. It could therefore turn out that nearly half of reprivatized assets would have to be transferred abroad, as this is where many people eligible for reprivatization now live.

As in the case of the Acts on Enfranchisement and on the Office of the State Attorney, the Act on Reprivatization was effectively vetoed by the president. But the unresolved problem keeps resurfacing in various forms. Many observers believe that the absence of appropriate regulations is dooming Poland to much greater expenditures in the form of compensation or property restitution in individual cases, as often adjudicated and too easily effected by the courts.

In writing about reprivatization, one cannot overlook one of its very important chapters: the incredible greed of Catholic Church officials coupled with the unfathomable submissiveness in this matter on the part of state officials—both from the right and from the left. Under a law enacted by the last communist government (on May 17, 1989), the state-church Property Committee (Komisja Majątkowa) was set up to deal with restoration of ownership of or compensation for property that had been seized by the authorities after the Second World War. The said committee has taken advantage of the right to adjudicate in closed session, and its decisions cannot be appealed. The Church would simply state what it wanted to acquire (land, schools, hospitals), designating the adjudicated compensation at a level many times below the actual value, to which the government officials would in turn consent. In this way the Church succeeded in gaining, mainly at the expense of municipal (local government) resources, greater assets than had been in its possession prior to the Second World War. There have even been instances when property forfeited in the nineteenth century was regained! A couple of years ago the SLD (Democratic Left Alliance) filed a complaint against the committee's activities to the Constitutional Tribunal, but there is visible delay in the issuance of a verdict even in such an obvious case. There are also numerous individual cases that contain criminal and corruption threads and have been directed to the Central Anticorruption Bureau and other organs of justice.

Foreign Capital and the "Subcontractor"

Passing over to the impact of foreign capital on Polish economy, it cannot be said that it brought the newest technology, or modernized the structure of our economy. Andrzej Karpiński, a brilliant man who published many studies on this matter, presents quite a gloomy picture (2008). He recalls "the unusually high state of penetration of Poland's own domestic market by imports. . . . The share of imports at 56 percent of sales in the domestic market places Poland among countries with relatively the highest import penetration in Europe." He also points to the technological weakness of our economy: "The position of modern elements in the country's economic structure is unusually weak, e.g. of high technology industry and other knowledge-based economy vehicles. The consequence is a high share of domains of the lowest technology, accounting for 36 percent of the entire industrial production. This means there is total domination of imitation processes and underdevelopment of the high technology sector, capable of competing at the innovation level."[3] His conclusion is that the strategic place and role of foreign capital is much, much greater than the general value of the influx of this capital. The country's assets have been sold very cheaply.

One such glaring example is the sale of the paper factory in Kwidzyń.[4] Its very modern machinery for basic production had been purchased for $400 million in Canada in the late 1970s. The same price had been paid for the grounds of the plant, the construction of buildings and the infrastructure. For a time the plant manufactured half of the paper used by the press in Poland and was one of the largest cellulose manufacturers in Europe, with 3,600 employees.

The Kwidzyń plant was bought by the U.S.-owned International Paper Group Inc. under the following terms: 80 percent of stocks went for $120 million and 20 percent was allotted to the employees. The new owner's tax exemption reached $142 million. Three years later, in 1993, C. C. Early, business development manager for International Paper Inc., would say in an interview for *Journal of Business Strategy* (March–April 1993): "The price was at such a level that we believe we are going to have an attractive income. . . . The Government of Poland has probably spent three to four times as much to build the factory. . . . This factory is fully modern, designed in accordance with totally modern western models. It meets all standards we would expect from any factory in the world."

This evoked an objection from the Society of Engineers and Technicians of the Paper Industry and the Sejm Committee for Ownership Transformations. One of the former ministers, Waldemar Kozłowski, lodged a protest to Prime Minister Hanna Suchocka and President Lech Wałęsa. In response he received an explanation from Minister for Ownership Transformations Janusz Lewandowski that the deal was advantageous due to the outdated character of the plant and in effect its possible bankruptcy.

During this time there appeared a Polish translation of an interview with the manager of the International Paper Group, published in the left-wing daily *Trybuna* (no. 110, 1993). Subsequently, Minister Waldemar Kozłowski filed a charge to the Prosecutor General against Minister Janusz Lewandowski's unpardonable negligence that caused a $500 million loss to the state. Unfortunately, shortly after filing the charge, Kozłowski died suddenly of a heart attack. The case was taken to the public prosecutor in Elbląg, which sent it to the NIK (Supreme Audit Office) agency in Gdańsk, and the latter forwarded it in turn to the NIK Central Office in Warsaw. And here it got stuck without further progress.

In the end, International Paper bought out the 20 percent of stock held by the employees at an extremely low price and in this way became the owner of the entire plant, in fact for free, if one takes into account the amount of exempted taxes (Gargas, 1995).

The grotesque crowning of this pathological deal was the resolution of the Municipal Council of Kwidzyń, on the motion of the Solidarity Trade Union Workplace Committee and all other trade unions of workplaces, bestowing on Minister Janusz Lewandowski the title of honorary citizen of Kwidzyń(!).*

At least this factory continues to operate. But the Polish authorities also sold off many enterprises as if unaware that many "hostile takeovers" by foreign capital were designed to eliminate domestic firms from the market. In this way many "shell companies" came into being.[5] Many firms were shut down, in others operations were drastically cut to benefit foreign importers. This was one of the main reasons, if not the main reason, for the premature deindustrialization of the Polish economy, increased unemployment, and a permanent foreign trade deficit with the accompanying debt growth.

The level of the price at which privatized state firms have been sold continues to be the subject of heated disputes and will probably remain so for a long time. The author, in taking up this subject, is faced with great approximations that allow for merely a very general orientation in the problem. Nevertheless, as we shall see, there is a growing agreement that this price has been much below the real value.

The discussion concerning this issue was rekindled by the Polish-American economist Kazimierz Poznański (2000), who for years has argued for gradual transformation. He showed that Poland has become rid of an immense portion of state assets for the price of about 10 percent of their true value, and this mainly to benefit foreign capital. Some economists have refused to acknowledge the calculations. But it soon turned out that even Ryszard Bugaj (2000), the most ardent critic of this emigrated economist, presented a not much better opinion, supported by a series of numbers. In his article,

---

*The story of this case is entirely based on the book by Witold Kieżuń, *Patologia transformacji* (The Transformation Pathology; 2012). The author, a specialist in management, has lectured in Poland, the United States, and Canada. For several years he was United Nations expert in Burundi (Central Africa). He is convinced that the systemic transformation in Poland assumed the form of "neocolonization," in resembling the earlier neocolonization of African countries.

turned down by *Gazeta Wyborcza* but published in *Trybuna*,[6] we find the following calculation: state proceeds from the privatization of the state sector were (at that time) not more than PLN 50 billion (the equivalent of about USD 17 billion). From this one must subtract the immense loss of taxes from the privatized firms. "At the same time, it can be cautiously assumed that the privatized assets make it possible to generate at least 1/3 of the GDP, i.e. in today's prices no less than PLN 250 bn. . . . Moreover, the beneficiaries of the 'sale with a discount' and various rebates have been for the most part foreign buyers." Poznański could well interpret the meaning of these numbers and statements as an unintended approval for his estimations.

To bring the problem closer, I shall refer to two kinds of numbers: the level of State Treasury proceeds from privatization and the investment outlays made for the privatized enterprises. The Ministry of Treasury informs that total proceeds (including those from Polish investors) were more than PLN 70 billion by the end of 2001.[7] Their report[8] in turn tells us that revenues from foreign investors from indirect (via the transformation of traditional state firms into Treasury Commercial Companies) privatization alone, from the sale of stocks and shares of privatized firms, amounted to PLN 38.6 billion. The investment obligations carried out during purchase by foreign investors totaled PLN 11.1 billion. To these sums we should add the (relatively small) share of foreign capital in directly privatized firms, mainly in employee companies (of the American ESOP type). The total proceeds from privatization (including proceeds from Polish investors) totaled only about PLN 70 billion by the end of 2001.

The role of foreign capital in Poland was much better rated by Maciej Bałtowski,[9] who based his views mainly on Main Statistical Office [GUS] data. Until 2000 the outlays of foreign capital totaled PLN 95.5 billion, of which PLN 42.5 billion went into the state budget. According to him, the estimated net profit for the year 2000 was only 4 percent, which gives the amount of PLN 6.2 billion. Such low profitability in the so-called emerging markets, with a fifteen-year period of return, would border on philanthropy. If, however, one adopts a ten-year period of return and on this basis calculates the business (income) value of assets invested by foreign capital in Poland, then it would amount to only about two-thirds of the total investment sum (PLN 62 bn : 95.5 bn). This crude calculation was enough for Bałtowski to consider the calculations of Kazimierz Poznański as absurd.

Unfortunately, the whole matter was not researched thoroughly, and Bałtowski himself soon unwillingly disavowed his calculations. The CASE compendium contains two of his monographs (he is co-author of the second), differing in meaning.[10] In them he subjects to separate study foreign capital enterprises formed from privatization and green-field (newly emerged) enterprises and reflects on why the former have better net earning capacity and profitability than the latter.

I cannot cite data directly questioning the barely 4 percent profitability calculated by him, since in the monographs, for reasons unknown, Bałtowski does not employ profitability, but relative indicators. The following fragment in an obvious way furnishes information to contradict this fifteen-year period of return: "New private enterprises attain somewhat higher (by 16 percent) labor productivity than privatized enterprises. But at the same time they show a decidedly lower earning capacity in comparison with privatized enterprises, particularly those privatized with the participation of foreign capital. This difference increases even more in the group of the biggest enterprises privatized with the participation of foreign capital."[11] "The earning capacity of enterprises privatized with foreign capital is at 8.69 percent in the group of the 200 biggest enterprises, whereas the earning capacity of green-field private enterprises with foreign capital only 4.6 percent."[12] One of the explanations for this turn of events was to be the not very convincing greater facility of concealing gains (among other things, the infamous transfers of profits abroad in the form of so-called transfer prices) in new enterprises than in privatized ones. On the other hand, the explanation could be very simple: foreign capital bought out the best enterprises in Poland with the best earning capacity and profitability.

If one even accepts the initial estimates of Bałtowski as close to reality, then there is still the questionable rationality of the policy of successive Polish governments with regard to foreign capital because they subordinated the Polish economy to it for a price at a fraction of the annual GDP. In addition, transnational corporations have taken hold of strategic positions in the Polish economy. Particularly striking is the privatization of banks. In 2003, the share of foreign capital in this sector was already about three-quarters of bank capital. This far-reaching privatization of a sector so sensitive for the operation of the national economy brought revenues in the range of PLN 16 billion to the State Treasury. The result is very different from a picture of lower prices and free competition. The banks operating in Poland offer very expensive services, at times being the most expensive in Europe. The interest-rate spread between deposits and credits is one of the highest and often was the highest among the countries of the European Union.

And in addition, both of the above opinions have been reaffirmed from an unexpected source, Jan Krzysztof Bielecki, formerly prime minister, and what makes his opinion more piquant, president of the largest foreign bank in Poland. Common sense induces him to object to an excess of foreign capital: "We needed things from abroad in order to catch up technologically and in management, but we cannot just be sub-contractors, as we will lose all management skills. If we remain proud only of the Polish plumber abroad—with all due respect for this trade— we are not going to build a modern country, because we need engineers, IT experts, high-class specialists."[13] So as not to dwell much longer on the issue of foreign capital, I shall note an equally categorical opinion of Bielecki on the Polish banking system: "Our program for restructuring banks in 1991 was not made to sell to foreign investors. . . . I was deeply convinced that the most important thing was to raise knowledge and this is why the West was needed by us like oxygen, but this did not mean that everything could be sold to them. Speeded up privatization served to patch up the budgetary gap. The development of infrastructure has also turned out to be catastrophic."[14]

All this is the result of a programmed negligence of structural industrial policy and of a naïve faith in market automatism of developmental processes.

It is time to evaluate the role of foreign capital in the process of privatization of the national economy and its strategic significance.

Irrespective of the political aspects of this problem, specialists not involved in politics also see the uncontrolled influx of foreign capital as one of the greatest shortcomings of systemic changes in Poland. I have already cited the opinion of an economist-practitioner with far-ranging management experience in transnational corporations—Stefan Dunin-Wąsowicz. He claims that the deliberate strategy of the great foreign corporations and the lack of experience and skills of Polish business and politicians in defining the needs of the market have made the Polish economy to a large extent dominated by sales channels determined by foreign firms; that markets have become for the most part divided between global concerns; that this defines the strategy of development of products and services, the channels of distribution, and prices; and that all this has transformed Poland's economy into a "subsidiary economy."[15] In these and several more publications, he reflected on how to best make use of the role of "subcontractor" and the possible directions of operation of Polish business that would increase its range of activity and the degree of independence. He was too late with his efforts to debunk the belief in the magic power of the market and to turn instead toward an active investment-oriented policy, at least within the scope practiced in the United States and Great Britain.[16] The pleas of many scholars for withdrawal from a policy of drastically low outlays for R & D, much lower than in the old EU countries, are encountering a similar fate.

Polish economists and politicians do not seem to be much concerned that the absence of an appropriate economic policy with a clear strategy has resulted in the development of a dependent economy, doomed to the role of subcontractor.

Society and the Ruling Class—Two Different Perspectives

The creation of the Polish version of capitalism is perceived by the people as alien and contradictory to their interests. The authorities in turn complain that the essence of the changes is not understood properly by an immature society contaminated by a sense of egalitar-

ianism and paternalism. Then again, when forced to certain self-criticism, the authorities say that the government has been unable to
explain to citizens what their true interests are.

The methods of privatization have formed a deep precipice
between what the people feel and the establishment. This can be easily
illustrated by the words of one of the classical diehard "privatizers,"
Piotr Kozarzewski. Referring to the data of CBOS from 2005, he wrote:

> Only 25 percent of respondents felt that privatization is advantageous
> for the Polish economy and 16 percent—for themselves personally.
> And, respectively, 40 percent and 46 percent that it is disadvanta-
> geous. . . . At the same time, the decided majority of respondents are
> in favor of a paternalistic role of the state in the economy and in the
> life of citizens, an egalitarian economic policy. In society there is a
> prevailing sense of being the losers of transformation and that it, and
> especially privatization, benefited above all dishonest individuals. . . .
> What is particularly alarming is the negative attitude among Poles
> who have obviously managed to adjust to the new system and who
> could become the social and political base of reforms, and also among
> the young people.[17]

A very interesting explanation of the reasons for this "alarming"
situation is given. It turns out that the "egalitarian attitudes and support for state paternalism make it impossible for society to redefine the
fundamental values in accordance with the principles of the new
system. The formed economy based on private ownership is by its
nature 'unjust,' if one applies egalitarian criteria: someone will be the
owner, and someone will not."[18] But the author also finds a deeper
cause that explains the lower than possible standard of living and
increased income disparities: "In Poland . . . the most important
source of the decline in support and increased disapproval for reforms
and particularly for privatization was most probably the slowing down
of ownership transformations. . . . This slowing down has led to . . .
extremely slow raising of the living standard of society and the growth
of income disparities."[19] This simple (or crude?) explanation relieves

Kozarzewski and the remaining authors of the need for deeper reflection over who exactly these new owners are, how they have become what they are and, most important, what kind of reality and work relations they have concocted for workers and what prospects they have created for young people.

Public distrust of privatization may have other, more profound, causes. Currently a dispute is under way over the further privatization of the hard coal mining corporation and the copper producing giant KGHM, which dominates over a substantial region of Poland. The resistance of the workers may result from their concern about their future fate, as pointed out by Żyżyński.[20] Exhaustible resources mean a limited supply, and what happens when these end? So long as a company belongs to the state, it can be bound to create a special fund for the needs of future restructuring of the region. Privatization essentially rules this out. Resistance against privatization of the coal mines can have similar background causes.

Maybe the current crisis, with some delay, can change the attitude of the government, provided public opinion exerts enough pressure. The Polish authorities owe to the people substantial fulfillment of the 1997 constitution, which promises (guarantees in its provisions) a new order based on the principles of a social market economy, social justice, and full employment. Unfortunately, none of the successive government coalitions has attempted to meet these promises, tolerating a highly unethical constitutional hypocrisy. In socioeconomic matters, the "binding" provisions have nearly the same value as the famed communist constitution of 1952. Until the great exodus abroad, unemployment was rising, as were income disparities and even absolute poverty, although the national income showed rapid growth. Following EU entry, this anachronistic system was confronted with the neighboring economies of the greater majority of the continent, which observed the principles of a social market economy, and especially with the Scandinavian countries, which combined the highest level of taxes and social security with the most modern dynamic economies. This is what inclined two Austrian economists, Karl Aiginger and Michael Landesmann (2002), to call the

Scandinavian countries "centers of economic excellence" and to reflect over whether this was not the appropriate model to follow by other European countries.

PART THREE

Looking Ahead

12. Ownership in Different Types of Capitalism

If as much pains as has been taken to aggravate the inequality of chances . . . had been taken to temper that inequality by every means not subversive of the principle itself; if the tendency of legislation had to favor the diffusion, instead of the concentration of wealth—to encourage the subdivision of the large masses, instead of striving to keep them together; the principle of individual property would have been found to have no necessary connection with the physical and social evils which almost all Socialist writers assume to be insepa-rable from it. Private property, in every defense made of it, is sup-posed to mean, the guarantee to individuals of the fruits of their own labor and abstinence.

—J. S. MILL, *The Principles of Political Economy*, 1848

As discussed in Part Two, the main architect of the Polish systemic changes, Leszek Balcerowicz, treated property as one of the basic pil-lars of economic systems. Let us take a closer look at his views, this time to consider not only his perspective on capitalism as such but also its variety.* He expressed his reflections in the 1989 monograph *Systemy gospodarcze* (Economic Systems) and in a separate study on property in 1997.

Although the final version of the 1997 study came into being many years after the collapse of the socialist system, it did not cease to be weighed down by the confrontation of (market) capitalism with (really existing) socialism. Perceiving property in this way may be odd, since the system which is now history in Europe has obviously failed in economic terms. It lost in the rivalry with capitalism because of its deeply rooted systemic defects. This truth became indisputable at the turn of the 1980s. Market socialism, or at least recognized as such in the versions we are familiar with (Yugoslav), had to lose as well. Even those who believe (and I am one of them) that this theoretical model has never been tried out anywhere, do not suggest it can be implemented in the foreseeable future. The spectacular breakdown of real socialism, together with the decentralized Yugoslav version, calls for caution in suggesting comprehensive system proposals. And so it is hard to believe that Balcerowicz is analyzing property in terms of a confrontation of capitalism with socialism (or more precisely—with communism) because he still thinks it is possible for the old system to return, even if in a corrected form. It is more likely that Balcerowicz feels that such a form of public discourse is the best way to present and defend *one* version of capitalism, the capitalism of free competition, that is, a capitalism that I believe belongs to remote history.

Such an approach strongly affects the way in which Balcerowicz perceives the American theory of property rights. When, in the spirit of the property rights theory, he describes its multidimensional spectrum of many variables, everything falls into place. But when he moves on to an analysis of the different types of ownership, the property rights theory becomes useless for him, as he limits its analysis to only

---

* Economists engaged in comparative analysis frequently use the notion of economic systems for what is better known to non-specialists as different types, variants, or models of capitalism. This may be confusing, because capitalism and socialism are often termed as systems. I suggest we call these mega-systems.

two essential notions: the entrepreneurship regime and the ownership structure. But these terms also turn out to be of little use when he presents his view regarding private, state-owned, self-managed, or cooperative enterprises. He simply says that the state is a "bad owner," that is to say, not worse than a private owner, but simply bad. The more a firm is an individual-private firm, the more efficient it is. But if Balcerowicz were shown anonymously the operations and efficient performance of two world-known French automobile companies, Renault and Peugeot (private and public), he would have great difficulty in recognizing the "bad owner." What is more important, today's ownership relations are becoming more and more complex; they overlap each other.

Balcerowicz's study (1997) contains many sentences of this sort: "Command socialism generates . . . much hidden unemployment and market socialism creates fewer jobs than competitive capitalism. . . . The former systems would tend to be plagued by stronger inflationary pressures." Just like the proverbial army general waging a war gone by. Such black-and-white thinking prevents him from reflecting on the real issue at hand, namely what kind of capitalism serves people best, ensuring the lowest unemployment and the lowest margin of social exclusion. Focusing only on what, according to him, creates the foundations of a rational order prevents him from understanding contemporary systemic differentiation. His typology of economic systems is limited only to market capitalism, distorted capitalism (quasi-capitalism), and to more or less liberal transition economies.

In fact, the actual choice of system does not boil down to an alternative between market capitalism and distorted capitalism, or quasi-capitalism. Obviously, the very term, distorted capitalism, suggests that it is an unwanted system, at most an unpredicted result. The real problems of today begin when we ask: What kind of capitalism is viable from a social point of view?

One could have imagined that the new global circumstances without Soviet-type socialism would free Balcerowicz from a bipolar perception of the highly differentiated world of "different capitalisms" based on different ownership forms. If, however, the "choice" of capitalism is limited to the "real" or "distorted" kind, then this is no longer a matter of a sensible choice. In perceiving the alternative in this manner, Balcerowicz imperceptibly negated the need for the development of comparative economics, and thereby his own pioneering role. His train of thought can be referred to the bitter remark made by the well-known researcher of common pool resources, Elinor Ostrom: "It's pathetic and at the same time dangerous that scholars are inclined to suggest radical institutional changes without a strict analysis of the ways of practical operation of different institutional combinations. The main weakness of the social sciences has become the absence of subtle analyses of the operation of alternative institutional combinations."[1]

Even the Gdańsk conservative and, like Balcerowicz, enthusiastic proponent of the Anglo-Saxon system, Jan Szomburg, understands that "comparative analyses do not predetermine the superiority of one form of capitalism over another. A more modest observation would be fitting here, that there are absolutely no most efficient capitalist-market systems and that the key prerequisite to their 'efficiency' is general cultural adequacy."[2]

After acknowledging that ownership is just one of the determinants of economic efficiency, Balcerowicz lists the following institutional fundamentals of growth: "an open regime of entrepreneurship, a capitalist ownership structure, flexible labor markets, a low or moderate tax/GDP ratio, a stable macroeconomy, and a stable political system."[3] This is a fine set of attributes of the old free-enterprise capitalism. Meanwhile, Balcerowicz suggests that these are attributes of the capitalism that is prevalent in today's world. Here is a surprising conclusion: "It is the existence of an especially large scope of such fundamentals and not any single factor, say, a special type of government intervention or a special type of investment, which explains economic miracles, be it in West Germany in the 1950s or East Asia since the early 1960s."[4]

It would be difficult to uphold such an interpretation for the two greatest systemic innovations of the postwar period: the German social market economy and the different versions of the economies of the "East Asian tigers," and especially the Japanese, South Korean, and Taiwanese economies. When we admire a musical virtuoso, we wonder about his character (talent, diligence) and not the common biological attributes of human beings. It is obvious that in the Asian countries the "fundamentals" mentioned by Balcerowicz exist on a smaller or greater scale. The question is, would these countries have achieved any "miracle" by listening to Leszek Balcerowicz or the commandments of the Washington Consensus.

With the systemic fundamentals arranged in such a way, it is not possible to reconcile such facts as a greater share in investment of the West German state than of private business (in the years 1953-54) and in housing construction, where the financial involvement of the federal and local authorities, reached about 70 percent. In Japan after the Second World War the policy of full employment was pursued so consistently and was so multidimensional, and the staff policy was so highly regulated, that at times it was hard to say whether there existed a labor market in Japan at all, not to mention a "flexible" one.

In South Korea and in Japan, the process of accelerated industrial modernization began with essential changes being made in the ownership structure with the help of political coercion. A radical agricultural reform was carried out in South Korea, eliminating the great estates in favor of small peasant holdings. A similar agricultural reform was executed in Japan, with the dismantling of the great land-industrial estates (*zaibatsu*). In their place, radically different corporations were created, having a cross-ownership structure with a considerable state share (*keiretsu*). Japanese corporations were (and continue to be) more of a community than a stock market commodity. For decades foreign capital had no access to the countries referred to above. Thus these were "half-open" regimes, to use Balcerowicz's language, but despite this, or maybe because of this, they experienced a great leap forward in economic growth.

It would have been even harder for Balcerowicz to explain the success of the Scandinavian countries drawn from the Swedish model. As we know, it is based on the theory of functional ownership, which defines ownership as a bunch of functions divided among various entities. According to this concept, capitalist ownership can and should be gradually socialized, divesting capitalist owners of successive ownership functions. It is because of these limitations that the firm Volvo did not lay off workers during (and because of) recession until at least the mid-1990s. Where, then, was a flexible labor market here? The Swedish ownership concept is theoretically similar to the American property rights theory referred to, only the Swedes drew entirely different practical conclusions from it. And it would be hardest to explain in Balcerowicz's categories the success of the Chinese economy, which, contrary to the common canons of economic theory, has been the fastest-growing economy in the world for the longest time, for over thirty years now. There is no flexible labor market there, and property is far from the ideal of "indivisible and fully transferable" property complying with the property rights theory.

Distribution of Property Rights

The structure of ownership is obviously closely related to social justice issues. Yet a scholarly approach to these problems is often viewed with suspicion, in the belief that it would be doomed to mere subjective evaluations. The opinion of the philosopher Leszek Kołakowski[5] is surprising to me. Though he defends the benefits stemming from the concept of social justice as a counterbalance to social Darwinism (this radically distinguishes him from Balcerowicz), he nevertheless feels that it is just as vague as the concept of human dignity, and "there is no way of defining it in economic categories." Whereas it undoubtedly does produce economic effects, "it is not possible to even approximately deduce their type."

This is not the place to elaborate further on this subject. I shall therefore limit myself only to saying that more and more economists, for example, those presented in the two volumes of *Economic Justice*,[6] treat the economic dimension of justice as a significant part of social justice, as well as justice in general. Thus economics should include it within the range of its interest in the belief that it can and should be dealt with in a scholarly fashion. What is more, quite a few authors are convinced that this phenomenon can be measured, although obviously it is still poorly defined, and understood in different ways. But on economic grounds this notion can be expressed in a more precise manner, even though it is a part of several other social sciences. In a similar way, liberty is also a normative notion and at least as vague as social justice. Yet many researchers have managed to establish quite widely accepted criteria for measuring it. In effect, various ranking lists are drawn up, so far limited mostly to economic liberty.

The most celebrated author of the contemporary theory of justice, John Rawls, firmly believed that justice in general, and distributive justice in particular, may and should be the subject of scholarly investigation. According to this philosopher of politics, among several of the most important values lies property (most often called wealth) as one of the social values that should be equally distributed. He explains the general concept as follows: "All social primary goods—liberty and opportunity, income and wealth, and what forms the basis of self-respect—are to be distributed equally unless an unequal distribution of any or all of these goods is to the advantage of the least favored."[7] In his reasoning, "distribution" is an unusually capacious notion and covers practically all "social values" that affect liberty and equality, both of which form social justice. Here property is treated as one of the factors determining equality and at the same time a factor shaping the economic system.

Ironically, this last issue was articulated in the clearest and most distinct way not by social democrats or Marxists, but by the leading theorists of modern liberal thought. Rawls was not the only one. There was the political scientist, jurist, and liberal thinker Bruce Ackerman, whose postulate of "future liberal revolution" is based on the belief that past implementation of liberal programs had been a failure. "A system based on the principles of laissez-faire on the one hand accepts immense concentration of hereditary wealth, and on the other allows for the existence of an uneducated class, deprived of any property. Such a systematic faulty distribution of wealth makes equal political participation a farce. It also coincides with all forms of market deception: the creation of cartels, environmental degradation, widespread exploitation of consumer ignorance. No thinking liberal, regardless of what Hayek says, will be happy to look at such evident injustice."[8]

Ackerman, like Rawls, postulates that ownership be subordinated to the needs of equality. According to him, "Even in property ownership the new system should aim at equal justice. . . . For contemporary liberalism the property right is not the most sacred. Unlike the nineteenth-century laissez-faire liberals, the aims of contemporary liberalism are more noble: the idea is . . . to enable the citizen to develop his character in conditions of liberty and equality."[9]

Rawls on Property-Owning Democracy

John Rawls's famous work *A Theory of Justice* (1971/1994/2005) probably contributed the most to the restitution of theoretical liberalism, or more precisely of social liberalism. Widely known as a liberal thinker, his leftist leanings are limited to his thinking that neither Karl Marx nor socialism is an expression of aberration. To the detriment of economic thought in Poland, this work has remained unnoticed by our economists.* What is interesting is that Rawls probably most distinctly expressed his view on the existing and postulated socioeconomic system in the preface to the Polish edition of his work.

After conceding that if he were to rewrite his book, he would more sharply differentiate property-owning democracy from the welfare state concept, he specifically says:

> Note here two different conceptions of the aim of political institutions over time. In a welfare state the aim is that none should fall below a decent standard of life, and that all should receive certain protections against accident and misfortune—for example, unemployment compensation and medical care. The redistribution of income serves this

---

* With probably the only exception being Leszek Balcerowicz (more about this in a moment).

purpose when, at the end of each period, those who need assistance can be identified. Such a system may allow large and inheritable inequities of wealth incompatible with the fair value of the political liberties . . . as well as large disparities of income that violate the difference principle. While some effort is made to secure fair equality of opportunity, it is either insufficient or else ineffective given the disparities of wealth and the political influence they permit.

By contrast, *in a property-owning democracy, the aim is to carry out the idea of society as a fair system of cooperation over time among citizens as free and equal persons. Thus basic institutions must from the outset put in the hands of citizens generally, and not only of a few, the productive means to be fully cooperating members of a society.*[10]

Interestingly, Rawls knowingly formulated a pre- or supra-systemic theory of justice. It left "open the question whether its principles are best realized by some form of property-owning democracy or by a liberal socialist regime. This question is left to be settled by historical conditions and the traditions, institutions, and social forces of each country."[11] These meaningful words were written by Rawls in 1993, quite a few years after the declaration of an "end to history," which was to be manifested in the ultimate victory of liberal capitalism. He demonstrates here a restraint toward the unknown future worthy of the founder of liberalism, John Stuart Mill.

Three tenets can be drawn from the described position.

1. For Rawls equality is a key principle, and this means equality of *all* primary goods, not only streams of incomes, but also wealth. On the level of the general principle, Rawls focuses his attention not on secondary redistribution of incomes, but on primary distribution. But he refers to reality when he places emphasis on "steady dispersal over time of the ownership of capital and resources by the laws of inheritance and bequest, on fair equality of opportunity, secured by provisions for education and training."[12] To emphasize once again: for Rawls, the postulate of equal distribution of *incomes* goes hand in hand with the postulate of such dis-

tribution of *wealth*. This is a very significant attribute, as income is a stream, and wealth what has already been accumulated.

2. Any deviation from the principle of equality—may I stress of both income and wealth, as well as liberty and equal opportunity—is to be considered in terms of advantages to the least fortunate.

3. The next difference is perhaps the most important—for Rawls, the term *of advantage to the least fortunate* may be (and is!) understood in two ways. One is as an excuse for production-motivation inequalities, that is, inequalities in remuneration so as to attain greater production effects, but also as giving more to those who not through their own fault are suffering deprivation or are exposed to barriers against taking advantage of *fair equality of opportunity* (Rawls's favorite expression). For example, more funds should be *given* for the education of children from slums, otherwise they will inherit the slums' status, similarly as when parents shower with private tutoring a less talented child, because a talented one will manage fine by himself. Only when they reach a more or less equal start in being prepared for life (graduating high school or university) and as adults will be able to account for themselves, can they be treated (for example, in a will) equally.[13]

Reasoning like this can be carried over to underprivileged groups, regions, and the like. This train of thought needs to be remembered in today's Poland, where nouveau-riche circles are arrogantly clamoring for the right to an entirely different, contrasting inequality, a right to unlimited wealth. The most vivid example of this is the annulment of the tax on inheritance and gifts for members of the immediate family.

Rawls's work, attacked by some and elaborated by others, not only helped stimulate liberal thought, but socialist thought as well. His theory gave rise to the much discussed concepts of liberal socialism (the Italian thinker Norbert Bobio). Mainly because of his methodological individualism, he is rightly regarded as a liberal thinker. But in the spirit of the liberal thought of John Stuart Mill, he does not denounce socialism, does not write it off as a dream of *homo sovieticus*, but calmly writes about it as an alternative, without putting in quotation marks social justice or exploitation.

Contrary to popular belief, Rawls did not limit himself to general descriptions of his theory. In his work we find a concretely outlined picture of the organization of a state that should ensure social justice, or a high level of it. The list of "supporting institutions" in a "properly organized democratic state" comprises a just constitution that secures liberty of conscience and freedom of thought, equal citizenship, the fair value of political liberty, and—again "fair" as opposed to formal—equality of opportunity, especially in education and culture, and finally freedom in the choice of occupation and in undertaking economic activity. Apart from ordinary regulations governing the conduct of firms and associations, the authorities are obliged to prevent the formation of monopolistic restrictions and barriers to the more desirable positions. The government would guarantee a social minimum through benefits or negative income tax.

Rawls proposed four "branches" to maintain the desirable social and economic conditions that make up a good state:

1. The *allocation* branch is to ensure a competitive system of prices, preventing the formation of unreasonable market power. The duties of this branch, however, extend beyond the conventional understanding of allocation of resources. It would also diagnose departures from the principle of efficiency, resulting from the fact that prices do not reflect the social benefits and costs and would act to correct them. This would be achieved not only through taxes and subsidies but also through a revision of the scope and definition of property rights.

2. The *stabilization* branch is to steer "strong effective demand," enabling "reasonably" full employment and free choice of occupation.

3. The *transfer* branch is responsible for the social minimum. The idea here is not only securing a decent living standard and respecting claims resulting from needs, but also maximum improvement of the situation of the least advantaged.

4. The *distribution* branch has a long-term task. The idea is "gradually and continually to correct the distribution of wealth and to prevent concentrations of power detrimental to the fair value of political liberty and fair equality of opportunity." One of the ends is wide dispersal of property to ensure "the fair value of the equal liberties."[14]

All these branches together will form a system in which land and capital are in possession that is not necessarily equal, but nevertheless in the possession of wide ranks of society, and not of a small group controlling the majority of resources. Only such a system of distributive justice, according to Rawls, disqualifies most of the arguments socialists give against a market economy. And again he astounds with his "supra-systemic" objectivism when he writes: "But it is clear that, in theory anyway, a liberal socialist regime can also answer to the two principles of justice."[15] The condition, however, is a form of ownership where firms are managed by employee councils or managers designated by them.

It is surprising that in many interpretations, the descent Rawls makes from a highly abstract level to the level of practical proposals, creating something like a realistic utopia of a more humane and more community-oriented type of capitalism, did not raise much interest. After all, it takes both parts to make up a certain thought-out whole.

It would seem that the systemic framework outlined here would incline toward a more in-depth and radical critical evaluation of both the Polish transformation and the emergent socioeconomic order, with its characteristic arrangement of proprietors. It turns out, however, that Rawls's radically egalitarian theory of justice has also been applied in attempts to legitimize the existing inequalities.

How Balcerowicz Abused Rawls's Theory

It is a paradox that the only Polish economist who took up the task of reinterpreting Rawls's theory was Leszek Balcerowicz. He did this in the book *Wolność i rozwój. Ekonomia wolnego rynku* (Freedom and Growth. Economics of Free Markets) (1998). In it, he formulates his own sharply contoured view on inequalities in a direct reference to the works of Rawls, in his words "the author of today's probably most influential theory of justice."[16] "In accordance with this concept," writes Balcerowicz, "out of the various possible income disparities, the best one is that with which the situation of the poorest improves the fastest."[17] However, this only summarizes the idea of the American thinker. The following is the decisive fragment of Balcerowicz's view:

> Simplifying and contouring the problem somewhat, we can say that there exist two different normative positions in the matter of social inequalities:
> 1. Emphasis is placed on static income inequalities, i.e. existing in each given period. It is desirable to diminish these inequalities, irrespective of their initial level and without association with any distinct and justified norm. I shall call this position *non-normative egalitarianism*.
> 2. First and foremost there is the ideal of equality of opportunities. The income inequality norm is inferred from this ideal with the additional assumption of broad economic liberty or the Rawls criterion. I shall call this position *dynamic egalitarianism*.[18]

The author of *Wolność i rozwój* devotes further argumentation to a critical rejection of "non-normative egalitarianism," defined also as "redistributionism," and to an elaboration of his own concept of dynamic egalitarianism.

In my belief, the interpretative "liberty" applied by Professor Balcerowicz is recklessly audacious, to say the least. Here we have the architect of the shock therapy plan placing the free market and economic freedom in the foreground, many times resorting to the views of F. Hayek and M. Friedman, complaining that the necessary, according to him, Polish income inequalities have "low legitimization." And he, undoubtedly, wanted to raise it by presenting his program as a version of one of the most egalitarian concepts given forth by liberal thought of the last half century.

It is hard to believe that anyone in good faith would elaborate on the above "Rawls criterion" basing it on a legal(?!) understanding of equality of opportunities, with the "additional" assumption of a broad definition of economic liberty. Of decisive importance here is the hidden assumption that in conditions of willful exchange of services, everyone, rich and poor alike, will benefit from an unequal distribution of gratification. With such boldness of interpretation, Balcerowicz might as well have referred to Karl Marx, with of course one "additional" stipulation, that it is not the capitalists who are exploiting the workers, but the other way around.

Among the achievements named as an example of the implementation of the reformulated concept of Rawls, Balcerowicz listed: "We succeeded in making considerable progress in several factors within the model of dynamic egalitarianism, economic liberty, privatization of the economy, opening up to the world, competition, monetary stabilization. Although there is still a lot left to be done: first of all privatization must be completed and great reforms must be carried out in areas maintained from taxes."[19]

When the book edition quoted here appeared in 1998, Balcerowicz was again deputy prime minister and minister of finance, this time because he was chairman of the Union of Liberty Party. His program of medium-term financial strategy called for downsizing all state expenditures from nearly one-half to one-third of GDP. To put it in plain language, social security transfers (of the welfare state) were to be drastically cut. In mid-term he left the government, because he arrived at the conclusion that his program was not being carried out radically enough.

Let us recall those times (detailed information can be found in other chapters). All basic indicators related to social justice were definitely negative (with a large margin of poverty) and several reflected deterioration of the social situation of the basic social groups. The continuously high unemployment began rising again, the number of unemployed persons receiving benefits decreased, and a growing number of persons were living below the social minimum and minimum of subsistence. Extreme poverty affected children most of all. Then the acute problem of one to two million undernourished children was disclosed, which Marcin Król (2003) would aptly call a political scandal. Not only that, this contradicted an elementary sense of social justice and was in glaring violation of the Constitution of Poland. All this happened with a relatively high national income growth rate.

If this was supposed to be yet another wave of sacrifices for the good of future growth, then how does one explain that toward the end of the rule of the coalition of the Union of Liberty and Solidarity Election Action the investment rate started to fall drastically, ending with one percent GDP growth for two successive years at the start of this century?

To set the record straight, what Balcerowicz describes as dynamic egalitarianism is nothing else but a no-alternative, dysfunctional elitism, while the presented attempt to usurp Rawls's justice theory has nothing to do with a scholarly approach. It is the result of manipulation to achieve immediate political goals.

Not long ago, Balcerowicz founded the Civil Development Forum, targeted at combating myths. He announced: "In social awareness there are opinions that have not much to do with facts. We shall regularly combat them." One of the objectives of this project is to consistently defend a social order based on growing inequalities, to prove that inequalities, and even their intensification, are in the end beneficial for all, including the poorest.

Many alleged myths are contested by the master economist himself. Quite often he is replaced in this by an economist of the forum, Andrzej Rzońca. According to him, "Inequalities are okay."[20] This was one of the first public declarations of the forum. Rzońca not only argues that "inequalities in incomes are natural and beneficial for the economy," but he also accepts that they will continue to grow. In doing this, he is creating new myths, which should in turn lead to the creation of an anti-forum, so as to combat myths in the style of Balcerowicz and Rzońca. Here are a few of the most glaring ones.

1. When speaking of growing inequalities in Poland, the author claims that "this is so not because growth pushes some people into poverty, but because it does not pull out everyone at once from it." Yet here are some figures, easily accessible in official statistics, to negate this. In the years 1996 to 2005, the number of people living below the biological subsistence level rose repeatedly from year to year. Within a decade, it increased nearly threefold, from 4.3 percent of the population to 12.3 percent, even though the national income rose during this time by more than a third!

2. Denying the opinion that in Poland "we have one of the greatest social disparities in Europe," the myth-buster (this term is taken from the forum website) replies: "Disproportions are not the biggest in our country and in recent years have even decreased somewhat. According to the World Bank, the differences in earnings of Poles are smaller than in eight countries of the European Union." The author unfortunately does not cite the source. It is not hard to find facts to negate this. In the two-volume collection of studies on social inequalities (Klebaniuk, 2007) we find a graph showing that in wages, the Gini index in Poland has reached the level of 0.40![21] Zachorowska-Mazurkiewicz refers to the newest report of Bank Kadr TEST, according to which Poland has the highest level of income inequality among the EU countries! The situation is similar with the spread of incomes. According to data from Eurostat-Database (of 25 EU countries in 2005), both the Gini index and the quintile share ratio (S20/S80) position Poland on the same level as Lithuania and Latvia, with only one country having higher inequality indicators—Portugal. The same source ranks Poland in the last place in the poverty rate. And Main Statistical Office (GUS) data also show that Poland is one of the most inegalitarian countries. Thus the saying of the economist-sociologist Lidia Beskid still holds true: "Against the background of other countries of Central Europe, Poland is implementing one of the most elitist models of income division."[22] In the Internet-available *Human Development Report 2007/08*, we see that in the Czech Republic, in

Slovakia, and in Hungary, the Gini income index is respectively: 0.25, 0.26, 0.27, but in Poland it is 0.34 (in other publications an even higher indicator was cited for Poland). What is also important is that this leap forward in income inequality occurred within a very short time.

3. The same source contains data refuting the statement made by Rzońca, that "all Asian countries" have a higher inequality rate than Poland. But something else is even more important. During their great leap forward, the East Asian countries radically leveled out income and wealth disparities. In both countries mentioned here, a radical agricultural reform was carried out. In Japan between the wars, the span between the wage of a rank-and-file worker and heads of corporations reached a hundred-fold level. Around 1980, the span dropped to fourteen-fold before tax and seven-fold after tax. It is true that in recent years the wage inequalities in Japan have grown substantially, but it is well known that today the bosses of Toyota earn a fraction of what the heads of General Motors or Ford earn, and certainly no one can say that the Japanese firm manufactures cars of poorer quality.

In answering a reporter's question on when disproportions are bad, the author again creates a myth: "Today the most widespread form of depriving people of a portion of their income generated is raising taxes for the richest. The poor majority puts pressure on the government to 'punish' the wealthy, to force them to share their wealth." And what proof is there for that? "We have heard in the preceding term of the Sejm ideas for a 50 percent personal income tax." But the road from "we have heard" (from representatives of a small opposition party) to "depriving people . . . of income" is still very long. This pressure is minor in comparison with the pressure to recklessly lower taxes, with general silence about the effects such an operation would have on government transfers. That is why for years now the state has been practicing a "planned scarcity of funds," in the words of one of our ombudsmen (T. Zieliński), when it comes to payment of statutory social obligations.

Another piece of political acrobatics is when Balcerowicz says to the audience of the Business Center Club (!) that "an expanded social state is the result of bad and immoral policy. Its advocates and architects have no right to demonstrate a moral superiority over those who oppose them. On the contrary, they deserve to be morally condemned."[23] Are these not the words of a general who is waging an outdated (nineteenth-century) war?

I realize that this is a heavy accusation. But the overinterpretation of Rawls described here is not an isolated case. How seriously, for example, can we take an author who cites the economies of Japan, South Korea, Taiwan, Singapore, or Malaysia as empirical evidence for the effectiveness of the "set of factors" that make up his "model of dynamic egalitarianism," without saying a word about not only far-reaching state interventionism but also that next to the Nordic countries these countries have for many years had the smallest degree of income and wealth inequalities in the world? It was this experience that inclined two successive vice presidents of the World Bank, M. Bruno and J. Stiglitz, and many other Western authors to reject the famous Kuznets law,* which still lies at the base of Balcerowicz's reasoning.

The Scandinavians
Have a Free Lunch for Poland

Balcerowicz's mentor, Milton Friedman, and his followers popularized the saying, "There is no such thing as a free lunch." In other words, a welfare state entails necessary costs, since high taxes and social spending must have a negative impact on the national income growth rate. But today there are already many facts that negate this view. Many Scandinavian, and especially Swedish authors, have been

---

*In his study of industrial modernization in several countries, Kuznets concluded that in the early stages of industrialization, income inequalities tend to increase (Kuznets, 1955). Later on this was called Kuznets' law. He was hoping, however, that after economies have been modernized, we would be witnessing the reverse tendency.

demonstrating this for a long time now. I shall refer to studies that show something quite the opposite: the welfare state does resemble a free lunch.

The American scholar Peter H. Lindert (2003, 2004, 2007) presented the developments and role of the social transfers sector from the eighteenth century until recent years. The point of departure of his reasoning is the "econometric consensus" concerning the effects of social spending: contrary to traditional belief, these studies do not find the existence of costs of slowing down GDP growth caused by a large share of tax-based social transfers in GDP. Similarly, Lindert's research leads to the conclusion that "as an economic species, the welfare state has shown strong survival instincts in the countries where it emerged in the twentieth century. Within the expanding OECD, the number of welfare states is stable or expanding."[24] It is true that with the adoption of the borderline for the share of social transfers (specifically defined, for example, excluding government and military pensions) in GDP at 20 percent, some countries have left this group. However, Switzerland took the place of Ireland, which greatly reduced its social spending. There is also a large group of countries that are almost in the "club."

I shall not describe here the many features of welfare states that do not stifle economic growth, and even intensify it. Let one important example suffice for Poland. Mothers with children are more willing to take up work when they have within reach affordable or free daycare centers and kindergartens, when benefits are enough not only for subsistence but also for education, or for participation in community life. It is obvious that the smaller the inequalities, the better the social security, or the utilization of human capital and the other way round.[25] Social capital can develop more easily. Even people involved in business feel better in secure, stable, and cultural surroundings.

From the point of view of Poland's future potential systemic choices, important information and statements can be found in a study drawn up by two Austrian economists, K. Aiginger and M. Landesman (2002). In terms of economic dynamism, they divided the EU countries into two groups. One included large countries:

Germany, France, and Italy, which have a low economic growth rate. The other included the smaller Northern European countries, which are doing quite well and are even in the foreground in the most modern sectors. The two economists called them "centers of excellence" and reflected over how much they could serve as a future model for other European countries. The following questions were put forward for consideration: "It would be interesting to analyze why Sweden and Finland—and with some qualifications—the Netherlands and Denmark invested into the 'growth drivers' while many other countries did not. And whether a 'new European model' is coming up, not defined by welfare and comprehensive social coverage only, but by investment into and fast diffusion of new technologies. . . . None is a low-cost country, all have rather high taxes and did face serious problems at some time in the early 1990s (afraid of losing markets or competitiveness). This is a parallel to the U.S. fear in the early 1990s of losing competitiveness to Japan."[26] We should add that this is despite that U.S. taxes and social transfers are almost half of those in the Scandinavian countries.

The above facts implicitly undermine the view that "over socializing" the German or French economy slowed down growth, since countries with a much higher level of taxes and welfare expenditures are in stable condition, and there is nothing to suggest that they would depart from the welfare state model. And though I do not think they will become an example to follow for the rest of Europe, for Poland they pose a challenge. They force us to think about whether our mission of further liberalization and deregulation of EU economies can be backed by sensible reasoning. We should rather consider which countries we can look to for models for ourselves.

Socialist Values

To understand the place of Balcerowicz's enunciations on the map of contemporary liberal thought, it is worth looking into the socialist adventure in the output of the liberal economist Joseph Stiglitz. In the early 1990s, he published three studies devoted to criticism of market socialism. They open with two Wicksell Lectures, circulating only in photocopied form under the title *Whither Socialism*, delivered in May 1990 at the University of Stockholm. This was an attempt to directly answer why the hitherto existing concepts of market socialism had failed. His reply being not a simple rejection of socialist ideas in general, but an indication where the mistakes lay in both the concept of market socialism itself, and in the more fundamental assumptions of neoclassical theory upon which this concept was founded.

Without going into the details of his criticism, I shall refer only to Stiglitz's final message, which in my opinion makes us aware not only of the meanders of socialism, the limitations of the popular versions of those times, but also of the lost opportunity. For this reason, it deserves to be recalled:

> There is a poem by the great American poet, Robert Frost, that begins: *"Two roads diverged in a wood, and / I took the one less travelled by / and that has made all the difference."* As the former socialist countries embark on the journey, they see many paths diverging. There are not just two roads. Among these there are many that are less traveled by—where they end up no one yet knows. One of the large costs of the socialist experiment of the past seventy years is that it seemed to foreclose exploring many of the other roads. As the former socialist countries set off on this journey, let us hope that they keep in mind not only the narrower set of economic questions that I have raised in this book but the broader set of social ideas that motivated many of the founders of the socialist tradition. Perhaps some of them will *take the road less travelled by, and perhaps that will make all the difference, not only for them, but for the rest of us as well.*[27]

This is a surprise coming from another world: during the height of success of turbo-capitalism preaching, otherwise known as Reaganomics, this American economist not only has the courage to speak up for socialist ideals for countries embarking on the path to a new socioeconomic order, but also to express hopes that these ideals could change the lives of both the post-communist societies and people in the West. And it is unfathomable for today's Polish imagination that with such views Stiglitz not only became chief economic advisor to President Bill Clinton, but was also nominated first deputy president of the World Bank.

Neither the final part of Stiglitz's lectures nor his later book contains any coherent outline of a vision based on the "broader set" of social ideas. He did, however, formulate eight "commandments," which, when read today, resound like sharp criticism of the Polish transformation. As an example, I shall merely quote those which, even following the commencement of the great "jump" into the market, in May 1990, would not have been a delayed suggestion. They concern the privatization of the public sector, still not begun on a great scale. Starting out with the earlier proven premise on the erroneousness of separating justice from efficiency and on the social and economic benefits stemming from a more egalitarian distribution of wealth, Stiglitz was turning to the post-socialist countries with a message concurrent with the earlier cited concept of property-owning democracy of Rawls.

> The former socialist economies are in the perhaps unique position of being able to obtain a degree of equality of ownership of wealth unattained, and perhaps unattainable, in other market economies. The often-noted goal of a "people's capitalism" may indeed be within their reach, in a way that most countries cannot even remotely approach, given their concentrations of wealth. They should not lose this opportunity. . . . From a strictly political perspective, the long-run legitimacy of democratic government would, I suspect, be enhanced if they could succeed in maintaining a more egalitarian wealth distribution.[28]

13. The New Order—
A Civilization of Inequality?

Capitalism does not merely mean that the housewife may influence production by her choice between peas and beans; or that the youngster may choose whether he wants to work in a factory or on a farm; or that plant managers have some voice in deciding what and how to produce; it means a scheme of values, an attitude toward life, a civilization—the civilization of inequality and of the family fortune.

—JOSEPH SCHUMPETER, 1994

What kind of civilization do Poles need? This is the question posed in Jerzy Jedlicki's book (1988) and is also its title. The question is about the characteristics of the new social order that has emerged after twenty years of transformation, as compared with the desirable order.

The author of a book about the social costs of the transformation, *Trauma wielkiej zmiany* (Trauma of a Great Change),[1] among these traumatic events, places unemployment in first place. This was "a situation unknown in the era of communism, when everyone had guaranteed employment, even if low-paid and not very satisfying. . . . Unemployment has become a subject of serious concern for 70 percent of the population—so many have ranked it highest on the list of problems plaguing the country in 1995. . . . In another survey, as many as 58 percent of respondents were worried about the possibility of losing their job as a result of bankruptcy."[2]

Massive and continuously high unemployment is the most socially distressing phenomenon, and greatly determines the remaining characteristics of the social order. The relevant figures are known, and show that until entry in the EU, the average unemployment rate was about 16 percent. What was most painful and alarming was that this took place in accordance with the vision of the main architects of the new order. In chapter 6 I recalled the projection of the main economic indicators for the years 1990–2000, drawn up in the Department of Economic Analyses of the Ministry of Finance. These were made public by Stanisław Gomułka (1990), the leading advisor to the minister of finance. Two rows of figures are especially noticeable, the first projecting a high, 7 to 8 percent growth rate of GDP and the other, the extremely high and hardly declining unemployment rate, alongside the high national income growth rate. Even for as late as the year 2000, an unemployment rate of 16 percent was forecast! In some way, this must have been a reflection of the mindset of the board of the Ministry of Finance, the organ determining the course of economic policy in the existing government. It makes you wonder.

The concurrence of the figures is striking—unemployment as projected and as extremely accurately "executed" (may I point out that this is the only projection of the first non-communist government that was carried out to the dot with surgical precision). Naturally, the concurrence only concerns registered unemployment. But some people without work do not register at all. A large portion is hidden among old-age and disability pensioners. This shows great inactivity in society, making Poland rank last, or last but one, in the EU in terms of occupational activeness or the employment rate.[3] One of the outcomes has been the so-called *pomostówki* (transition state pensions), over the scope of which a battle is being waged. Another development is what Mieczysław Kabaj and myself have called the "neoliberal welfare state."[4] This fitting term underscores the paradoxical fact that under the banner of efforts to create a minimal state in regard to the proportion of people living off the state coffers, a bloated state machinery has evolved, incapable of or unwilling to fulfill the social obligations imposed on it by the constitution.

Of course, this does not mean that all successive government cabinets deliberately strove toward high unemployment. The essential decisions defining the course of systemic changes were taken during the economic rule of Leszek Balcerowicz, in the governments of Tadeusz Mazowiecki (1989–90) and Jan Krzysztof Bielecki (1991). Later we can merely observe some sort of adaptation of the successive governments to the situation created through the shock operation. In all of this, there was no reaction among the authorities to the ideas of Jacek Kuroń to imitate Roosevelt's New Deal.[5] The successive governments of Jan Olszewski (1992), and especially the government based on a dispersed coalition, the quite exotic cabinet of Hanna Suchocka (1992–93), did not manage to come up with any promising program for combating unemployment.

Exceptions here were the cabinets of Józef Oleksy and Włodzimierz Cimoszewicz, when the economy was mainly the responsibility of deputy prime minister and minister of finance, Professor Grzegorz Kołodko, an outstanding personality in more than one respect. In those years of the SLD-PSL (Democratic Left Alliance and Polish Peasants' Party) coalition (1994–97), efforts were taken to lower unemployment, and a considerable advance was made in this. It is true that the coalition was lucky enough to govern during a boom in the world economy while the exact figures of unemployment decline (down to 10 percent) may be questioned.

Less fortunate was the subsequent coalition government of AWS-UW (Solidarity Election Action and Union of Liberty) (1998–2001) of Jerzy Buzek (as of this writing still chairman of the European Parliament), with the return of Leszek Balcerowicz as his deputy, unsuccessful in both respects—employment and growth. The public declaration of Longin Komołowski (1999), the former S. activist, then minister of labor, that the natural unemployment rate in Poland is between 8 and 10 percent, best shows the acceptance of the doctrine justifying high unemployment. The government encountered unexpected external shocks (the echoes of the Asian and Russian financial crises) and was unable to cope with them. The government of the SLD + PSL + UP (Labor Union) coalition (of Leszek Miller and Marek Belka as prime ministers), in its attitude to unemployment, resembled the cabinet of Tadeusz Mazowiecki—it planned unemployment growth and it kept its word (the 20 percent level was reached). The rate of labor force activity fell below 50 percent!

The equivalence of predicted unemployment and actual unemployment in the year 2000 seems to be important in that it rules out the treatment of this development as an accidental result of unforeseen circumstances, in contrast to the imagination and aims of the ruling elites. A fundamental question comes to the fore: How is it possible that any political formation—left, right, or central—can come up with the idea of projecting unemployment at such a high level, for such a long time? When wondering about the reasons behind this feat, it would be interesting to look not only into the minds but also into the hearts of its authors. But does this apply to the authors only? After all, the idea appeared in the form of an extensive elaboration in a periodical of the economists (*Gospodarka Narodowa*). And yet nobody protested? Nobody was indignant? Nobody pointed out the many pathologies that could easily be inferred from making such an idea real? In some way, this weighs hard on everyone involved in the changes (including the author of these words). It also shows the "spirit of the times."

Most of the architects of the concept of Polish economic transformation are still alive. Can they be counted on to honestly unveil the premises of their reasoning? Maybe at least they could do this in memoirs published posthumously. The following hypothesis of mine is meant to encourage such memoirs. Radical as it may sound, my view is that this is how a shock operation, Margaret Thatcher–style, was conceived. The Iron Lady saw no possibility of guiding Great Britain onto the path of more rapid growth without breaking the resistance of the miners. Were our Thatcher disciples guided by similar premises and similar motivations? There was the time (1980–81) of the terrible experience, when, for the first time after the war, the GDP dropped by almost one-fifth and the economy went into anarchy. Did this not suggest that the condition for systemic reforms toward a free market, along with a labor market, was to break down something much more powerful than the British trade unions—the reemerging, once nearly ten-million-strong, S. movement?

I also think that this is how one should understand the well-known opinion of Jacek Kuroń (1994), that the S. social movement was "destroyed by the government and administration in the years 1989–93." In Poland this task was made easier. There was no need for any confrontation. It was enough that—once again I quote Kuroń— "The collapse of real socialism did not bring freedom and self-management opportunities for workers. On the contrary, they lost not only privileges, but also prestige."[6] And S. backed the program that led to this, while its prestige suffered because its advisors and activists were the ones who had created this program and implemented it.

Were these visionaries not aware of the social consequences of unemployment? Probably not. They reasoned in abstract, macroeconomic categories. And the author of these words knows very well from his own experience of the early 1950s that inconvenient conclusions tend to be pushed aside subconsciously.

The Manifold Effects of Unemployment

Let us try to draw up a list of the effects of unemployment, as should be done by these visionaries. Naturally, the matter concerns massive and very high unemployment which:

- raises work discipline;
- weakens the bargaining power of employees and their representatives, the trade unions;
- worsens the working conditions (health and safety at the workplace), enhances authoritarianism of managers, reduces mobility of workers;

- leads to stagnation or wage reductions, with all the consequences of this both for the employee and for the economy, reducing the domestic purchasing power;
- discourages innovation;
- burdens the state with excessive expenditures, as opposed to full employment, which would increase GDP and in the longer run would be the surest way to solve public debt;
- gives rise to poverty and social exclusion, raises the number of prisoners, that is, develops many pathologies—frustrations and psychological ailments, the *blokersi* youth subculture in prefab-housing settlements;
- deepens gender inequality, because women lose out more than men;
- deepens regional inequalities;
- leads to the loss of acquired qualifications, also qualifications of those who out of necessity consent to work but not in their own profession;
- produces obvious demographic consequences, with resignation from or delays in procreation, in addition to malnutrition and even hunger of children; provokes many unfavorable political developments.

In Poland, where massive and high unemployment coincides with an exceptionally high demographic boom and with a rapid rise in the number of persons acquiring a higher education, the massive exodus of young people abroad means there is no chance for the emergence of a large, modern middle class. As we can see now, only a small portion of emigrants return and even fewer enter the ranks of this class.

In fact, mass and permanent unemployment rules out wide legitimization of the existing social order. Since the unemployed do not vote, the politicians do not bother with them. This is the groundwork of political hypocrisy: creating an illusion that countervailing measures are being taken, with disregard for the constitution, which in Poland obliges the government to ensure maximum employment.

A sad analogy comes to mind. Many people condemn the 1944 Warsaw Uprising, among other things due to the massive loss of the capital's intelligentsia, which had to have a negative impact on the condition of Polish society after the Second World War. The number of persons who lost their lives then reached about 200,000. Our new emigration totals over two million people. From a purely economic point of view, was not the loss of "society's blood" following the last exodus much more grave?

In the light of this long list, can there be any doubt that, even from the traditionally liberal point of view, the social, economic, and political price of such massive and long-lasting unemployment is much greater than the "benefits"?

At least two more detailed comments to this list are pertinent. The first one follows immediately, and the second is discussed at the beginning of the next section.

Unemployment, not only when it already affects someone, but also potential unemployment, creates a sense of hopelessness. In the peak years of 2003 to 2004, unemployment directly affected every third family in Poland. This leaves a deep imprint on a considerable portion of young people, becoming particularly distressing as the children of the last demographic boom become adults, with unemployment among young people exceeding 40 percent.

One of the best illustrations of the *blokersi* subculture can be found in an essay by Marcin Kula describing the observations of a teacher of the Vocational School of Construction in Łódź. In a polemic with one of the intellectuals, who attempted to explain the sources of violence among radical youth groups, the teacher K. Jurek wrote that he does not agree with the saying that

> those who manifest this dissatisfaction are "bums and derelicts." Many of them are students and graduates of elementary and vocational schools, as there are no jobs for them. Some already in the course of their education realize that they are lost. Entire classes of vocational schools take up social benefits after school. Once again let me repeat this—these are not "bums and derelicts." They try to find a place for themselves in life. But various goods are tempting. Hence the high crime rate, especially of car burglaries and theft. And—a car thief is highly rated: he has a luxury car, girls, money. Many would

like to be one, but not everyone can. For this group of young people society has nothing to offer. It would be best if they just vanished into thin air. They have no jobs, housing, and—worst of all—no prospects. This is why they are very vulnerable to any radical agitation, including the nationalist type. . . . In society there are enclaves of people who are unable to adapt to the new circumstances. These are people who feel deprived already at the start. Someone may take advantage of their dynamic power and strength. . . . Among the many kinds of writing on the walls of our towns there is the word "Kaszana" [blood sausage] or "Kaszana forever." "One of my students," continues the discoverer of the new Promised Land,* "explained to me its meaning. Society is divided into two groups: for some there are elegant cars, villas and ham; for others tramways, prefab housing and blood sausage [kaszana]. Kaszana. Kaszana forever."[7]

Of course, among them there are also exceptionally talented individuals who are able to break away from their hopeless situation and become successful, for themselves and for society. The "syndrome" of this generation has been finely portrayed by a writer who has successfully made it to the top:

I was going through this phase in my life when gone was the brief enthusiasm over obtaining the title of Master of Arts. And what followed was depression resulting from the ordinary everyday life of an unemployed person without any right to a benefit. I used to wait in enormous lines in Labor Offices, it was like scenes from *The Promised Land*. There was no light in the tunnel, I wouldn't have anything to live on if it weren't for my parents. I was ready to go down into the sewage canals, anything just to earn something. This is the syndrome of my generation—just after graduation people suddenly

*The title of the novel *Ziemia Obiecana* (The Promised Land) by Nobel Prize–winner Władysław Reymont. Also the title of Andrzej Wajda's film, both showing the period of the origins of capitalist Łódź.

panic and send out hysterical motivation letters to hell itself. . . . We all have fingers cut up from the razors we clutch at in desperation.[8]

Indeed, how many potential Kuczoks will not succeed in crossing the Rubicon, will not make it, will not be blessed with a lucky opportunity?

A Destructive Imbalance:
Poor because of Defenselessness

The second comment concerns the barrier of creating a social balance, necessary for more or less normal operation of the economy.

Several years ago, Wiesława Kozek (2000) carried out an analysis of how trade unions were pictured in political journals, mainly in *Gazeta Wyborcza, Polityka*, and *Wprost*. The trade unionists were regularly portrayed as egoistic destructors. Currently, employee trade unions are being reactivated in several branches, mainly in the teaching, mining, and railway sectors. At the same time, the negative portrayal of trade union activists has resurfaced in two of the weeklies. The cover of *Polityka* carries the title: "Protest szoł. Liderzy związkowi chcą wstrząsnąć Polską, a przynajmniej telewidzami" (Protest Show. Trade union leaders want to shake up Poland, or at least television viewers). Then there is the article by Marcin Kołodziejczyk and Cezary Nazarewicz (2008), "Teatr zwany strajkiem" (Theater Called a Strike), full of bitterness toward trade union activists and ending with an "in-depth" diagnosis by one of the key leaders of S., senator of the Civic Platform, Jan Rulewski: "The trade union movement has been replaced by good legislation that defends an employee better than an organization, so people are not so keen on trade unions." The same trend can be found in *Wprost,*[9] in the attacks on teachers' trade unions. Both periodicals aim at eliciting a negative view of public opinion toward trade unions in general. In these articles we find no attempt to understand even the simple fact that pursuing reforms that reduce incomes of large social groups during an economic slowdown is a pro-recession measure, something by now understood by nearly the whole Western world. In these circumstances is it worth resorting to voices of reason? Do they have any chance at all to break through the fanatically one-sided media?

The untiring researcher of employment relations in Poland Juliusz Gardawski,[10] describes the existing nineteenth-century employment relations, particularly in small enterprises (employing less than fourteen persons), although in many supermarkets they are no better either. Similarly, the National Labor Inspectorate for years has been alarming the authorities and public opinion about the repeated violation of the Labor Code. Gardawski[11] adds that work relations often tumble down "into the ruts of the autocratic style, allowing for work supervisors to ignore the rank-and-file workers." One of the reasons for this was that, before EU entry, in Poland, next to Ireland, the proportion of wages in value added had declined the most.

In these circumstances, to speak and write of good legislation that protects the workers is an expression (N.B., by a former top activist of S.!) of extreme ignorance or equally extreme political cynicism. Following the brief *intermezzo* created by entry in the European Union during a prosperous turn of the economy, hard times are here again. How easy it is to use the crisis as an excuse for cuts and limitation of rights. An obsessively neoliberal state does not want to and is unable to do something about the shortsighted reduction of labor costs, which also reduces aggregate demand. Strong trade unions could prevent this shortsightedness.

Irrespective of market fluctuations, Gardawski believes (and so do I) that trade unions are needed for reasonably normal economic development in capitalism. We have before us two alternatives: consent to the disappearance of an institutionalized representation of employee interests and deregulation of work relations, which carries the danger of "appearance of an alienated working class susceptible to anomie, deprived of an organization with which it could identify itself."[12] Or instead: "The political elite can take up the difficult task of supporting trade unions, helping to reform them, to educate leaders, and at the same time the trade unions can assume a responsible attitude, similar to that of certain trade unions of Western Europe during a crisis."[13]

Unfortunately, successive administrations are not going in that direction. After the 2007 election, Gardawski's pessimism is even more justified. There is the fear whether this path will not turn out to be "too difficult for our political, economic and trade union elites." Moreover, certain actions are going in the opposite direction. Exempting a considerable group of small enterprises (employing fewer than twenty persons) from the obligation of having payroll and work regulations could not be anything other than extension of the limits of admissible lawlessness.

One more thing can be added. Gardawski writes only about elites among the political and the trade union authorities. But to a large extent this path is a difficult one because of the conduct (isolation) of our intellectual elites. I shall give one example here. Many Western countries are familiar with the role of trade union economists, who regularly take up problems beleaguering the trade union movement. In some countries, for example in Sweden, these are outstanding economists of this profile and research area (Gosta Rehn, Rudolf Meidner, Walter Korpi). In Poland, one can find a few sociologists or academic social politicians of this sort, but not economists. This is one of the reasons the trade unions do not have their own research base, especially in economic issues, and therefore cannot present their own postulates on the basis of their own analyses and forecasts.

For academic specialists in social policy and employment, or for sociologists, the list of the effects of unemployment presented by me may seem to be too abbreviated and incomplete, or even trite and obvious. But it is enough to reach into the books of economists describing the Polish transformation to see how little attention is paid to these issues. The book by Leszek Balcerowicz (*Socjalizm, kapitalizm, transformacja*—Socialism, Capitalism, Transformation, 1998) need not be the only unfavorable example. In the book by a member of the Democratic Left Alliance (who has just joined the conservative-liberal Platforma Obywatelska—Citizens' Forum), Dariusz Rosati, *Polska droga do rynku* (The Polish Road to Market, 1998), the above issues occupy but marginal space. The rich bibliography does not include even a single academic publication on social problems. In the theoretical literature on the Polish economic transformation, they are virtually absent.

Obviously, there is still a strong tendency to marginalize the weight of these pathological phenomena, alongside poverty and inequalities. Getting accustomed to an unemployment rate of 16 to 20 percent has dulled sensitivity toward the continuously large scale of the problem. This is probably best illustrated by *Gazeta Wyborcza* (July 4, 2007) in an article by two journalists, with a table that shows over 10 percent unemployment in Poland, positioning it in the last place in the EU. Yet the title of the article reads: "Polska wyszła z bezrobocia" (Poland Has Overcome Unemployment). And this is not an isolated case, although it does rank highest in its stupidity.

But even assuming that Poland could overcome unemployment, making it one of the lowest in the EU, and could have at least an employment rate at an average EU level, it would still have to grapple with the long-term social effects of unemployment for years to come. Sociologist Leszek Gilejko aptly writes about the "civilizational dimension" of the fear created by unemployment, and even of a "civilization of unemployment."[14]

Mass unemployment and the absence of a strong employee organization in the private sector are also the main sources of all other characteristics of the new order, above all the sudden rise in the poverty level. In Poland, it is much more acute than in the other countries of Central Europe. Many researchers, with the application of various poverty lines, concede that at the outset of the twenty-first century we have twice to three times as many families living in poverty as fifteen years ago. Alongside unemployment itself, there is also the excessively stringent social policy toward the unemployed. Its most striking element is depriving the great majority of registered unemployed persons (in recent years—over 85 percent) of the right to a benefit. To add to this, many unemployed persons do not register at all. Most of the population is now below the minimum subsistence level (according to GUS, in 2003, persons living below this minimum accounted for 58 percent; later GUS stopped publishing these findings altogether). What is hard to accept is the already mentioned very rapid increase in the number of persons living in poverty. As shown above, in the years 1996 to 2005 the number of persons living below subsistence level tripled, while the GDP rose by more than one-third! Neither the SLD-UP-PSL coalition nor its remnants have drawn any lessons from this fact, unprecedented in Europe west of Ukraine and Belarus.

Peasants have fallen into deep indigence in Poland. According to various estimates, the average income of a farmer dropped by nearly three-fifths in 1990–91 and, even in the late 1990s, was 40 to 60 percent of the average income of wage earners (in 1988 this parity was at about 100 percent). The villages have been affected by unemployment the most, becoming its repository.

An inevitable consequence of these developments has been one of the highest coefficients of social inequalities in Europe. On the one side, there is the great portion of poor people, and on the other, great fortunes, usually at the interface of the public and private sector. What is particularly striking is the greed of the executive management groups (CEOs). Once again I shall refer to a study that has led one economist-sociologist to the following conclusion: "Poland has the most unequal distribution due to the extremely low concentration of low incomes with a high (higher than countries richer than Poland) concentration of high incomes. In other words, against the background of other countries of Central Europe, Poland is implementing the most elitist model of income distribution."[15]

Especially in the mid-1990s, the general picture was quite dismal. Poland came out shamefully backward also in terms of social and political discrimination against women. International comparative research (in 1995) revealed that the sum of monthly earnings (main and additional jobs) of a working woman was only 57 percent of a man's earnings. This indicator was the worst from the six investigated countries, worse not only than Hungary and the Czech Republic, which might have been expected, but also of Slovakia, Bulgaria, and even Russia. Similar ratios referring to compensation for the main job did not look any better (here at least we outdistanced Russia).[16] One after another public preschools and kindergartens were closed down, diminishing job opportunities for mothers.

As other groups hardest hit by the economic crisis, women are having a hard time in the labor market. They are the ones more likely to be included in layoff plans, or in outsourcing schemes where employees are discharged, to be rehired anew as employees of an agency. This is more profitable for the company, but divests an employee of social rights (to sick leave, paid vacations, a state pension). When hiring new employees, businesses are often more willing to accept men than women, in the unfounded belief that they will prove to be more capable. This is in spite of the fact that, statistically speaking, women are better educated than men and more of them complete higher-education programs. To add to this, the new capital pension system generally projects much lower old-age pensions for women than for men, since women have fewer years of employment or have part-time employment and more often receive lower pay, with the retirement age being lower for women than for men (sixty for women and sixty-five for men). Not without significance here is the traditional approach to the role of women as the guardians of the family hearth, while men are perceived as the principal breadwinners. Yet life carries its own perverse arrangements, a not uncommon sight being that of a woman holding a job and at the same time running the house, while supporting an unemployed husband. Add to this the frequent drinking problems, and you have an ironic combination of traditional roles and modern reality.

Recent times, however, have brought some hope for a better future through a better public awareness of the problems. We can at last talk about a true women's (feminist) movement, of different political hues, ranging from liberal businesswomen to feminist anarchists. And in recent years, women's discrimination in employment and on the political scene has encountered strong contestation. Two consecutive Women's Congresses have been held, both closely followed by the media. Efforts to introduce a 50 percent parity on all levels of electoral lists were backed by 120,000 signatures. The Sejm, though still dominated by conservative rightist factions, under pressure ratified a law on a 35 percent minimum for men and women on ballot lists. This was received as an "absolute novelty comparable to the 1918 right for women to vote in parliamentary elections,"[17] but demands for the 50 percent parity are still upheld.* The annual manifestations of women's rights (called *Manifa*) have also become more popular. It seems that what is most needed now is for politicians to shift their priorities from building sports stadiums and monuments to focusing on programs that provide affordable housing and kindergartens.

The housing barrier remains a distressing problem for many families. The widespread practice is to build expensive housing for the rich, with the nearly total disappearance of inexpensive municipal housing construction, especially for the more than half of all families with income below the social minimum. Thus, two separate ways of life have emerged, two different community types, separated from each other by high fences, private police, elitist schools, and menacing watchdogs. The welfare state is also being downsized; nineteenth-century employment relations are becoming predominant in the newly emerged private sector (apart from the portion of privatized state firms). And finally, there is the pervasive corruption and clientelism, manifesting itself with particular force in privatization processes.

These developments should be viewed as characteristics making up the system, which will be with us for many years. They can be called resultant systemic characteristics, although the new system can be perceived as a blend of specific institutional-organizational schemes that produce these results. A system that creates the characteristics referred to has an institutional-organizational structure that is radically different from, for example, the Swedish or Austrian system.

To recapitulate, Polish capitalism is characterized on the one side by massive unemployment, a large portion of people living in poverty, and high and constantly rising wage and income disparities. On the other side there is a diverse group of those who hold wealth and power, with strong clientelist or corruption links among its members. Both sides are the result of not so much uncontrolled market

*In the last parliamentary election (October 2011), the number of women parliamentarians turned out to be much lower (by nearly one-half) than the 35 percent written into legislation.

processes as deliberate activity (or inactivity, depending on the circumstances) of the state. All this convinces me even more that Poland has created one of the most unjust social and economic systems of the second half of the twentieth century, and with this system, it has entered the European Union. A good illustration can be found in the ranking drawn up by the two authors of the Index of Social Justice.[18] The index is based on seven indicators describing social welfare: poverty prevention, education, labor market performance, social expenditure on health and cohesion, income distribution, and intergenerational justice and anti-discrimination policies. Countries were ranked on a scale ranging from 1 (lowest justice level) to 10 (highest). On this scale all Scandinavian countries are at the top of the list. Then come the old continental states—Germany, France and others, followed by Slovakia (14th), the Czech Republic (15th), and Hungary (16th). And where is Poland? All the way down at 26th, which is worse than all Anglo-Saxon countries, including Great Britain (21st) and the United States (24th).[19]

The inglorious record Poland has achieved is also reaffirmed in the database of where in all of the three aforementioned Central European countries as well as Slovenia the Gini index ranges from 0.24 to 0.28, whereas in Poland it is above 0.36, the highest among the ten new members of the EU, and 4 percentage points higher than the average.[20] These data refer to 2005. Other research shows an even higher Gini index for Poland. For instance, according to Golinowska (2008) it is 0.38, and apart from Portugal it is the highest in Europe.

What Kind of Capitalism: Managerial?

Three California sociologists have formulated the view that in Central Europe a managerial, not property-owning or political, capitalism is being formed. This, according to them, is a "capitalism without capitalists," in the sense that great proprietors are not predominant in it. It seems that, for such a type of capitalism, the concept of managerial capitalism would be too narrow. We are dealing here with an unfettered, nineteenth-century type of capitalism, with its focus on the primitive accumulation of capital. Nevertheless, I shall recall this concept because it facilitates understanding of the very beginning of the restoration of capitalism, made "by design."

The essence of the Californians' concept has been described as follows:

> The most distinctive characteristic of post-communist social structure in East Central Europe is the absence of a capitalist class. Private property rights are in place, markets in labor and capital exist, these economies are open to world markets, and they have strong relationships with international financial institutions. However, there is no organized group of major capitalists. . . . Indeed, the result of privatization in most of the region has been highly diffused property rights. This is the puzzle we seek to understand: what explains the distinctive class structure of the fledgling capitalist economies of East Central Europe? In the absence of a capitalist class, who has power?[21]

As opposed to Western countries, especially the United States, where the economically dominant class technostructure* creates a recruitment base for the political power elite, in Poland, the Czech Republic, and in Hungary, these groups—according to Eyal, Szelenyi and Townsley—belong to different social milieus. The collapse of communism has allowed the technocratic-managerial elite to assume leading positions in the economy, but it "was not in a position to make a bid for political power. The key positions of political power were taken by humanistic intellectuals. They quickly organized a tight ruling group, or 'politocracy,' which only later formed an alliance with the new technocratic-managerial elite."[22]

This description does not contradict the Polish reality, but only in the sense that central power is in fact mainly exercised by "humanistic intellectuals" (provided we can call professors of economics "human-

---

*Notion introduced by John Kenneth Galbraith to denote the powerful group of professional managers in great corporations.

istic," which I am not too sure about). At the outset of Polish capitalism, there was, in fact, a distance between the technocratic-managerial group and what the authors call the politocracy. However, this concerned the very highest level of the central authorities. Ironically, many agree that business had the most say during the last communist cabinet of Mieczysław Rakowski. The most important offices were taken by two businessmen (non-intellectuals). Ireneusz Sekuła became the deputy prime minister in charge of preparing the reform package and Mieczysław Wilczek, an adamant advocate of radical and speedy privatization economy and the free market, became minister of industry. Only briefly, in the cabinet of Hanna Suchocka, the office of minister of industry was held by an assistant professor in economics, Henryka Bochniarz, president of the company NIKOM. But in general, deputy prime ministers (sometimes even prime ministers: Włodzimierz Cimoszewicz, Jerzy Buzek, Marek Belka) responsible for economic matters, particularly ministers of finance, the treasury, and industry (also of the economy), were neither key managers nor wealthy proprietors, but professors or academics of lower rank.

However, in light of the above functions of the mutual exchange of services and gains, such a genetic differentiation of these two groups, and especially defining the system with the help of one group, seems to be of little cognitive value. It obliterates the social aspects of this system, exaggerates the role of managerial professionalism, and underestimates the bureaucratic imprint of the emerging system. I do not see much sense in separating the role of the managerial group from other holders of power.

Most probably, seeing in managers the "dominant class" was based on the authors' belief that current and systemic economic policy is determined by a small number of important decisions influenced by this politically dominant group. Meanwhile, in the process of transformation, and especially privatization, the matter is much more complex. There are hundreds of thousands of decisions concerning personnel, credit, taxes, and customs (also deferring, for example, the execution of overdue credits, taxes, insurance premiums, customs duties, demolition of illegally erected buildings). All these constitute the closely interconnected power apparatus, along with the administration and local self-government, with great and small businesses. These links are hidden and harder to research than the official lines of policies declared by the government or parliament.

It also does not seem that the time sequence between the establishment of the "politocracy" and the moment of "concluding the alliance" with the technocratic-managerial staff would be of importance, as the authors write. This is especially so when the initially evident contradictions between the objectives of the authorities and the interests of this proto-technostructure turned out to be short-lived. Włodzimierz Wesołowski (1992) called the initial systemic actions of the authorities "transgressive interests." They were to consist of the implementation of the organization and legal rules of a healthy capitalist economy subjected to free competition, of wealth based on entrepreneurial work, innovation, and the ability to carry on an economic calculation. Since there was yet no distinct capitalist class in existence, the political authorities acted in the name of an "imaginary" middle class that was supposed to create the foundations of the liberal-democratic order. Leszek Balcerowicz often enumerates the features of such an imaginary system, which happen to concur with the Washington Consensus. Some foreign commentators perceive this as a description of Polish reality. These visions of an ideal system conform more to the main centers of Western economic thought, the referred-to Washington Consensus and the Maastricht Treaty, than to the interests of domestic businesses, which have strong protectionist inclinations. The latter are more interested in subventions and rebates than liberalization and hard budgetary constraints. This is especially true in the case of managers and new owners with *nomenklatura* enfranchisement roots, accustomed to paternalistic policy.

There is, nonetheless, a large sphere of economic policy that is not transgressive. In three areas, the declared objectives of the authorities are absolutely concurrent with the interests of the new proprietary class. These are lowering taxes for enterprises and for the affluent, efforts to downsize the welfare state, and further "flexibilization" of the labor market.

Of the Corruption-Clientelism Kind?

So far, we have mostly dealt with one end of the social spectrum, that of massive unemployment and increased poverty, the rapid decline in individual incomes of peasants, the slow growth of average real wages, the unusually wide wage disparities, nineteenth-century employment relations, and downsizing the welfare state. But to answer the earlier questions on the Polish version of capitalism, we also have to take a closer look at the opposite end, the less numerous but more influential group of power and property. Whereas the former are the object, the latter are the beneficiaries of the systemic changes. The successive lists of the wealthiest Poles are well known, and certain names, such as Jan Kulczyk, Ryszard Krauze, and Aleksander Gudzowaty, are a symbol of great fortunes created at the interface of the public and private sectors.* Due to their influence among the authorities, they are often called oligarchs, and the process of mutual interaction of great business and the authorities is called oligarchization. The horrendously high, for Polish conditions, salaries and severance pay of the presidents and chief executives of great firms, counted in millions, are

---

*A researcher of the business and political elites summarizes this process: "The early 1990s were the best. . . . A businessman represented a person capable of managing well in life. . . . People became rich quickly and lost their fortunes just as fast. The well-known king of the Tri-City (Gdańsk, Gdynia, Sopot), Janusz Leksztoń, who created the Elgaz empire, went bankrupt within two years and is in prison today. In the first years of the transformation businesspeople were not yet a social group with specific attributes. It was only in the mid-1990s that the stratification began. Communist symbols that gained from enfranchisement in the privatization of state companies fell from their pedestals—Dariusz Przywieczerski or Ireneusz Sekuła. Their place was taken by those who topped the lists of the wealthiest: Solorz, Krauze, Gudzowaty, Kulczyk, Niemczycki. They became active on a greater scale only in the reality of the Third Polish Republic, making their fortunes on privatizations and dealings with the state. They can be regarded as the symbolic core of Polish business. Poles began losing their faith in this group toward the end of the 1990s when the names of businesspeople began to be associated with scandals. . . . This had an impact on the entire business sphere, being a businessperson was eyed with suspicion." Jasiecki, "Biznes rządzi" (Business Reigns), *Newsweek* (Polish version), August 16, 2010.

hard to accept, and, given the stagnation of low wages, evoke social indignation. Sociologists (Gardawski, Gilejko, 1999) name as beneficiaries, next to managers and individual proprietors of fortunes, two other social groups: people of the political authority and state administration and the petit bourgeoisie, based on small business.

Contrary to the declarations of the authorities (and to the Balcerowicz Plan), pledging withdrawal of the state from the economy and limitation of its influence, the state administration expanded quickly during the entire transformation period. In 1990, public administration employed 159,000 and six years later, 290,000 persons. The state administration (excluding local governments) grew even more, doubling in size. The most rapid growth occurred in the central administration (by a factor of more than two and a half). To understand the character of the system that was created, it is most important to perceive the role of this social group in public administration, which the sociologists referred to above call the *transformation class*. In their opinion, these people have taken advantage of the *transformation rent*, which is, of course, but a euphemism for corruption and clientelism.

Many sociologists have written about corruption and clientelism, but they admit that these phenomena are hard to research on a regular basis. Though agreeing with this, I shall refer not to their views but to what Jacek Kuroń said, in my opinion presenting the most realistic analysis of these phenomena. I have written about the transformation of a considerable portion of the old *nomenklatura* apparatus into businesspersons. Kuroń recalls the beginnings of this self-enfranchisement of the power apparatus at the end of the 1980s and adds that in the general rush to get rich quick, bosses of state enterprises would set up deals with *nomenklatura* companies of acquaintance, bringing great losses to the enterprises, but immense gains for themselves.[23]

These deceitful activities were later dubbed the "red cobweb." But as opposed to many politicians of the right wing, who only see this phenomenon on the side of the old post-communist *nomenklatura*, Kuroń has demonstrated that this model of self-enfranchisement of the new power elites continued well onto the whole period of systemic changes.

The above quoted statement is from early 1997. In autumn of that year, the post-Solidarity coalition (Solidarity Election Action and the Union of Liberty) came to power and one of the slogans of its electoral campaign had been fighting corruption. Less than two years later, corruption and its milder form, clientelism, were already the most highlighted topics of the day. This happened not because the administration took up the battle against corruption, but because it was accused of favoring it. The opinions of sociologists leave no doubt that these are deeply rooted and growing phenomena. One sociologist who is also a politician (former senator and deputy of the Union of Liberty) ended a description of the commonplace nature of corruption by saying that his attempts to intervene, all the way up to the level of the general public prosecutor, as a rule were futile.[24] He also complained that in the social circles of the political elites, touching on this subject was not the thing to do.

Another sociologist writes that after the last administrative and local-government reform, the local administrators also turned out to be "efficient builders of the next *nomenklatura*. . . . At the level of local communities, all posts—beginning with the director of a kindergarten in a small town—are political, i.e. apportioned for their own kind, regardless of competence, qualifications or social merit. Any hopes for justice have probably vanished for good . . ."[25]

Organized Anger Was Lacking

What does public opinion say about all this? What about the trade unions and non-governmental organizations? And where are normally functioning organs of public scrutiny? These questions are answered indirectly by the American political scientist David Ost. Although he has left-wing views, he decided, in a way, to set them aside and look at the systemic changes in the post-communist countries, primarily in Poland, where he spent many years as a researcher. Ost analyzed the systemic changes in countries of this region in the light of older experiences of liberal democracy in capitalist countries, mostly in the

United States. The guiding line of thought of the book *The Defeat of Solidarity* is presented in the form of six theses, which can be cited word for word:

1. The emotions generated by capitalism, or what I call "economic anger," need to be organized along some lines or cleavages.
2. For liberal democratic outcomes, economic anger is best organized along class lines, meaning that economic conflicts get expressed as economic conflicts, rather than as ethnic, racial, national, or religious ones.
3. In post-communist societies, class sensibilities are extremely low, due to the legacy both of communism and of the struggle against communism.
4. East European [for Ost, Central Europe is also "East"] liberal parties are reluctant to promote class cleavages, because they see class only as an anti-capitalist identity rather than a politically liberal one.
5. Liberals are reluctant to mobilize emotions, because they see them as a threat to their interests.
6. Illiberals, who are always anxious to mobilize around emotions, are able to score great successes as they organize economic anger along non-economic cleavages.[26]

Ost wrote this book before the spectacular victory of the populist and nationalistic party of the Kaczyński twins.* Since Ost's book was published in Polish during their rule, it is no wonder that it became very popular. Ost predicted the victory of opponents of political liber-

---

*The legend of the Polish non-communist Left, Karol Modzelewski (2006) starts his evaluation of the Kaczyński victory in the following way: "Demonstrators chant: 'Thieves, thieves!' There had to appear a party that says: 'Yes, they are thieves and we are sheriffs who are going to introduce some order.'" Modzelewski also poses the question: "What will happen when the people realize that once again they have been cheated?" (Modzelewski K. 2006, "Chóry i pienia" (Choirs and Chants)), *Gazeta Wyborcza*, July 29–30). Fortunately, people realized this two years later, when unexpectedly the Kaczyński brothers lost their power in the election.

alism, who were able to harness the anger of considerable social groups around national slogans and claims.*

There is, however, one lasting value of Ost's research. He proved that by acting against a certain class equilibrium between capital and labor, and even destroying it, the Polish version of capitalism and democracy does not fulfill even the minimum liberal-democratic criteria. Thus when I describe Polish capitalism as an Anglo-Saxon capitalism I have in mind the variant that developed in the United States and Great Britain following the confrontation and weakening of the trade unions by the government of Ronald Reagan (breaking the strike of the air traffic controllers) and Margaret Thatcher. In Poland, the trade unions were weakened even more and in a more subtle way. Instead of having a head-on confrontation, it was enough for the trade unions to become involved in support of anti-employee systemic changes and the shock operation. That is why rebuilding the strength of the trade unions in Poland is going to be an extremely difficult task.

*An interesting study was presented by the economic historian Jacek Kochanowicz (2010) about the role of the leading daily newspaper *Gazeta Wyborcza* (all that time under Adam Michnik). Gazeta "was adamant in supporting not only the market transition in general, but also the particular form it took under the Balcerowicz Plan. In the process of convincing its readership, it argued, in a manner similar to the early nineteenth-century classical economists, that it was the only way to achieve an efficient economy and that the social costs and suffering—however lamentable—were impossible to avoid. In the longer run, the paper argued, the reform would benefit the poor as well. . . . They wanted reforms fast and swift, as they were afraid that pain and suffering would mobilize resistance. . . . They believed that the sooner economic rebuilding produces success, the more the support for the reforms would build up. . . . In the Enlightenment vein, they also believed that rational arguments had the force of convincing even those whose immediate interests were threatened by the short-term effects of systemic change. The danger they were the most afraid of was the right-wing, nationalist populism. Ironically, the type of policies they advocated actually led to marginalization and social exclusion, with few provisions how to institutionalize re-inclusion. Thus, as we see from looking around East Central Europe politics, in the longer term they were leading exactly to what *Gazeta* was the most afraid of."

A Shock Therapy for Iraq

The leap into the market performed in Poland in accordance with the wishes of the IMF and the World Bank and propagated by the major mass media in the country, became a model to follow for other post-communist countries. However, in no other country with a similar historical background (with the exclusion of the countries of the former USSR), were the social effects of this leap so profound and long-lasting as in Poland. In Hungary and in the Czech Republic unemployment remained half that in Poland; income disparities and the range of poverty were much lower. This was also the case with Slovakia, which did experience very high unemployment, but within a shorter time than Poland. In all these cases we can only speak of the Polish leap as a model. But there was one instance where Poland became very much involved in exporting this model. This was the inglorious participation of Poland in the occupation of Iraq and in the systemic transformation of that country's economy.

The Polish-British journalist Ewa Jasiewicz, author of *Podpalić Gazę* (Razing Gaza; 2011), devoted a separate chapter to the role of Poland and particularly its involvement in Iraq.* She writes:

Prior to any military alliance with the U.S.A., Poland had to prove itself as pliant to U.S. economic foreign policy. From 1988 until today, Poland is an ongoing laboratory for an increasingly aggressive neoliberal free-market capitalism. U.S. Free Marketers were busy putting together a historical piece of legislation to smooth the path from a cen-

*Ewa Jasiewicz supplied me with the unpublished English version of this chapter. This part of the book is heavily based on it. The name of the chapter, "Israel in Europe," mainly shows that Poland was to play a role similar to that of Israel—of the closest U.S. ally in Europe. However, after several years disappointment was evident. President Barack Obama announced the withdrawal of the U.S. bid to build missile defense system silos in Poland. Polish foreign minister Radosław Sikorski (2009) responded by saying that this decision would end the "deep-rooted illusions in some of the country's ruling circles that Poland would become an 'Izrael nad Wisłą'—an Israel upon the Vistula River, a kind of Israel in Europe—for the USA."

trally planned economy to a neoliberal free -market one in as quick a period of time as possible. The Support for European Democracy Act (SEED) passed by Congress in 1989 was the ultimate free-market Structural Adjustment Program cemented into U.S. law.

$ + technical assistance

The list of recommendations of this law was even more far-reaching than the decalog of the Washington Consensus, embracing privatization of economic entities; establishment of full rights to acquire and hold private property, including land and the benefits of contractual relations; simplification of regulatory controls regarding the establishment and operation of businesses; dismantlement of all wage and price controls; removal of trade restrictions, including on both imports and exports; liberalization of investment and capital, including the repatriation of profits by foreign investors; tax policies that provide incentives for economic activity and investment; establishment of rights to own and operate private banks and other financial service firms, as well as unrestricted access to private sources of credit; and access to a market for stocks, bonds, and other instruments through which individuals may invest in the private sector.

Despite SEED being limited by law to former Central and Eastern European countries, 15 years later its core elements were lifted wholesale and rewritten into the new laws and regulations of Iraq—a country militarily occupied by multinational troops, led by the United States. Poland was chosen as an economic model for this country. The U.S. regent in Iraq, Paul Bremer III, publicly praised Poland for its most energetic development of the private sector among all the post-communist countries.[27]

It is no wonder that the man designated to carry out this task was the newly installed Director of Economic Policy at the Coalition Provisional Authority, former Polish deputy prime minister and minister of finance, professor of economics Marek Belka. He became responsible for the implementation of Paul Bremer's Order No. 39, which allowed for the wholesale privatization of Iraqi state companies, assets and services and 100 percent profit repatriation for investors. Over 200 state-owned enterprises, including the electricity, telecommunications and pharmaceuticals sectors, were privatized, and thousands of workers summarily sacked. Other orders restructured the rate of corporate taxation, slashing it from 45 to 15 percent.

The economic reforms were described by *The Economist* as "a capitalist's dream," yet it was a dream that had been dreamed before and piloted before in Poland. Only in occupied Iraq, the privatization process was illegal—leading the UK's attorney general Lord Peter Goldsmith to inform the then prime minister Tony Blair that "the imposition of major structural economic reforms would not be authorised by international law."[28]

The process, initiated and implemented under direct occupation—prior to the installation of a pro-occupation "sovereign" Iraqi government in June 2004—was illegal under international law and constituted a process of pillage under the Hague Regulations of 1907 and the Geneva Conventions of 1949. Under Article 55 of the Hague Regulations, an army and administration of occupation is only "an administrator and usufructuary" of a territory and its property under the laws, and though authorized to use crops and buildings to sustain itself, has no right to "alter the substance" of, for example, state assets.*[29]

Belka was more than an "advisor" to Bremer, as has often been quoted in the Polish media. He was one of the primary architects of Iraq's shock-therapy fire sale. Between June 2003 and October 2004 he was chairman of the CPA's Council for Coordination, the body responsible for coordinating the restructuring of the Iraqi Economy with the IMF, the World Bank, the UN, and international donors.

Belka's responsibilities were the control of funds earmarked for the reconstruction of Iraq, coordination of humanitarian aid, and overseeing other steps aimed at the reconstruction of the country. This was the first body that supervised the setting up of structures and levers to bring in privatization. Belka was named Director of

---

*Journalist Naomi Klein described the principles of usufruct at the time as the house-sitter's rule, i.e.: "If you are a house sitter, you can eat the food in the fridge, but you can't sell the house and turn it into condos. And yet that is just what Bremer is doing: what could more substantially alter 'the substance' of a public asset than to turn it into a private one?" (Klein, 2004).

Economic Policy in August 2003, and the following month was appointed to the Iraq Strategic Review Board, along with the Iraqi ministers of finance and planning.

The board was tasked with approving project proposals and control of all donor activities including "the prioritization of projects." Under Belka, privatization picked up speed and from December 2003 until the end of his term in March 2004, new orders on finance were passed on Tax Strategy; the Trade Liberalization Policy; on Tariffs and Public Debt, a Central Bank Law, Amendments to the Company Law 1997; and a Board of Supreme Audit was also set up, all under a direct occupation administration and without any democratic mandate or process.

The dramatic state of the Iraqi economy is a well-known picture. To this day the country is unable to cope with supplying water and electricity. Moreover, at times one hears the words "on the brink of disaster." When thinking about the causes, it is hard to separate the effects of war and occupation from the effects of an imposed systemic transformation. The truth is that barely two decades after the outburst of Solidarity, carrying so much hope for the world, Poland has contributed to the state of things in Iraq in the military as well as economic aspect.

First in Class

One of the negative outcomes of the victorious strikes of August 1980 and the Solidarity movement was a strong belief that Poland was to play a special role as pioneer of socioeconomic transformations in the post-socialist world. The Polish elites have claimed the role of the vanguard in formulating models first for the post-socialist region, and today even for the whole European Union. And the Balcerowicz Plan was considered to be a pioneer source of pride (some feel this way to this day). To recall, Jacek Kuroń, after the first defeats from which he drew far-reaching political conclusions and wrote about them with genuine frankness, nevertheless continued to see Poland's mission in paving the way for our part of Europe. In referring to the experience of S., he wrote: "It's us, Poles, who for ten years have been paving the way for all nations of Central and Eastern Europe. It is very difficult, we may not like it, but that's how it is."[30] He was arguing for a radical turn of systemic changes, looking for examples from across the ocean: "The United States responded with the New Deal to the Great Depression . . . and this was a social policy program. This program protected the weaker ones, but at the same time stimulated the market, was beneficial for production, profits, and wages. Now it is our turn."[31] In this spirit, Kuroń submitted proposals, where housing was highest on the list: "Housing construction is not only a problem for those who do not have a roof over their heads or live somewhere on the side. It also provides employment for many people, a sales market for enterprises from all branches of the economy. Employees of construction enterprises and all those who work for housing construction—will earn money. They will also buy goods. This will be the driving force of the entire economy."[32] Intuitively, but aptly I think, he also focused on the stimulation of foodstuff production.

After twenty years, we must say that Kuroń's concept found its perverse fulfillment. First, the Polish transformation of "shock therapy" indeed became a model for other countries of the Soviet bloc, although not in promoting something that would resemble Roosevelt's New Deal, but rather, diminishing employment and workers' rights. Even the most elementary rights are being broken. In the *Biuletyn Dialogu Społecznego* (of the Ministry of Economy and Labor) we read: "In the Polish version of market economy, not paying for work is becoming commonplace. This has in fact become a pathology of the system. The Pope called it 'a sin that cries to heaven for vengeance.'"[33]

Yet in these circumstances there are more and more voices saying that the mission of Polish authorities and Polish parliamentarians in the EU should be efforts to "desocialize" the economies of the European Union, making them even more free-market oriented.

A characteristic article in this mood was written by Jan Szomburg (2002), suggesting the guidelines of Poland's integration strategy in the EU. They are based on two premises, which, in the face of facts, are difficult to uphold. The first premise was the allegedly excessive interventionism of the EU. In his words: "[The EU] with one foot is already in the world of global competition, and with the other still in the old regulatory-institutional framework, in the old mentality and in state-intervention models that are already ineffective today." The other premise was that as a result of excessive intervention, the EU economy was developing more slowly than the American economy: "Low systemic competitiveness has caused that in the 1990s the EU developed more slowly than the United States." The economist blamed the EU for excessive social transfers, and especially for wage surcharges. He wrote: "There is too little market and entrepreneurship there and too much state and social protection. . . . Social protection systems are not only too costly, but they also destroy the labor markets." Szomburg also felt it was a bad thing that the EU was spending so much on public help to firms (1.25 percent of GDP, while in the United States this was only 0.25 percent), which allegedly "disturbs rational capital allocation." That is why the Forum of the EU stated: "From the beginning of membership Poles should decidedly speak out in favor of deregulation and liberalization, breaking all visible and invisible barriers to unconstrained economic activity while limiting public assistance, and opposing the hoisting of technical, social and environmental standards."

Szomburg used these two premises to build the future strategy for Polish authorities and the country's role as the harbinger of further marketization of the EU, modeled after the United States. The concept presented by him and the Gdańsk Institute for Market Economics chaired by him became the basis of the Polish Lisbon Strategy Forum, created in 2003, together with the Office of the Committee for European Integration. The forum was to publish a White Paper each year, containing information and recommendations concerning implementation of the Lisbon program of a "new social model" strikingly similar to the American one, and to Americanize the entire EU. Thus it was not only U.S. Defense Secretary Donald Rumsfeld who juxtaposed the "new Europe" (the countries of Central

Europe) against the "old" one, treating the latter as a sclerotic creation. This was also being done by conservative circles in Great Britain and some politicians of this "new Europe."

The following are two telling examples.

Two authors once expressed an opinion in the *Wall Street Journal Europe* that "some candidate countries, such as Poland, have always felt close links with the United States and the American model of capitalism suited them better."[34] Following EU entry, the candidate countries will "press for liberalization of the social sphere and the labor code" both at home and in France and Germany. They observed that Great Britain, as an advocate of greater liberalization, may become "a powerful ally of the new members." Similar views were expressed by the conservative shadow minister of state in Great Britain, Lord Howell. He compared the countries of the New Europe, "bristling of dynamism," against the German "spiral of unemployment."[35] In this, he was seconded by the chief economist of London's European Bank of Reconstruction and Development (EBRD).

As can be seen, Poland's pioneer role in systemic transformations contains much more ambitious content matter than the initial justification of the high costs of being in the lead. But the older pioneer role can be at least partly excused. Poland happened to be the first to take the plunge into the unknown. Hence it was easy to "overshoot," to apply excessively strong measures, to amass them in a very short time.

In my opinion, the authorities should rather be blamed for their inability to at least partly withdraw from this stance so as to diminish social distress. And now it is high time to draw conclusions from the unfortunate, miscalculated jump into the free-market economy. The continued desire to be in the lead in the European Union cannot but be acknowledged as a great, obvious incongruity. Here is a country with an economy weighed down under the greatest burden of unemployment, poverty, injustice, and violation of elementary employee rights, yet displaying an ambition of being the leader in shaping a "new economic order" for the entire EU. This looks like an unprecedented manifestation of vanity and ideological insensibility.

There was something unusually arrogant already in the
Balcerowicz Plan. It was visible in the lighthearted responses of certain officials to questions about unemployment: we do not know how
high it is going to be, "maybe a million, maybe two, maybe three, or
maybe not at all." The government of that time unanimously picked
the farthest-reaching of the three variants presented by the IMF
experts. It is also known that lifting customs barriers in 1990 went so
far as to make Poland one of the most laissez-faire countries of the
world (as said, directly after Hong Kong). But later on as well, Poland
moved to the forefront in commercialization and privatization of certain areas.

Until recently, Poland was nearly the only country in Europe west
of Ukraine where agricultural production was not subsidized. This
was one of the reasons why until 2004 farmers' incomes were almost
half of what they had been fifteen years earlier. The argument raised
against this statement, that KRUS (pension fund for farmers) is over
90 percent paid for from the state budget, is misplaced in that most
often recipients are old-age pensioners who even if they are running a
small farm, treat it as complementary to their subsistence. The
absence of subsidies for market producers created a glaring asym-
metry in the competition of farm produce from Poland with the highly
subsidized produce from Western Europe.

In many Western countries the old-age pension system is changing
due to the aging of populations and the slowdown of economic
growth. However, the pay-as-you-go public pension system is still
prevalent. Even if reforms in some EU countries are being carried out
in the direction of the greater individual involvement of citizens in
financing pensions, increasing the capital premium pillar, this is being
done gradually and usually voluntarily. But Poland chose to implement a reform with a very high proportion of capital fund pensions,
probably the highest in Europe, dependent on the situation in the
stock market. This immensely expands the range of insecurity in
society and in the lives of individuals.*

---

*The implementation of this pension system became one of the reasons for the

At the close of the last century, Poland already had one of the highest shares of the private sector in the health services, and if you add unregistered services, quite possibly the highest. And yet both the 1999 reform and competitive programs aim at further prompt privatization of the health services.

Two other initiatives merit attention. The attempt to introduce the flat-rate tax as proposed by Leszek Balcerowicz as finance minister failed. Later, however, serious thought was given to it by prime minister Leszek Miller. All countries of the "old EU" have more or less progressive taxes. But among the Polish authorities, the idea of income tax at the same rate for all is alive and well in both liberal and central-left parties.

Current ambitions are aimed at making the Warsaw Stock Exchange the most significant financial center of Central Europe and one of the biggest in all of Europe. Leszek Balcerowicz stubbornly harps on about the alleged "oversocialization" of Western European economies. And with this ideological baggage, we have entered the European Union, proud that we are going to change it in the spirit of the "civilization of inequalities." Obviously, Reaganism and Thatcherism, which in the Western countries sound obsolete, have remained firmly rooted in the minds of the Polish authorities.

---

growth of state debt, since public finance now had to cover two systems—the old one and the new one—at the same time. When the debt and budgetary deficit growth was accelerated by today's global crisis, the government felt it was necessary to lower the contribution paid into the Private Pension Funds. This in turn evoked the fury of the defenders of the capital reform, with Leszek Balcerowicz in the lead.

14. Start a Debate on Poland and the European Union

We are clearly in the midst of a global crisis and this forces the authorities, political parties, and non-governmental organizations (trade unions) to reflect on the situation in the world, in the European Union, and in Poland. What they do and how they behave will depend on how they assess the situation, not only as it is now, but also the processes and events of the past. Those who had been planning festivities to celebrate twenty years of Poland's transformation have now been forced to at least change their tune. The crisis is what throws a new light on the recent past.

The Meanders of Globalization

The principal decisions defining the form of the emerging system and the structures of our economy were made in Poland at a time of the greatest popularity of the free-market ideas of Reaganomics, or its even worse edition, the naively monetarist policy of Margaret Thatcher, and in theory, the free-market concepts of Friedrich A. Hayek and Milton Friedman. Poland eagerly succumbed to the myth of these concepts.

Only a few years ago, Leszek Balcerowicz wrote with visible pride about the universal applicability of the American model. In a way, he justified the expansion of the only world superpower under the banner (the title of the volume) *Reaganomics Goes Global*, and—at least in Polish conditions—delineated the framework of public debate. In the Preface to this publication, he wrote, after a Polish-American conference organized by the Warsaw School of Economics:

> A distinct departure from this statist trend, i.e. a reduction of these areas of state activity, took place during the times of President Ronald Reagan.... Together with Prime Minister Thatcher ... they outlined the course, sooner or later ... to be followed by other countries of the West.... Although in some periods the American model leaned in the direction of statism, for nearly the whole time it secured a broader scope of basic individual liberties, especially economic liberty, than the decided majority of systems in other countries. This was and is, I believe, the main reason for the successes of the United States. By expanding the scope of economic liberty (lowering taxes, reducing administrative barriers to economic activity), within the existing (or emerging) state under the rule of law, the course is in some degree in the direction of the American model. And in this way it is the course of economic success.[1]

The Civil Development Forum founded by Balcerowicz appears to define the basic way of thinking of the media in Poland.

In Polish public opinion, the concept of globalization that developed in the first half of the 1990s continues to prevail, with small exceptions. In brief, it goes like this: the world economy is becoming globalized, heading in the direction of a single, world socioeconomic system, with the elimination of national borders and states. This is so irrespective of whether anyone has read books by Kenichi Ohmae (1990, 1995) or believes in his vision of a world "without borders" and "without a state." The final result is preceded by regional integration, the examples of which are NAFTA and the European Union. This was most vividly expressed by an economist from Columbia University,

Andrzej Rapaczyński. In the article "Niepotrzebne państwo narodowe" (National State Not Needed),[2] he expressed the belief that
national identities are "something like an appendix—an organ whose
role boils down to provoking an inflammation once in a while."

Notoriously no heed is taken of the equally strong, and recently
even stronger, tendency toward systemic diversification of today's
world, including the European Union. Processes of integration and
convergence are understood in a similarly one-sided way, where opposite processes, phenomena of disintegration and divergence, are
ignored or overlooked.

To perceive both the possibility and the need for a systemic reorientation in Poland, it is necessary to take a look at the international situation, which has changed radically since the early 1990s. Today the
decline of these integration concepts is amazingly widespread, except
in Poland. Here are the most pertinent examples. Germany is—at least
in public rhetoric—returning to its social market economy. Spain has
withdrawn from its neoliberal policies. Jose Zapatero has for a couple
of years been viewed as the most leftist prime minister in Europe. He
failed, however, in trying to rescue the financial sector in typical IMF
style. The Swedish right-wing government came to power in 2006
under slogans of better protection of the Swedish model than by the
Social Democrats.

Several countries in South America have broken off with the doctrine of the Chicago Boys, exercising more or less left-wing policies.
Created by eight countries, the Bolivarian Alliance for the Americas
seems to promise better rules of cooperation than the EU. Two demographic and developing economic giants have entered the world arena,
namely China and India, with economic systems still not yet clearly
defined, but showing distinct features, which are not merely cultural.
One of the most important developments of recent years is the emergence and reinforcement of what the authors of *Comparative
Economics*, J. B. Rosser and M. V. Rosser (1996), call the "new tradition-
alism," that is, the economy and economic policy of Islam and other reli-
gions, which has not only created a barrier to globalization of the Anglo-
Saxon style, but has also intensified conflicts in today's world.

There are many new developments in theory as well. Though still shallow, a widespread reversal from market fundamentalism can be seen in favor of Keynesianism. Even Milton Friedman made adjustments to his promotion of market liberty and monetarism, which had been untarnished by realism. For the former free-market advocate Jeffrey Sachs, the Scandinavian model has become more attractive than the American way of doing business, meaning he has orphaned his blind followers of the 1990s. And by now his criticism[3] of the quarter-century reign of Reaganomics is one of the harshest. Even Francis Fukuyama (2009) calls for a rejection of Reaganomics, assuming correctly that the causes of the current crisis stem "directly from the Reagan model."

Highly noteworthy in economic writings is the theoretical output, presented in many publications, of the former chief advisor to President Bill Clinton, former first vice president of the World Bank, Joseph Stiglitz. And the greatest achievement of this Nobel Prize holder is opening the eyes of a large portion of economists and other scholars of social science to the thought that the old dilemma (of Kuznets-Lewis-Okun) of the choice between efficiency and equality has become outdated in the light of the experience of the East Asian tigers (and, may we add, of the five Scandinavian countries). To recall: Simon Kuznets was convinced that the natural price for capitalist industrialization is an increase in income disparity. Meanwhile, Japan, South Korea, and Taiwan began this process with a reduction of property and income inequalities. It turned out that greater equality, both in incomes and in property, can be (in general is) a factor encouraging economic growth. And this is not only because it facilitates social peace, but also because it contributes greatly to develop human capital.

The second part of the Kuznets hypothesis, that at a high level of industrialization these inequalities will decrease, has not come true, at least in the major countries of the Western world. Following a period of a certain leveling out of incomes in the first twenty-five years after the Second World War, the United States, Great Britain, and many other countries returned to a "civilization of inequality"—with stagnation or even a drop in incomes in the groups below the national average, and with simultaneously rapidly rising family fortunes. A "new poverty" emerged, even among full-time workers. What is more, taking advantage of the strength of the only superpower, the American "oligarchic triad" (the U.S. Treasury Department + Wall Street + the IMF) and the transnational corporations successfully began to impose a "civilization of inequality" on the world. They imposed not only free trade but also the unconstrained movement of capital (together with derivatives), for which the Third World countries in particular were not ready.

Aware of the superpower weight of the American economy and policy in the world, Stiglitz subjected to comprehensive criticism the faults of the socioeconomic order of the United States, the deregulatory frenzy and the political and ideological hypocrisy of the establishment. He devoted much attention to defending the poorer countries against the neocolonial aspirations of his own country. With this, he contributed to a rebirth of the ethos of economics, the duty of which is to serve the truth and interests of the global community, even when the truth is at a certain moment inconvenient or unfavorable for one's own country.

Another development is the writings of the former financier-profiteer now turned philosopher and philanthropist, George Soros. On the occasion of the previous recession, he pointed out that if no way is found to significantly stimulate the world economy and if pressing social issues are further disregarded, globalization processes will not last. At the time, it appeared to many that he was exaggerating when he wrote: "We have become aware that our civilization is in danger. It therefore becomes pointless to try to improve the position of our social system, if the system itself is drifting toward a catastrophe."[4] And soon enough, the catastrophe came without warning. "We are in the midst of a financial meltdown the world has not seen the likes of since the times of the Great Depression. . . . This situation will have far-reaching consequences. This is no ordinary crisis, but the end of the current era."[5] Many other authors write in a similar way. Especially now, when we clearly see that Barack Obama, who was seen as a new Franklin D. Roosevelt, has not risen to the occasion.

The above words of Soros are taken from a book devoted to financial markets, which narrows down the subject matter (intentionally). The issue, in fact, concerns the crisis of our civilization, which makes the tasks standing before the authorities and society immeasurably harder.

The Limits of Integration

I believe that for Poland, two acknowledged facts are of supreme importance. First, globalization has slowed down in general and in regard to its tendency to eliminate systemic differences, it has been stopped by the erosion of the myth of the American model and with the launching of various forces of resistance (alterglobalism, terrorism, numerous manifestations of cultural resistance). As early as the mid-1990s, Robert Boyer suggested that "the 1990s and the next century, too, are likely to be still the epoch of nations. The complex set of contradictory forces that are pushing simultaneously toward convergence and divergence are far from moving toward a single best institutional design."[6] He was seconded in this, in the same book, by Robert Wade,[7] who wrote a piece titled "Reports of the Death of the National Economy Are Greatly Exaggerated." What is more, many economists agreed that globalization brought the greatest advantages to the economies of countries in which the role of the state was strong.

The second acknowledged fact is that within the EU there persistently exists systemic diversity. The EU economies do not form a single socioeconomic order, and for a long time to come they will remain highly diversified in this respect, which should inspire Poland to once again take up the debate on choosing a better social order than the one practiced until now. The prerequisite for such debate is—and this I repeat—doing away with the mistaken belief of many politicians and economists that the EU is now, or is quickly becoming, a single economic organism. This is a difficult task, since apart from a few exceptions, the entire group of economists not only do not deal with problems concerning systemic diversity or comparative economics, but also ignore the already substantial trend of research of Western economists. Today's world, with the exception of waning communist enclaves, is divided, according to most of our economists, into the group of countries with a developed market economy and "emerging markets." This view is reinforced by an entire bureaucratic machinery, locally and in Brussels. The "free" market is written and talked about as if it were the existing state of things, and not a thing of the remote past. Yet a free market in times of domination by multinational corporations is rather "wishful thinking."

An exception here is academic social politicians, who have acknowledged the idea of the diversity of social systems as obvious, at least with regard to their field of interests (mainly analysis of different aspects of social protection). But it is enough to look at the topics of publications in periodicals of both of these groups—economists and social politicians—to notice that communication between them is very limited. The latter have no impact on the narrow approach of economists and economic politicians. The barriers between economists and sociologists are most probably smaller than between economists and social politicians, but sociologists are more involved with yesterday's problems and less with the future.

The systemic classifications are diverse, but probably the most popular of all in the Western countries is that of Bruno Amable (*The Diversity of Modern Capitalism*, 2003). In the EU itself he distinguished four types of capitalism: *liberal market* (Great Britain, Ireland), *social democratic* (Scandinavia), *continental European* with German predominance, and the *Mediterranean* (patrimonial) kind.

The debate on joining the eurozone should become an occasion to make up for this oversight and to define the model closest to the preferences of the Polish people. Furthermore, the matter also concerns *mutatis mutandis* the actions of institutions specific to the European Union. During the 2000–2002 recession, the EU's inability to act jointly was revealed. It turned out that the reigning principle then was: every man for himself—each country individually. Even Sweden, not a member of the euro zone, had reason to complain at the disgraceful breaking of the Amsterdam Treaty by the leading EU countries. And now the situation has become quite dramatic.

Unexpectedly, the most serious, thought-provoking statement on this subject until now has come from an adamant admirer of Hayek-Friedman economics, Witold Gadomski, in his article "Kapitalizm do remontu" (Capitalism for Renovation).[8]

> Europe, which for half a century now has been on the road to integration ... this time stands before perhaps the most difficult examination since the creation of the EEC. It is still too early to say whether the global financial crisis will speed up integration, or reverse this process by several decades. I am rather betting on the latter option. The problem is that from the moment that the banking crisis hit Europe ... the main role in conducting rescue missions has been played by the governments of the individual countries and not by European institutions, which are nearly invisible.... The stimulation packages, in effect increasing the debt of the individual countries, collide with the common monetary policy conducted by the European Central Bank. If one country increases its debt and issues bonds, this affects the interest rates of bonds in other countries of the eurozone. In other words—countries that become more indebted do this at the price of their neighbors.... If there were no common currency, the countries that are doing worse would allow for a lowering of the value of their domestic currencies, so as to raise competitiveness in this way (at the cost of lowering the living standard).... Spain, Greece and Ireland—may soon have problems with the repayment of their debts. Not long ago this would have been unthinkable. Entering the eurozone was thought to be a 100-percent guarantee of stability. The world crisis has painfully verified these views. On the whole, Europe, and especially the eurozone, is in danger of chaos.... Not more than a year ago, rumors of a possible exit of certain countries from the eurozone could have been regarded as political fiction. Today this cannot be ruled out.

It is interesting that even the extreme free-market advocate Milton Friedman had a highly critical view regarding fast adoption of a common currency. Before the introduction of the euro, he expressed the opinion (as in the title of his article): "Monetary Unity to Political Disunity."[9] For him, the United States "is an example of a situation favorable to a common currency." But two features determine this: a common language and high mobility of the workforce, which allows for prompt adjustments in the event of unexpected shocks. Another important feature is that the federal government has an adequately large budget to mitigate any possible shocks. The situation is diametrically different in the European Union. According to Friedman, the EU "exemplifies a situation that is unfavorable to a common currency." This is because of the different languages, cultural differences, and national loyalties, as well as a very limited budget. He relaxed his view with regard to Germany, the Benelux countries, and Austria, which were for a long time practically linked to the German mark. Overall, he felt that it was much too early for this in Europe. "Political unity can pave the way for monetary unity. Monetary unity imposed under unfavorable conditions will prove a barrier to the achievement of political unity."

Diversity Is a Value

The coexistence and competition of different types of capitalism is not an expression of an unfinished process of integration or immaturity that the EU needs to overcome. Moreover, I believe that preservation of institutional-organizational diversity is a prerequisite for the viability of the European Union. Excessive pressure to integrate may produce quite the opposite effect—arouse or strengthen "reactive nationalism."

To support my view, I shall resort to the opinion of one of the leading British economists, the Nobel Prize laureate James Meade. In his opinion, systemic diversity is a value worth defending. It is likewise feasible and desirable. He writes that it is "unlikely that all European countries would select exactly the same set of arrangements." However, he felt it an important research task to look for an answer to the question on "how far and by what international means can diversity of experiments be made compatible with freedom of movement of goods, capital and people between the members of the Community."[10] In another essay he directly and categorically speaks out against the centralist-unifying trends of the EU. Assuming there is "almost infinity of various diverse ways in which the production of goods and services may be organized, planned and managed," he expresses the belief that "it would be a great obstacle to progress if changes in these structures could be tried out only on a uniform basis in every European Country simultaneously."[11]

It seems that it would be difficult to carry out this systemic experimentation, at the same time taking a great leap toward integration with the implementation of a common currency. And if this is hard to reconcile, should not priority be given to more essential systemic changes and only after these are in place the most suitable moment for joining the eurozone be sought?

This reasoning calls for a closer look at political processes in the European Union. The observed readiness of governments to rescue the financial sector on a grand scale and the manifestations of increased protectionism should be taken advantage of by the Polish authorities, encouraging them toward better negotiations and a more consistent return to an industrial policy. The structure of our economy could be modernized. The example of Finland should be particularly instructive for us. Within just a few years, this country has not only overcome deep recession and high unemployment, but its economy has been modernized, through the replacement of the recent exports of wood and wood-like products, mainly to Soviet Russia, with an electronic invasion of the whole world.

Changing the Fate of the "Subcontractor"

I have already written about the consequences of the uncontrolled influx of foreign capital, regarding this to be one of the biggest shortcomings of Polish systemic transformations. I have already referred to the opinions of the experienced manager of international corporations, Stefan Dunin-Wąsowicz, an unquestioned authority on the strategies of transnational corporations. According to him, the strategists of Western corporations have taken advantage of the lack of experience and skills of Polish business and Polish politicians to dominate the channels of wholesale trading, transforming the Polish economy into a "subsidiary economy," pushing it into the role of subcontractor.[12]

For years now, Andrzej Karpiński has been writing in the same spirit, being familiar with the Polish economy inside out. In his last book (2008), he recalled "the unusually high state of penetration of Poland's own domestic market by imports. . . . The share of imports at 56 percent of sales in the domestic market places us among countries with relatively the highest import penetration in Europe." He also pointed to the technological weakness of our economy: "The position of modern elements in the country's economic structure is unusually weak, e.g. of high-technology industry and other knowledge-based economy vehicles. The result is a high share of domains of the lowest technology, accounting for 36 percent of the entire industrial production. This means there is total domination of imitation processes and underdevelopment of the high sector that could compete at the innovation level."[13]

Are Dunin-Wąsowicz, now a member of the neoliberal CASE, and Andrzej Karpiński, until recently secretary in the Committee of the Polish Academy of Sciences Poland 2000 Plus, both exaggerating? Hardly so, as Karpiński's book is based on many years of statistical-comparative studies, and the opinions of Dunin-Wąsowicz result from many years of experience in transnational corporations and confrontation of this experience with the Polish reality.

And, besides, both of the above opinions have been corroborated from an unexpected angle by Jan Krzysztof Bielecki, formerly prime minister and, which makes his opinion more piquant, president of a foreign bank in Poland. Above we have shown that common sense made him stand against an excess of foreign capital.[14] Currently he is acting in this spirit as chairman of the government's consultative body of the Economic Council.

All this results from the programmed negligence of structural industrial policy and from a naïve faith in market automatism as far as developmental processes are concerned. Dunin-Wąsowicz highlighted the faults of the Polish economy and the economic policy for the purpose of changing the situation. He pointed to the need to expand the area of operation and to increase the degree of self-reliance of Polish business. He stressed that even such liberal countries as the United States and Great Britain "are after all pursuing a pro-investment policy."[15] He treated as "pathology" the "reduction of the dimensions of local research and development activity, and thereby reduction of the foundations of autonomy of growth," suggesting the course for counteraction.

The abundant diagnostic and postulative output of the Committee of Forecasts Poland 2000 Plus, also in the form of "supplications" to the authorities, shows the persistence of the efforts of this body, as well as their futility. The doctrine of the "magic role of the market," to use the language of Dunin-Wąsowicz, provided grounds for opening the gates to all foreign investment, above all in the form of participation in privatization. Successive governments continue to pay homage to this doctrine.

Maybe the current crisis can change the attitude of the government, if enough pressure is exerted by public opinion. The Polish authorities owe to the people substantial fulfillment of the 1997 constitution, which promises (guarantees in its provisions) the new order based on the principles of a social market economy, social justice, and full employment. Unfortunately, none of the successive government coalitions has attempted to meet these promises, tolerating a highly unethical constitutional hypocrisy. In socioeconomic matters, the "binding" provisions have nearly the same value as the famed communist constitution of 1952. Until the great exodus, unemployment was rising, as were income disparities and even absolute poverty, although the national income showed a rapid growth. Following EU entry, this anachronistic system was confronted with the neighboring economies of the greater portion of the continent, which observed the principles of a social market economy, and especially with the Scandinavian countries, which combined the highest level of taxes and social security with the most dynamic modern economies. This is what inclined two Austrian economists, Karl Aiginger and Michael Landesmann (2002), to call the Scandinavian countries "centers of economic excellence" and to wonder whether this was not the appropriate model to follow.

Chronology

August to September 1980—workers' mass strikes in Gdańsk and Szczecin shipyards, the railways, Silesian coal mines, and elsewhere end with several agreements between the political authorities (Communist Party and government) and the strikers, legalizing the independent and self-governing trade union Solidarność (Solidarity), until 1990 chaired by Lech Wałęsa. This mass social movement soon counted almost ten million members.

October 1981—ratification of the pro-market and pro-syndicalist Solidarity Program titled "The Self-Governing Republic."

13 December 1981–Summer 1983—martial law de-legalizing Solidarity and restricting certain human and civil rights.

January 1982—economic reform drastically reduces central planning, but preserves the rationing of assets and funds, creating a system often called "neither plan nor market."

February to April 1989—the Round Table negotiations between the political authorities and the repesentatives of a broad opposition circle (dominated by Solidarity) accomplish an agreement on some liberalization of parliamentary elections (one-third of seats in Sejm and free election to a newly created Senate), legalization of Solidarity, and radical economic reforms.

4 June 1989—unintended by the political authorities and unexpected by the opposition, spectacular victory of Solidarity in parliamentary election.

September 1989—formation of a non-communist government led by a Catholic, Tadeusz Mazowiecki. It is dominated by Solidarity activists, but some communists are included. Leszek Balcerowicz is appointed deputy prime minister and finance minister, and Jacek Kuroń is appointed minister of labor.

22 December 1989—the government's and Polish Central Bank's Letter of Intent and Memorandum of Economic Policies is sent to the IMF.

End of December 1989—parliamentary ratification of government's ten bills containing the so-called Balcerowicz Plan, called by opponents "shock without therapy" or "Big Bang." These laws came into force on January 1, 1990.

January 1990—dissolution of the Polish United Workers' Party and creation of a much smaller Social-Democracy of the Polish Republic (SDPR). Soon the Democratic Left Alliance (SLD) is formed, a non-Solidarity federation of trade unions and some two dozen other political and social units, clearly dominated by SDPR.

13 July 1990—law on privatization is ratified (subsequently amended many times).

January 1991—after Wałęsa's victory in presidential elections, creation of new cabinet of Jan K. Bielecki. Balcerowicz keeps his posts.

Autumn 1991—the first free parliamentary elections. Twenty-nine parties, most newly created, have a seat in Sejm. Main parties on the left: Democratic Left Alliance (SLD), Polish Peasant Party (PSL), Union of Labor. Main parties on the right: Union of National Christians, Alliance of the Center, Liberal Democratic Congress, Democratic Union chaired by T. Mazowiecki (later both were unified into Union of Liberty chaired by L. Balcerowicz). In 1991–93, there were several cabinets led by parties stemming from a split in Solidarity.

Spring 1991—Warsaw Stock Exchange created.

Spring 1993—Hanna Suchocka's cabinet loses parliament's vote of confidence and new elections are called.

September 1993—at the elections, the SLD and other parties in opposition gain a majority in parliament. Several post-Solidarity and right-wing parties do not reach a newly fixed minimum of 5 percent of the votes and remain outside parliament. Between 1993 and 1997, a coalition of the SLD and the PSL is in government. Surprisingly, the IMF-supported "market friendly policy" is with some minor changes continued.

1991 to 1994—Polish government's agreement with the Paris Club (representing Western governments) and the London Club (representing private banks) concerning foreign debt reduction—by about half.

22 November 1996—Poland becomes full member of OECD.

25 May 1997—the constitution of the Polish republic is ratified in a referendum. The Constitution states that the foundation of the economic system is "social market economy based on freedom of economic activity, private property, solidarity, dialog and cooperation of social partners" (art. 22) and that the republic realizes "principles of social justice" (art. 2). The constitution was an outcome of a great compromise between four main parliamentary factions, but furiously attacked by Solidarity and the right-wing parties that were outside parliament.

September 1997—electoral victory of Solidarity Election Action (AWS), which is an alliance of the Solidarity trade union and many Christian right-wing parties. A coalition of AWS and Union of Liberty forms a government headed by Jerzy Buzek (prime minister, former Solidarity activist, now ending his presidency of the EU parliament) with Leszek Balcerowicz as his deputy and minister of finance.

1999—Poland becomes member of NATO.

1 May 2004—following long negotiations ending in 2002, Poland becomes a member of the European Union.

2006—Poland ratifies the Lisbon Treaty, replacing the earlier rejected Constitutional Treaty, and, like Great Britain, excluding the Charter of Fundamental Rights.

Bibliography

A.K.K., "Rozdanie świadectw w 1994 r.," *Rzeczpospolita*, August 20, 1992.

Ackerman B., *Przyszłość rewolucji liberalnej*, Warsaw 1996.

Adler-Karlsson G., *Functional Socialism, the Swedish Experience*, Stockholm 1989.

Aiginger K., Landesman M., *Competitive Economic Performance: USA versus EU, Research Report WIIW*, Vienna 2002.

Aleksandrowicz P., "Program dostosowawczy," *Gazeta Bankowa* no. 28, July 10–16, 1989.

Amable B., *The Diversity of Modern Capitalism*, Oxford 2003.

Andreff W., *Comment*, in UNDP & Koping-Datorg, *Privatization in the Transition Process. Recent Experiences in Eastern Europe*, Geneva 1994.

Ash T. G., Kis J., Michnik A., "Tysiąc słów," *Gazeta Wyborcza*, July 10, 1989.

Baehr J., *Companies with Employee Participation*, Poznań 1993.

Baka W., *Zmagania z reformą*, Warsaw 2007.

Balcerowicz L., *800 dni. Szok kontrolowany*, Warsaw 1992.

———, "Gospodarka z kulą u nogi," *Puls Biznesu*, March 29, 2006.

———, "Mam zdjąć okulary?," *Gazeta Wyborcza*, August 17, 1991.

———, Preface, in Bieńkowski W., Radło M. J. (eds.), *Amerykański model rozwoju gospodarczego. Istota - efektywność możliwości zastosowania*, Warsaw 2006.

———, *Socjalizm, kapitalizm, transformacja*, Warsaw 1997.

———, *Socialism, Capitalism, Transformation*, Budapest 1995.

———, *Spór o pojęcie celów społecznych*, Warsaw 1984.

———, *Systemy gospodarcze*, Warsaw 1989.

———, Interview, *Rzeczpospolita*, June 22, 1990.

_____, "W stronę analizy własności," in L. Balcerowicz, *Socjalizm, Kapitalizm, Transformacja*, Warsaw 1997.

_____, *Wolność i rozwój. Ekonomia wolnego rynku*, Kraków [1995] 1998.

_____, "Tak poprawia się kapitalizm," *Gazeta Wyborcza*, October 1, 2008.

Bałtowski M., *Prywatyzacja przedsiębiorstw państwowych. Przebieg i ocena*, Warsaw 1998.

_____, (ed.), *Przedsiębiorstwa sprywatyzowane w gospodarce polskiej*, Warsaw 2002.

_____, "Rodowód własnościowy i udział kapitału zagranicznego a wyniki największych polskich przedsiębiorstw," in B. Błaszczyk, P. Kozarzewski (eds.), *Zmiany w polskich przedsiębiorstwach. Własność, restrukturyzacja, efektywność, Raport CASE*, Warsaw 2007a.

Bałtowski M., Miszewski M., *Transformacja gospodarcza w Polsce*, Warsaw 2006.

Bauer O., *Zwischen zwei Weltkriegen?*, Bratislava 1936.

Becker G., "Rule No. 1 in Switching to Capitalism: Move Fast," *Business Week*, May 29, 1995.

Berle A., Means G., *The Modern Corporation and Private Property*, New York 1932.

Berliner J., "The Gains from Privatization," in U.S. Congress, Joint Economic Committee, *The Economies of Former Soviet Union*, Washington D.C. 1993.

Beskid L., in Milic-Czerniak R. (ed.), *Gospodarstwa domowe w krajach Europy środkowej*, Instytut Spraw Publicznych, Warsaw 1998.

Bhagwati J., "An Interview," in *India Times*, December 31, 1997.

Bielecki J.K., "Ucieczka na Zachód," interview by Janina Paradowska, *Polityka*, January 31, 2009.

BIPS [Press Information Bureau of Solidarity] *Statut. Uchwała Programowa z Aneksem. Dokumenty Zjazdu*, Gdańsk (n.d., 1981?).

Biuletyn, "Sprzedaj chatę, daj wypłatę," *Biuletyn Dialogu Społecznego* no. 5, 2004.

Błaszczyk B. et al., "Secondary Privatization in Poland" (Part II): Evolution of Ownership Structure and Performance in National Investment Funds and Their Portfolio Companies," CASE, Warsaw 2001.

Błaszczyk B., Nawrot W., "Postępy prywatyzacji w Polsce w latach 1991–2006 a sektor nie sprywatyzowany," in B. Błaszczyk, P. Kozarzewski (eds.), *Zmiany w polskich przedsiębiorstwach. Własność, restrukturyzacja, efektywność*, Report 70, Warsaw 2007.

Bobrowski C., "Rozwój planowania w Polsce Ludowej," (n.d., 1964?), (photocopied text in my possession).

Bochniarz H., Wiśniewski A., "Godzina prawdy," *Rzeczpospolita*, February 5, 1999.

Bolesta-Kukułka K., *Gra o władzę a gospodarka polska 1944–1991*, Warsaw 1992.

Bornstein M., *Comparative Economic Systems: Models and Cases,* Homewood
    IL 1974.

Borodziej W., Garlicki A. (eds.), *Okrągły Stół. Dokumenty i materiały,* 4 vols.,
    Warsaw 2004.

Boyer R., "The Convergence Hypothesis Revisited: Globalization but Still the
    Century of Nations," in S. Berger, R. Dore, *National Diversity and
    Global Capitalism,* Ithaca NY and London 1996.

Brossio G., Hochman H.M., *Economic Justice,* 2 vols., Cheltenham and
    Northampton 1998.

Bruno M., "Stabilization and Reform in Eastern Europe, A Preliminary
    Evaluation," IMF Working Paper no. 92/30, Washington 1992.

Bruno M., Squire L., "The Less Equal the Asset Distribution, the Slower the
    Growth," *Transition* World Bank no. 9-10, Washington D.C. 1996.

Brus W., *Uspołecznienie a system polityczny,* Uppsala 1974.

———, "Demokracja a efektywność gospodarcza (spojrzenie po dziesięciu
    latach)," *Dwadzieścia jeden* no. 5, 1987.

———, "Refleksje o postępującej nieoznaczoności socjalizmu," in A. Jasińska et
    al., *Demokracja i socjalizm,* Wrocław-Warsaw-Kraków [1989] 1992.

———, "The Bane of Reforming the Socialist Economic System," *Banca
    Nazionale del Lavoro Quarterly Review* no. 187, December 1993.

Brus W., Kowalik T., "Socialism and Development," *Cambridge Journal of
    Economics* no. 3-4, 1983.

Brus W., Łaski K., *Od Marksa do rynku,* Warsaw [1989] 1992.

Brus W., Łaski K., *From Marx to the Market,* Oxford 1991.

Brzeziński Z., "Demokracja wobec globalizacji. Kilka refleksji na temat global-
    nych dylematów zwycięskiej demokracji," *Przegląd Polityczny* no.
    40-41, 1999.

Buchanan J., *Post-Socialist Political Economy,* Cheltenham 1997.

Bugaj R., "Kształt i warunki polskiej przebudowy," *Tygodnik Powszechny* no. 46,
    1988b.

———, "Widmo demokracji," *Tygodnik Powszechny* no. 22, 1988a.

———, "Postkomunizm z Ameryki," *Gazeta Wyborcza,* July 3, 2000.

———, "Prywatyzacja, biznes i media," *Trybuna,* July 22-23, 2002.

Bugaj R., Kowalik T., "The Privatization Debate in Poland," in *Privatization in
    Eastern Europe,* Vienna 1993.

Bujak Z., "Polityka i ambicje," *Gazeta Wyborcza,* September 8-9, 1990.

———, *Przepraszam za Solidarność,* Warsaw 1991.

Bukowski J., "Rola Ministerstwa Przekształceń Własnościowych w rozwoju
    udziału pracowników w prywatyzacji," in L. Gilejko (ed.),
    Partycypacja i akcjonariat pracowniczy w Polsce, Warsaw 1995.

Burnham J., *The Managerial Revolution,* New York 1941.

Bywalec C., "Poziom życia społeczeństwa polskiego na tle procesów transformacji
    gospodarczej (1989-1993)," study commissioned by INE PAN, 1995.

Castells M., *The Information Age: Economy, Society, Culture*, 3 vols., Oxford 1996–2001.

Celiński A., "Korupcja," *Nowe Życie Gospodarcze*, July 18, 1999.

———, "Trudno postawić konia przed wozem," *Życie Warszawy*, August 9–10, 1989.

Dahl R., *A Preface to Economic Democracy*, New Haven 1985.

———, *Polyarchy*, New Haven and London 1971.

Dahl R., Lindblom C., *Politics, Economics, and Welfare*, New York 1953.

Dallago B., "Systemic Change, Privatization and Entrepreneurship," in N. P. Ostojic and N. Scott (eds.), *Experiences and Results of Privatization in the Economies in Transition*, Belgrade 1998.

Dąbrowski M., "Czy w Polsce jest możliwy gospodarczy cud," *Gazeta Wyborcza* no. 77, 1989a.

———, *Podmiot przedsiębiorczości w różnych wariantach gospodarczych, referat na kongres PTE*, Kraków 1987.

———, *Program Sachsa i polskie konieczności*: komentuje. *Diagnoza społeczna*, Warsaw 2003, (photocopy).

Djilas M., *The New Class*, New York 1957.

Domański H., "Mobilność i hierarchie stratyfikacyjne," in H. Domański, A. Rychard, *Elementy nowego ładu*, Warsaw 1997.

———, "Wzrost merytokracji i nierówności szans," in H. Domański et al. (eds.), *Jak żyją Polacy*, Warsaw 2000.

Domański H., Rychard A., *Elementy nowego ładu*, Warsaw 1997.

———, "Nowe społeczeństwo klasowe?," discussion between R. Krasowski and J. Ostrowski, *Życie*, March 20, 1998.

Domarańczyk Z., *100 dni Mazowieckiego*, Warsaw 1990.

Dryll I., "Droga do raju," *Życie Gospodarcze* no. 40, September 10, 1989.

Dubiński K. (ed.), *Okrągły stół*, Warsaw 1999.

Dunin-Wąsowicz S., "Blaski i cienie 'gospodarki oddziałów,'" *Rzeczpospolita*, September 29–30, 200la.

Dunin-Wąsowicz S., "Komplikacje 'pooperacyjne'," *Rzeczpospolita*, December 8–9, 200lb.

———, "Pomoc na starcie. Czy państwo powinno wspierać inwestycje, a jeśli tak, to w jaki sposób może to robić," *Rzeczpospolita*, January 4–5, 2003.

Dyner J., Izdebski H., Szlajfer H., "Patologie prywatyzacji," *Życie Warszawy* no. 222, 1989.

Dzielski M., "Bez kontestacji," *Ład* no. 23, 1988.

———, "Gospodarcza racja stanu," *Polityka*, January 28, 1989.

Estrin S., Jones D., "The Determinants of Investment in Employee-Owned Firms," *Economic Analysis*, February 1998.

EuroMemorandum, 2008, available at http://www.euromemo.eu/.

Eyal G., Szelenyi I., Townsley E., "The Theory of Postcommunist Managerialism," *New Left Review* no. 222, 1997.

Eysmont E. et al., "Odejście tyrana," *Spotkania*, May 8, 1992.

Federowicz M., *Trwanie i transformacja*, Warsaw 1992.

Frasyniuk W., "Wracamy do gry," interview by W. Bereś, *Gazeta Wyborcza*, May 29–30, 2004.

Friedman M., "Walutowa jedność drogą do politycznego podziału," *Rzeczpospolita*, September 2, 1997.

Friedman T., *Lexus i drzewo oliwne. Zrozumieć globalizację*, Poznań [1999] 2001.

Friszke A., "Polityka i wartości," *Rzeczpospolita*, April 18, 2002.

Fukuyama F., "Obama musi przeprowadzić rewolucję idei," *Europa*, supplement to *Dziennik*, January 31, 2009.

Gadomski W., "Kapitalizm do remontu," *Gazeta Wyborcza*, January 2009.

Gajdziński P., "Balcerowicz na gorąco," interview by . . . , Poznań 1999.

Galbraith J. K., *American Capitalism. The Concept of Countervailing Power*, Boston 1952.

_____, "Don't turn the world over to the bankers," 2003 (photocopy in author's possession).

Gardawski J., *Przyzwolenie ograniczone. Robotnicy wobec rynku i demokracji*, Warsaw 1996.

_____, *Związki zawodowe na rozdrożu*, Warsaw 2001a.

_____, *Powracająca klasa. Sektor prywatny w III Rzeczypospolitej*, Warsaw 2001b.

_____, *Polacy pracujący a kryzys fordyzmu*, Warsaw 2009.

_____, *Working Poles and the Crisis of Fordism*, Warsaw, 2010.

_____, *Dialog społeczny w Polsce, Teoria, historia, praktyka*, Warszawa 2009.

Geremek B., *Geremek odpowiada, Żakowski pyta*, Warsaw 1990.

Gilejko L., "Praca-między przymusem a szansami awansu," in *Problemy polityki społecznej. Studia i dyskusje* no. 72, 2004.

Główny Urząd Statystyczny, *Prywatyzacja przedsiębiorstw państwowych 2003*, Warsaw 2004.

_____, *Rocznik Statystyczny 2006*, Warsaw 2006.

Gomułka S., "O czynnikach ekonomicznych w demokratyzacji socjalizmu i socjalizacji kapitalizmu," *Aneks* no. 15, 1977.

_____, "Kornai's Soft Budget Constraint and the Shortage Phenomenon: A Criticism and Restatement," *Economics of Planning* no. 1, 1985.

_____, "Specific and Systemic Causes of the Polish Crisis, 1980–82," *Slavic and Soviet Studies* 35/5, 1983.

_____, "Jak stworzyć rynek kapitałowy w Polsce i jak wykorzystać ten rynek do reformy systemu własności," July 1989 (photocopy typescript in author's possession).

_____, "Shock Needed for Polish Economy," *Guardian*, August 19, 1989.

_____, "Stabilizacja i wzrost: Polska 1989–2000," *Gospodarka Narodowa*, May 1990.

_____, "Stabilizacja i wzrost: Polska 1989–2000," in *Polityka finansowa—nierównowaga—stabilizacja,* Warsaw 1990.

_____, "Kornai's 'Road to a Free Economy' in Light of Polish Experience," *Journal of Comparative Economics* no. 16, 1992.

_____, "Polska reforma gospodarcza w latach 1990–91. Zasady, środki działania i wyniki reformy," in Instytut Nauk Ekonomicznych PAN, *Gospodarka Polska 1990–1993. Kontrowersje wokół oceny doświadczeń i polityki gospodarczej,* Warsaw 1994a.

_____, "Polityka stabilizacyjna w Polsce 1990–93: odpowiedzi na pytania," in Instytut Nauk Ekonomicznych PAN, 1994, *Gospodarka Polska 1990–1993. Kontrowersje wokół oceny doświadczeń i polityki gospodarczej,* Warsaw 1994b.

_____, "Demokracja a efektywność gospodarcza (spojrzenie po dziesięciu latach)," *Dwadzieścia Jeden* no. 5, 1997.

_____, *Transformacja ekonomiczna Polski 1985–2002, dokumenty i analizy,* Warsaw 2010.

Goodwin R. N., "Economic Justice Dies a Slow Death," *Los Angeles Times,* October 18, 1995.

Gordon D., "Conflict and Cooperation: An Empirical Glimpse of the Imperatives of Efficiency and Redistribution," in S. Bowles, H. Gintis (eds.), *Recasting Egalitarianism,* London-New York 1998.

Gotz-Kozierkiewicz D., "Jakie podatki płacą Szwedzi?," *Wektory Gospodarki* no. 9–10, 1989.

Graczyk R., "Jak obalono komunizm?," *Tygodnik Powszechny,* April 29, 2007.

GUS, Rocznik statystyczny 2006, Warsaw 2007.

Harrod R., "John Maynard Keynes," in *International Encyclopedia of Social Sciences,* vol. 8, n.d.

_____, "The Possibility of Economic Satiety, Use of Economic Growth for Improving the Quality of Education and Leisure," in *Problems of United States Economic Development,* New York 1958.

Hayek F. A., *Droga do zniewolenia,* Kraków [1944] 1996.

Heilbroner R. L., *Wielcy ekonomiści,* Warsaw 1993.

Her Majesty's Treasury, *The Modernization of Britain's Tax and Benefits System, Number Four: Tackling Poverty and Extending Opportunity,* London, March 1999.

Herer W., Kowalik T., Sadowski W., "Uwagi do programu dostosowawczego," 1989 (typescript in author's possession).

Herer W., Sadowski W., *Zderzenie z barierami rozwoju,* Warsaw 1989.

Hirsch F., *The Social Limits of Growth,* London-Henley 1977.

Howell Lord, "Is the 'Other Europe' Emerging?" *Wall Street Journal Europe,* February 12, 2003.

"International Assistance for Poland," Gdańsk 1989 (photocopy in author's possession).

Innes J., "US and UK Action in Postwar Iraq May Be Illegal," *The Scotsman*, May 22, 2003.

Janczak H. [S. Kurowski], *Reforma gospodarcza w PRL. Trzecie podejście*, Wydawnictwo CDN, Warsaw 1986.

Janicki M., Władyka W., "Salon podwinął rękawy," *Polityka*, August 2, 2008.

Jarosz M., *Władza, przywileje, korupcja*, Warsaw 2004.

Jasiewicz E., *Podpalić Gazę*, Warsaw 2011.

Jasiński P., *Z powrotem do kapitalizmu. Problemy przekształceń systemowych i własnościowych*, Warsaw 1994.

Jasiński P., Szablewski A.T., Yarrow G., *Konkurencja i regulacja w przemyśle energetycznym. Brytyjskie doświadczenia a polskie problemy*, Warsaw 1995.

Jedlicki J., "Cywilizacja przedmurza," interview with . . . by Marek S. Szczepański, *Wprost*, September 10, 1989.

———, *Jakiej cywilizacji Polacy potrzebują?*, Warsaw 1988.

Jeziorański T., "Jaka własność," *Życie Gospodarcze* no. 8, 1990.

Jones D. C., Svejnar J., *Advances in the Economic Analysis of Participation and Labour-Managed Firms*, 2 vols., Greenwich-London 1985, 1987.

Józefiak C., "Optymalne tempo," in P. Gajdziński, *Balcerowicz na gorąco*, Poznań 1999.

Kabaj M., "Założenia umowy społecznej w zakresie tworzenia miejsc pracy," in A. Wratny, *Umowa społeczna*, IPiSS, 2006.

Kabaj M., Kowalik T., "Who Is Responsible for Post-Communist Successes in Eastern Europe?," *Transition Newsletter*, August 1995.

Kaminski M., "The Hare Always Wins: Economic Reform Can't Afford to Wait," *Wall Street Journal*, January 2, 2004.

Karpiński A., *Przemiany strukturalne w procesie transformacji Polski 1989–2003–2025*, Warsaw 2008.

Karpiński A., Paradysz S., "Nowe tendencje w przemysłach wysokiej techniki," *Przyszłość. Świat-Europa-Polska* no. 2, 2007.

Katznelson I., *Krzywe koło liberalizmu. Listy do Adama Michnika*, Wrocław 2005.

———, *Liberalism's Crooked Circle: Letters to Adam Michnik*, Princeton NJ, 1996.

Keynes J. M., *Collected Writings*, vol. 26, London-Basingstoke n.d..

———, *Ogólna teoria zatrudnienia, procentu i pieniądza*, Warsaw [1936] 1956.

Kieżun W., "O lepszą Polskę," in Askanas W. et al., *Koźmiński reaktywacja*, Warsaw 2011.

———, *Patologia transformacji*, Warsaw 2012.

Klebaniuk (ed.), *Oblicza nierówności społecznych*, vol. I, Warsaw 2007.

Klein N., "Iraq Is Not America's to Sell," *The Guardian*, November 7, 2003.

Kochanowicz J., "Co pozostało z państwa opiekuńczego (po komunizmie)?," in *Indywidualizm a kolektywizm*, Warsaw 1999.

Kolarska-Bobińska L., "Jak krzyk dziecka," interview, *Życie Gospodarcze* no. 26, 1993.

Kołakowski L., "Po co nam pojęcie sprawiedliwości społecznej?," in *Moje słuszne poglądy na wszystko*, Kraków 2000.

Kołodko G., *Wędrujący świat*, Warsaw 2007, available at http://www.tiger.edu. pl/kolodko/ksiazki/GWK-Cele_rozwoju_a_makroproporcje_gosp.pdf.

Kołodziejczyk M., Nazarewicz C., "Teatr zwany strajkiem," *Polityka*, December 6, 2008.

Komołowski L., "Bezrobocie," *Wprost*, March 5, 1999.

Konsultacyjna Rada Gospodarcza, *Model szwedzki*, Warsaw, June 1989 (duplicated text).

Kornai J., *Anti-equilibrium. Teoria systemów gospodarczych. Kierunki badań*, Warsaw 1977.

————, *Contradictions and Dilemmas, Studies on Socialist Economy and Society*, Cambridge, MA–London 1985.

————, *Droga do wolnej gospodarki*, Warsaw [1990] 1991.

————, "The Affinity between Ownership Forms and Coordination Mechanisms: The Common Experience of Reform in Socialist Countries," *Journal of Economic Perspectives* no. 3, 1990.

————, *The Socialist System*, Princeton NJ 1992.

————, "Marx through the Eyes of an East European Intellectual," 2010, duplicated text.

Kowalik T. (ed.), *Zachodni spór wokół kapitalizmu i socjalizmu*, Warsaw 1990.

Kowalik T., "Prywatyzacja czy gospodarka mieszana," in W. Wesołowski (ed.), *Losy idei socjalistycznych i wyzwania współczesności*, Warsaw 1990.

————, "Sierpień—epigońska rewolucja mieszczańska," *Nowe Życie Gospodarcze* no. 37, 1996.

————, "Robotnicy i rewolucja," *Dziś* no. 5, 2006.

————, "Nierówności nie są OK," *Le Monde Diplomatique*, March 2008.

————, "Property Rights and Social Justice," *Studia Historiae Oeconomicae* no. 28–29, Poznań 2010–2011.

————, *Systemy gospodarcze. Efekty i defekty reform i zmian ustrojowych*, Warsaw 2005.

Kozarzewski P., "Prywatyzacja w Polsce w perspektywie porównawczej. Wyniki ilościowe i jakościowe," in B. Błaszczyk, P. Kozarzewski (eds.), *Zmiany w Polskich przedsiębiorstwach. Własność, restrukturyzacja, efektywność*, Report. 70, Warsaw 2007.

Kozek W., "Destruktorzy. Obraz związków zawodowych w tygodnikach politycznych w Polsce," address at 11th Sociological Congress, 2000 (typescript).

Kozłowska-Burdziak M., *Instytucjonalne uwarunkowania przekształceń własnościowych państwowych gospodarstw rolnych w Polsce w latach 1992–2002*, Białystok 2006.

Krajewski A., "Balcerowicz kandydatem do Nobla," *Gazeta Wyborcza*, June 28, 1991.

———, "Opodatkowanie sektora publicznego i prywatnego w Polsce," *Gospodarka Narodowa* no. 7-8, 1994.

Krajewska A., Krajewski S., "Ekonomiczno-finansowa kondycja przedsiębiorstw sprywatyzowanych," in M. Bałtowski (ed.), op. cit.

Krawczyk R., *Wielka przemiana*, Warsaw 1990.

Król M., "Skandal głodujących dzieci," *Rzeczpospolita*, April 12-13, 2003.

Krugman P., "America Revels in a Replay of the Gilded Age," *The New York Times*, October 26, 2002.

Krzemiński I., "Strategia rządzenia," *Rzeczpospolita*, July 31-August 1, 1999.

Kuczyński W., "Kłopoty z socjalizmem," in W. Kuczyński, *Agonia socjalizmu*, Warsaw [1988] 1996.

———, *Po wielkim skoku*, Warsaw 1980.

———, *Zwierzenia zausznika*, Warsaw 1992.

Kula M., "Czarnowski czytany ponownie," *Przegląd Humanistyczny* no. 3, 1996.

Kumor W., "Pakt został przedstawiony," *Gazeta Wyborcza*, September 24, 1992.

Kurczewski J., "Taka młoda a taka brzydka," *Gazeta Wyborcza*, January 27-28, 1985.

Kuroń J., *Moja zupa*, Warsaw 1991.

———, "Rzeczpospolita dla każdego. Myśli o programie działania," *Życie Gospodarcze* no. 21, 1994.

———, *Spoko! czyli kwadratura koła*, Warsaw 1992.

———, Żakowski J., *Siedmiolatka, czyli kto ukradł Polskę?*, Wrocław 1997.

———, "Trzech na jednego," An Interview with . . . , *Zdanie* no. 1-2, 2001

Kurowski S., "Wyjście z kryzysu - program alternatywny," in *Ruch Związkowy*, fascicles of OPSZ no. 1, 1981.

Kuznets S., "Economic Growth and Income Inequality," *American Economic Review* 45/1, 1955.

Kwaśniewski A., "Coś musi powstać za sprawą innej generacji. Trzech na jednego," *Zdanie* no. 1-2, 2004.

Lange O., "Maszyna licząca i rynek," in O. Lange, *Dzieła*, 1973.

———, "The Economic Operation of a Socialist Society," in O. Lange, *Economic Theory and Market Socialism*, Aldershot 1994.

Lange O., Breit M., "Droga do socjalistycznej gospodarki planowej," in O. Lange, *Dzieła*, vol. 2, Warsaw [1934] 1973.

Le Goff J., "Historia nie da się oszukać," *Gazeta Wyborcza*, April 2-4, 1994.

———, "Jedność w różnorodności," discussion between W. Fałkowski and A. Gałkowski, *Rzeczpospolita*, August 9-10, 2003.

Lewandowski J., "Msza przeciw prywatyzacji," *Gazeta Wyborcza*, January 15, 1999.

Lewandowski J., Szomburg J., *Strategia prywatyzacji*, Gdańsk 1990.

Lindblom C., *Inquiry and Change. The Troubled Attempt to Understand and Shape Society*, New Haven-London-New York 1993.

———, *Politics and Markets. The World's Political Economic Systems*, New York 1977.

Lindert P. H., *Growing Public: Social Spending and Economic Growth since the Eighteenth Century*, Cambridge 2004.

———, *Welfare State, Markets, and Efficiency: The Free Lunch Puzzle Continues*, Jerusalem Institute 2007.

———, *Why the Welfare State Looks Like a Free Lunch*, Working Paper 9869 NBER, Cambridge MA. 2003.

Lipiński J., "Najpierw ugasić pożar," interview by G. Garlińska, *Zmiany* no. 19, 1989.

Lipowski A., "Rynek a własność," address at conference: Systemy własności a proces gospodarowania, IRG SGPiS, Warsaw 1984 (photocopy).

Ludwiniak K. (ed.), *Pracownik właścicielem*, Paris 1989.

Lutkowski K., "Z czym do Funduszu," September supplement to *Polityka* no. 19, 1989.

Łagodziński W., "Strach przed biedą," *Rzeczpospolita*, August 27, 1999.

Łagowski B., "Trzech na jednego," interview by E. Chudziński, A. Komorowski, and W. Rydzewski, *Zdanie* no. 1-2, 1996.

Łagowski B., "Zniszczenie i pustka," in B. Łagowski, *Liberalna Kontrrewolucja*, Centrum im. Adama Smitha, Warsaw [1989] 1994.

Łaski K., Bhaduri A., Levcik F., "Od gospodarki planowej do systemu rynkowego: co się nie powiodło i co teraz trzeba zrobić," in *Gospodarka Polska 1990-1993. Kontrowersje wokół oceny doświadczeń i polityki gospodarczej*, Instytut Nauk Ekonomicznych PAN, Warsaw 1994.

Ławiński P., "Ile wytrzymacie?," *Tygodnik Solidarność*, September 29, 1989.

Maciejewicz P., "Jak Polska stala się statystycznym rajem," *Gazeta Wyborcza*, December 7, 2005.

Małachowski A., "Łzy cisną się do oczu," *Przegląd* no. 11, 2001.

———, "Rozliczmy współczesność," *Przegląd*, January 7, 2002.

Mate A., "Why the Privatisation of Iraq Is Illegal," *The Guardian*, November 7, 2003.

Mazowiecki T., "Na początku jest pustka," *Gazeta Wyborcza*, September 18-19, 2004.

McPherson C.B., "The Rise and Fall of Economic Justice," in G. Brossio and H. M. Hochman, *Economic Justice*, vol. 1, Cheltenham and Northampton 1988/1998.

Meade J., *Efficiency, Equality and the Ownership of Property*, London 1964.

———, *Different Forms of Share Economy*, London 1986.

———, *Liberty, Equality and Democracy*, Basingstoke-London 1993.

Meade J., *Liberty, Equality and Efficiency*, Macmillan and Houndmill, London 1993.

Mencinger J., "Słowenia: Alternatywna polityka gospodarcza w praktyce," in T. Kowalik et al., *Wokół polityki gospodarczej Unii Europejskiej,* Warsaw 2004.

Merkel W., Giebler H., "Measuring Social Justice and Sustainable Governance in the OECD," in Stiftung B. (ed.), *Sustainable Governance Indicators 2009,* Gütersloh 2009.

Michna W., "Bezrobocie na wsi," in *Encyklopedia Agrobiznesu,* Warsaw 1998.

Michnik A., "Wasz prezydent, nasz premier," *Gazeta Wyborcza,* July 5, 1989.

_____, "Związek zawodowy już nie wystarcza," *Gazeta Wyborcza,* July 6-8, 1989.

_____, "Gdzieś we wschodniej części Europy," *Tygodnik Powszechny* no. 35, 1993.

Milanovic B., "Poland's Quest for Economic Stabilization 1988-1991: Interaction of Political Economy and Economic," *Soviet Studies* 3/44, 1992.

Mill J. S., *Zasady ekonomii politycznej,* vol. 1, Warsaw 1965.

_____, *Principles of Political Economy,* vol. 1, New York 2006.

Miller S., Grow B., "Wolnorynkowa opcja w Unii rośnie w siłę," *Wall Street Journal Europe,* quoted from *Gazeta Wyborcza,* November 12, 2002.

Międzyzakładowa Struktura "Solidarności," *Raport: Polska 5 lat po sierpniu,* Warsaw 1985.

Ministerstwo Finansów, "Założenia i kierunki polityki gospodarczej," supplement to *Rzeczpospolita,* October 12, 1989.

Ministerstwo Skarbu Państwa, *Dynamika przekształceń własnościowych,* Warsaw 2002a.

Ministerstwo Skarbu Państwa, *Raport o przekształceniach własnościowych w 2001 roku,* Warsaw 2002b.

Minsky H., "The Transition to a Market Economy," Working Paper, J. Levy Economics Institute, Bilthwoods 1991.

Modzelewski K., *Dokąd od komunizmu?,* Warsaw 1993.

Morrison R., *We Build the Road as We Travel. Mondragon, A Cooperative Social System,* Philadelphia–Santa Cruz 1991.

Mrak M. et al., *Slovenia, From Yugoslavia to the European Union,* Washington D.C. 2004.

Nellis J., "Time to Rethink Privatization in Transition Economies?," *Transition* no. 1, 1999.

Nelson R. R., "Assessing Private Enterprise: An Exegesis of Tangled Doctrine," *Bell Journal of Economics* 12, 1981.

Nelson R. R., Winter S. G., *An Evolutionary Theory of Economic Change,* Cambridge MA–London 1991.

Nove A., *The Economics of Feasible Socialism,* 2nd ed., London 1991.

NSZZ "Solidarność" Region Warmińsko-Mazurski, *Porozumienia Okrągłego Stołu,* Warsaw 1989.

Ohme K., *The Borderless World,* London 1990.

_____, *The End of the Nation State,* New York 1995.

Olczyk E., Pilczyński J., "Prawo pracy coraz częściej łamane. W pracy bardziej niebezpiecznie," *Rzeczpospolita,* December 21–22, 1996.

Ost D., *Klęska "Solidarności": Gniew i polityka w postkomunistycznej Europie,* Warsaw 2007.

_____, *The Defeat of Solidarity. Anger and Politics in Post-Communist Europe,* Ithaca NY 2005.

Ostrom E., *Governing the Commons; The Evolution of Institutions for Collective Action,* New York 1990.

_____, *How Inexorable Is the "Tragedy of the Commons?" Institutional Arrangements for Changing the Structure of Social Dilemmas,* Bloomington IN 1986 (photocopy).

_____, *Institutional Arrangements and the Common Dilemma,* Bloomington IN 1987 (photocopy).

Ostrom E. et al., *Rules, Games & Common Pool Resources,* Ann Arbor MI 1994.

Ostrowska M., Szumlewicz K., "Polityka jest rodzaju żeńskiego, ale nie ma w niej kobiet," *Lewą Nogą* no. 16, 2004.

Panel, "Premierzy o 15 latach transformacji ustrojowej," statement by Marek Belka, *Gazeta Prawna,* February 21, 2005.

Passent D., "Anioł z pierwszej strony," *Polityka* no. 13, 1988.

Paszyński A., "Drogi i bezdroża reformy," *Tygodnik Powszechny* no. 50, 1988.

"Plan Sachsa," *Gazeta Wyborcza,* August 24, 1989.

Płowiec U., "Uwagi o gospodarczej i społecznej transformacji Polski w świetle wyzwań jej rozwoju w XXI wieku," in E. Mączyńska, Z. Sadowski (eds.), *O kształtowaniu ładu gospodarczego,* Warsaw 2008.

"Podziały w Solidarności. Dlaczego?," discussion with editors, *Życie Gospodarcze* no. 23, 1991.

Polak J., *Monetary Analysis of Incomes Formation and Payments Problem,* Washington 1957.

Porębski C., *Umowa społeczna. Renesans idei,* Warsaw 1999.

Poznański K., *Wielki przekręt. Klęska polskich reform,* Warsaw 2000.

Pryor F. L., *The Future of U.S. Capitalism,* Cambridge-New York 2002.

Przeworski A., "Demokracja to nierówność," interview by M. Nowicki, *Europa,* Sunday supplement to *Dziennik,* May 30–31, 2009.

Przychodzeń J. and Przychodzeń W.,"Szara strefa a nierówności dochodowe w gospodarkach posocjalistycznych," *Master of Business Administration* no. 2, 2009.

Putnam J., *The Modern Case for Socialism,* Boston 1943.

Rabska T., "W stylu starej epoki," *Życie Gospodarcze* no. 36, 1989a.

_____, "Statut 'wzorcowy' czy bezprawny," *Życie Gospodarcze* no. 45, 1989b.

Rakowski M., *Dzienniki polityczne 1987–1990,* vol. 10, Warsaw 2005.

Rapaczyński A., "Niepotrzebne państwo narodowe," *Rzeczpospolita,* March 23–24, 2002.

Rawls J., *A Theory of Justice*, Cambridge MA 1971.

———, *A Theory of Justice*, Oxford 1999.

———, *Teoria sprawiedliwości*, Warsaw 1994.

Rein M., "The Social Structure of Institutions: Neither Public nor Private," in S.B. Mamerman, A.J. Kahn (eds.), *Privatization and the Welfare State*, Princeton NJ 1989.

Rek M., "Nierówności społeczne w debacie prasowej: dyskusja o polskiej biedzie na łamach *Gazety Wyborczej*," in J. Klebaniuk (ed.), *Oblicza nierówności społecznych*, vol. 1, Warsaw 2007.

Roemer J., *A Future for Socialism*, Cambridge MA 1994.

Roemer J. et al., "Equality and Responsibility," *Boston Review* no. 2, 1995.

Rogoff K., "Dać upust złej krwi," *Forum*, September 22, 2008.

Roosevelt F.D., Belkin D. (eds.), *Why Market Socialism? Voices from Dissent*, Armonk-New York-London 1994.

Rosati D., "Ekstremista," *Przegląd Tygodniowy* no. 24, 1989.

Rosati D., *Polska droga do rynku*, Warsaw 1998.

Rosser J., Rosser M. V., *Comparative Economics in a Transforming World Economy*, Chicago-London 1996.

Rostowski J., "Chcieliśmy uniknąć powtórki z 1981 r.," interview by Marzena Kowalska, *Życie Gospodarcze*, June 26, 1994.

Rothschild K. W. (ed.), *Power in Economics*, Harmondsworth 1971.

Rowthorn B. et al., "Public Ownership and the Theory of the State," in T. Clarke et al., *The Political Economy of Privatization*, London-New York 1994.

"Rząd proponuje związkom. Pakt o przedsiębiorstwie państwowym," *Gazeta Wyborcza*, September 10, 1992.

Rzońca A., "Nierówności są OK," *Gazeta Wyborcza*, February 14, 2008.

Sachs J., "Nauka przetrwania," interview by Jacek Żakowski, *Polityka*, January 24, 2009.

———, *Poland's Jump in a Market Economy*, Cambridge MA 1993.

———, *The End of Poverty*, New York 2005.

Sachs J., Lipton D., "Program stabilizacyjny dla Polski," *Gazeta Bankowa* no. 33–34, 1989.

Sadłowska K., "Chcemy opieki państwa," *Rzeczpospolita*, May 6, 2003.

Savas E. S., *Prywatyzacja-klucz do lepszego rządzenia*, Warsaw 1992.

Schumpeter J. A., *Kapitalizm, socjalizm i demokracja*, Warsaw 1995.

———, *Capitalism, Socialism and Democracy*, London-New York 1994.

Semprich Ż., "Program powszechny z wyjątkami," *Rzeczpospolita*, December 15, 1998.

Sikorski R., "Polska to nie Izrael nad Wisłą," *Gazeta Wyborcza*, September 20, 2009.

Skalski E., "Koszty i ofiary," *Tygodnik Powszechny* no. 35, 1989.

Skarżyńska K., "Agresja na pokaz," interview by W. Maziarski, *Gazeta Wyborcza*, August 7, 2002.

Skidelsky R., "Economic Freedom and Peace," *Newsletter* (Institute for Human Sciences in Vienna) no. 67, 2000.

Słabek H., *Obraz robotników polskich w latach 1945–1989,* Kutno-Warsaw 2004.

Socialist Union, *Twentieth-Century Socialism,* London 1956.

Sombart W., *Dlaczego nie ma socjalizmu w Stanach Zjednoczonych?,* Warsaw [1906] 2004.

Soros G., "A plan for Poland," 1989c (typescript dated June 8, 1989).*

_____, "A plan for Poland" (typescript dated September 6, 1989d).*

_____, "A plan for Poland—stage two" (typescript dated December 19, 1989e).*

_____, "Wybrać musi społeczeństwo," interview, *Życie Gospodarcze* no. 52–53, 1989.

_____, "A plan to solve the economic crisis in Poland, expanded version" (typescript dated May 1, 1989).*

_____, "An East European Payments Union" (typescript dated May 4, 1990).*

_____, "An educational initiative for Eastern Europe" (typescript dated May 15, 1990).*

_____, *George Soros on Globalization,* New York 2002.

_____, "International economic assistance for Poland" (typescript dated March 24, 1989).*

_____, *Kryzys finansowy, Nowy paradygmat rynków finansowych i co to oznacza,* Warsaw 2008.

Staniszkis J., "Gesty jako argumenty," *Tygodnik Solidarność* no. 26, November 30, 1989.

Steingart G., "Plajta ostatniej utopii," *Forum*, October 6–12, 2008.

Stiglitz J., *Whither Socialism,* Wicksell Lectures, Stockholm 1990, mimeo.

_____, *Whither Socialism,* Cambridge MA 1994.

_____, "Some Lessons from the East Asian Miracle," *Research Observer* 11/2, 1996.

_____, "The Role of Government in Economic Development" (keynote address), *Annual World Bank Conference on Development Economics 1996,*Washington D.C. 1997.

_____, *More Instruments and Broader Goals: Moving toward the Post-Washington Consensus,* Helsinki 1998.

_____, "Development Thinking at the Millennium," in B. Pleskovic, N. Stern (eds.), *Annual World Bank Conference on Development Economics 2000,* Washington D.C. 2001.

_____, *Globalization and Its Discontents,* New York-London 2002.

_____, *Wizja sprawiedliwej globalizacji,* Warsaw [2006] 2007.

Strange S., *Casino Capitalism,* London 1986.

Strzelecki Jan, "Prywatyzujcie,prywatyzujcie! Rozmowa z Miltonem Friedmanem," *Res Publica* no. 10, 1990.

Suwalski A., "Ekonomiczno-Społeczne zagadnienia sporu o powszechne uwłaszczenie," *Ruch Prawniczy, Ekonomiczny i Socjologiczny* 1, 1997.

Szahaj A., *Jednostka czy wspólnota? Spór liberałów z komunitarystami a "sprawa polska,"* Warsaw 2000.

Szomburg J., "Jaki kapitalizm?," special issue of *Przegląd Polityczny*, 1993.

———, "Strategia integracji i rozwoju," *Rzeczpospolita*, December 16, 2002.

Sztompka P., *Trauma wielkiej zmiany. Społeczne koszty transformacji*, Warsaw 2000.

Szwarc K., "Radykalnie czy na oślep," *Życie Gospodarcze* no. 37, 1989.

Święcicki M., "Chciałbym reform radykalnych i odpowiedzialnych," *Życie Warszawy* no. 243, 1989.

Tawney R. H., *Acquisitive Society*, London 1921.

Tittenbrun J., *Z deszczu pod rynnę. Meandry polskiej prywatyzacji*, 4 vols., Poznań 2007.

Toporowski J., *The End of Finance: The Theory of Capital Market Inflation, Financial Derivatives and Pension Fund Capitalism*, London 2000.

Toporowski J., *Theories of Financial Disturbance*, Cheltenham-Northampton 2005.

Trembicka K., *Okrągły Stół. Studium o porozumieniu politycznym*, Lublin 2003.

Trzeciakowski W., "Teoretyczne przesłanki i założenia transformacji systemowej polskiej gospodarki," in M. Belka, W. Trzeciakowski (eds.), *Dynamika transformacji polskiej gospodarki*, vol. 1, Warsaw 1997.

Uvalic M., Vaughan-Whitehead D., *Privatization Surprises in Transition Economies, Employee-Ownership in Central and Eastern Europe*, Cheltenham 1996.

Vaughan-Whitehead D., "Employee Ownership on the Policy Agenda: Lessons from Central and Eastern Europe," *Economic Analysis* 1/2, 1999.

Wade R., "Globalization and Its Limits: Reports of the Death of National Economy Are Greatly Exaggerated," in S. Berger, R. Dore, *National Diversity and Global Capitalism*, Ithaca NY–London 1996.

Walicki A., "Liberalizm w Polsce," in A. Walicki, *Polskie zmagania z wolnością*, Kraków [1988] 2000.

———, *Marksizm i skok do królestwa wolności. Dzieje komunistycznej utopii*, Warsaw 1996.

Wałęsa L., "Oświadczenie. Dajmy rządowi uprawnienia nadzwyczajne," *Gazeta Wyborcza*, December 13, 1989.

Ward B., "The Firm in Illyria: Market Syndicalism," *American Economic Review* no. 48, 1958.

Warzywoda-Kruszyńska W., "Politycy nic nie wiedzą o biedzie," *Gazeta Wyborcza*, September 21, 2005.

Weisskopf T., "Market Socialism in the East," *Dissent*, Winter 1995.

Welfens P. J., Jasiński P., *Privatization and Foreign Direct Investment in Transforming Economies*, Aldershot 1994.

Wesołowski W. (ed.), *Losy idei socjalistycznych i wyzwania współczesności*, Warsaw 1990.

Wesołowski W., "Nowe spojrzenie na interesy," *Przegląd Społeczny* no. 11–12, 1993.

Wierzbicki P., "Przeklęte piętno," *Tygodnik Powszechny*, August 6, 1989.

Wilczyński W., "System funkcjonowania gospodarki—doświadczenia i warunki sukcesu," address at PTE Congress in Kraków, *Ekonomista* no. 2, 1988.

Winiecki J., "Źródła ekonomicznego sukcesu: eliminacja barier dla ludzkiej przedsiębiorczości," in *Pięć lat po czerwcu*, Warsaw 1995.

Wolf M., "Cutting Back Financial Capitalism Is America's Big Test," *Financial Times*, April 15, 2009.

Woś A., "Drogi restrukturyzacji rolnictwa," in Rada Strategii Społeczno-Gospodarczej, *Zasady i drogi restrukturyzacji rolnictwa*, Report 17, Warsaw 1996.

Woś A., Zegar J. S., "Skuteczność instrumentów polityki ekonomicznej wobec rolnictwa, w okresie transformacji," in Rada Strategii Społeczno-Gospodarczej, *Wieś i rolnictwo. Wyzwania i kierunki rozwiązań w obliczu integracji europejskiej*, Report 38, Warsaw 1996.

Wroński P., "Mocno bolało, ałe być musiało," *Gazeta Wyborcza*, June 6–7, 2009.

Wróblewski A., "List do George'a Sorosa" (typescript dated May 23, 1989).*

Wujec P., "Pejzaż przed PPP," *Gazeta Wyborcza*, March 17, 1993.

Wyczałkowski M., *Życie człowieka kontrowersyjnego*, PTE, Warsaw 2004.

Wygnański J., "Ekonomizacja sektora pozarządowego," *Ekonomia Społeczna* 1 /2), 2008.

Yarrow G., "Privatization in Theory and Practice," *Economic Policy* no. 2, April 1986.

Zachorowska-Mazurkiewicz A., "Społeczne implikacje dysproporcji ekonomicznych w zglobalizowanym świecie," in J. Klebaniuk (ed.), *Oblicza nierówności społecznych*, Warsaw 2007.

Zagrodzka D., "Czy Sachs powtórzy sukces Grabskiego?," *Gazeta Wyborcza*, August 23, 1989.

Zieliński M., "Nauczyciel z ulicy," *Wprost*, December 7, 2008.

———, "Prywatyzujmy, prywatyzujmy, prywatyzujmy," *ResPublica Nowa*, December 1992.

Zienkowski L., "Czy to już zmierzch gospodarki rynkowej?," *Gazeta Wyborcza*, February 3, 2009.

Żminda S., Bałtowski M., "Rodzaj inwestora zagranicznego a wyniki największych polskich przedsiębiorstw," in B. Błaszczyk and P. Kozarzewski (eds.), *Zmiany w polskich przedsiębiorstwach. Własność, restrukturyzacja, efektywność*, Report 70, Warsaw 2007.

Żyżyński J., "Niedocenione skutki prywatyzacji," *Master of Business Administration* no. 6, 2010.

*All typescripts made available by Stanisław Gomułka.

Notes

INTRODUCTION
1. Kowalik, 1996.
2. Ost, 2006.
3. Kabaj, 2006, 19.
4. Gilejko, 2008.
5. Wroński, 2009.
6. Wesskopf, 1995.

1. THE COLLAPSE OF "REALLY EXISTING SOCIALISM"
1. Nove, 1991, vii.
2. Putnam, 1943, 7.
3. Brus, Kowalik, 1983, 250. The author of this part of the article, and particularly of the term "conservative modernization," was Brus.
4. Kornai J., 1977, 357–63.
5. Diagnoza, 2003.
6. Lange, 1943.
7. Kornai, 1992.
8. Brus [1989] 1992.
9. Lange, 1938.
10. Lange and Breit [1934], 1973.

2. THE NEOLIBERAL ABOUT-FACE
1. Modzelewski, 1993.
2. Paszyński, 1988; Skalski, 1989.
3. Staniszkis, 1989.

4. Ławiński, 1989.
5. Ibid.
6. Ibid.
7. Ibid.
8. Ibid.
9. Michnik, 1989.
10. Wierzbicki, 1989.
11. Celiński, 1989.
12. Modzelewski, 1993, 10–11. Emphasis as in original.
13. Katznelson, 2005, 57.
14. Ibid., 58.
15. Walicki [1998] 2000, 37–38.
16. Ibid., 41.
17. Ibid., 39.
18. Dzielski, 1989.
19. Ibid.
20. Bugaj, 1988a.
21. Passent, 1988.
22. Dzielski, 1988.
23. Wesołowski, 1990.
24. Ibid.
25. Ibid., 52.
26. Ibid., 51.
27. Ibid., 58.
28. Ibid., 60.
29. Ibid., 60.
30. Ibid., 56.
31. Ibid., 57.
32. Ibid., 21.
33. Ibid.
34. Ibid., 45.
35. Ibid.
36. Ibid., 28.
37. Ibid., 29.
38. Ibid., 33.
39. Ibid., 35.
40. Ibid., 36.
41. Ibid., 43.
42. Ibid., 31.
43. Słabek, 2004.
44. Ibid., 384–85.
45. Ibid., 385.
46. Ibid., 399–400.

47. Ibid., 400.
48. Ibid., 384.
49. Paszyński, 1988.
50. Skalski, 1989.
51. Staniszkis, 1989.
52. Rabska, 1989a, 1989b.
53. Dyner, Izdebski, Szlajfer, 1989.
54. Kuroń, Żakowski, 1997.
55. Ibid., 119.
56. Ibid., 91–92.
57. Ibid., 127.

3. A BRIEF COMPROMISE: THE ROUND TABLE
1. Baka, 2007, 174.
2. Ibid., 52.
3. Baka, 2007, 200.
4. Borodziej and Garlicki, I, 2004, 307–8. Hereafter referred to as B-G.
5. Baka, 203.
6. Dubiński, 1999, 555.
7. B-G, II, 24.
8. Ibid., 26.
9. Transcript, 32.
10. Ibid., 21.
11. Ibid., 24.
12. Ibid., 27.
13. Ibid., 36.
14. Ibid., 50.
15. Ibid., 52.
16. Ibid., 55.
17. Ibid., 53.
18. B-G, IV, 18, 22.
19. B-G, IV, 15.
20. B-G, IV, 133.
21. Ibid., 132.
22. Ibid., 133.
23. Baka, 2007, 258.
24. Ibid., 213.
25. Ibid., 215.
26. Ibid., 226.
27. Ibid.
28. Ibid., 22.
29. Rostowski, 1994, 40.
30. "International," 1989.

31.   Dubiński, 557.
32.   Rostowski, 1994, 40.
33.   Jasiński, 1994, 120.
34.   Józefiak, 1999, 160.
35.   Geremek, Żakowski, 1990, 129.
36.   Ibid., 220–21.
37.   Kuczyński, 1992, 86.

4. FROM GRADUALISM TO "JUMP"
1.   Kuczyński, 1992, 54–55.
2.   *Kultura* 6, 1988.
3.   Kuczyński, [1988] 1996, 263-64. Emphasis as in original.
4.   Ibid., 266.
5.   Ibid.
6.   Bolesta-Kukułka, 1992, 141.
7.   Gomułka, 1989b.
8.   Brus, 1974.
9.   Gomułka, 1983.
10.   Soros, 1989a, in Kowalik, 2010, 398–99.
11.   Ibid., 406.
12.   Wróblewski, 1989, in Kowalik, 2010, 401–2.
13.   Conversation in Kowalik, 2010.
14.   Rosati, 1989.
15.   Rosati, 1998, 323–24.
16.   Ibid., 50.
17.   Ibid., 318–20.
18.   Ibid., 31, Figure 8.1.
19.   Stiglitz, 1996, 167.
20.   Sachs, 2005, 122.
21.   Ibid., 112.
22.   Ibid., 117.
23.   Ibid., 118.
24.   Sachs and Lipton, 1989.
25.   Dąbrowski, 1989.
26.   Dryll, 1989.
27.   "Podziały," 1991.
28.   Ibid.
29.   Dąbrowski, 1989.
30.   Lipiński, 1989.
31.   Święcicki, 1989.
32.   Szwarc, 1989.

5. GREAT SYSTEMIC CHOICES

1. Jedlicki, 1989.
2. Panel, 2005.
3. Friszke, 2002.
4. Kuczyński, 1992, 56.
5. Mazowiecki, 2005.
6. Eysymont et al., 1992.
7. Balcerowicz, 1984.
8. Balcerowicz, 1991.
9. Balcerowicz, 1990.
10. Balcerowicz, 2006.
11. Panel, 2005.
12. Kuroń, 1991, 10, 17–18.
13. Ibid., 111.
14. Ibid., 110.
15. Kuroń, 1994.
16. Ibid.
17. Kuczyński, 1992, 83–84.
18. Rakowski, 2005, 531.
19. Lutkowski, 1989.
20. Ibid., 1989.
21. Ibid.
22. Aleksandrowicz, 1989.
23. Kuczyński, 1992, 98–99.
24. Ibid., 100.
25. Balcerowicz, 1992, 47.
26. Gomułka, in Kowalik, 2010, 133.
27. Kuczyński, 1992, 109.
28. Kuroń, 1997, 76.
29. Quote after Kuczyński, 1992, 105–6.
30. Małachowski, 2001.
31. Małachowski, 2002.

6. THE BALCEROWICZ PLAN IN PRACTICE

1. Kuczyński, 1992: 107.
2. Ibid.
3. Gomułka, 1990.
4. Bobrowski, date not available. Copied text.
5. Gomułka, 1990.
6. Ibid., 7.
7. Domański, 1997, 56.
8. Skarżyńska, 2002.
9. Frasyniuk, 2004.

10. Kowalik, 2011.
11. Rostowski, 1990; Kowalik (ed.), 2011, xxx.
12. Ibid., 7.
13. Polak, 1957.
14. Ibid., 16.
15. Ibid., 19.
16. Ibid., 26.
17. Ibid., 27.
18. Ibid., 29.
19. Ibid., 47.
20. Gomulka, 1994a, 1994b.
21. Ibid., 120.

7. THE ALTERNATIVE AFTER THE SHOCK

1. Janicki, Władyka, 2008.
2. Ibid.
3. Ibid.
4. Kwaśniewski, 2004, 128–29.
5. Kozarzewski, 2007, 63.
6. Konsultacyjna, 1989, 3–4.
7. Ibid., 5.
8. Brus, 1993.
9. Kornai,1990, 101. Emphasis as in original.
10. Brus, Łaski,1989, 149.
11. Brus, Łaski, 1989, 139.
12. Hayek, 1946, 155.
13. Ibid., 156.
14. Sadłowska, 2003.
15. Gardawski, 2009-Polish, 2010a-English.
16. Gardawski, 2010a, 14.
17. Ibid., 14–15.
18. Gardawski, 2010b.
19. Ibid., 132–34.
20. Lutkowski, 1989.
21. Kowalik, 2010, 614.
22. Ibid., 488.
23. Kowalik, 2010, 462.
24. Graczyk, 2007.
25. Wroński, 2009.
26. Kowalik, 2011, xxx.
27. *Przegląd,* 1989.

8. OWNERSHIP: FROM TABOO TOPIC TO THE ROUND TABLE AGREEMENTS

1. Bornstein, 1974, 19.
2. Uvalic et al., 1996; Vaughan-Whitehead, 1999.
3. BIPS (Press Information Bureau of Solidarity), date of pub. unknown, 4.
4. Janczak (Kurowski's pen name), 1981, 86–87.
5. Brus, Łaski, 1991.
6. Międzyzakładowa, 1985.
7. Ibid., 59.
8. Ibid., 111.
9. Janczak, 1986, 60.
10. Lipowski, 1984, 19.
11. Wilczyński, 1988.
12. Ibid., 311.
13. Lindblom, 1993, 198–99.
14. Ostrom, 1986, 9–10.
15. Buchanan, 1997, 236.
16. Dahl, 1985, 55.
17. Lindblom 1977, 172–73.
18. Yarrow, 1986, 332.
19. Rowthorn et al., 1994, 65.
20. Ostrom, 1990; Ostrom et al., 1994.
21. Wygnański, 2008, 45.
22. Kornai, 1983, 102.
23. Rein, 1989.
24. BIPS, 1989, 14.
25. Jasiński, 1994, 120.
26. Jeziorański, 1990.
27. Ibid.

9. OPEN AND HIDDEN PRIVATIZATION STRATEGIES

1. Bałtowski and Miszewski, 2006, 233.
2. Berliner, 1993, 3.
3. Ibid., 10.
4. Stiglitz, 1998, 21.
5. Gomułka, 1985.
6. Gomułka, 1992, 290.
7. Kuroń, 1992, 224–25.
8. "Rząd," 1992.
9. Kuroń, Żakowski, 1997, 88–89.
10. Kuroń, 1993, 1994.

10. OWNERSHIP TRANSFORMATIONS IN PRACTICE

1. Krajewska, 1994; Federowicz, 1992.
2. Winiecki, 1995, 59; 1997, 135.
3. Kowalik, 1990, 94–101.
4. Tittenbrun, 2007, I, 35.
5. Domański 1997, 56.
6. Olczyk and Pilczyński, 1996.
7. Ibid.
8. Biuletyn, 2004.
9. Kolarska-Bobińska, 1993.
10. Błaszczyk and Nawrot, 2007, 97.
11. Tittenbrun, 2007, 4, 9.
12. *Gazeta Bankowa* no. 32, 1997. Quote after Tittenbrun, 2007, 4, 10.
13. Tittenbrun, 2007, 9–10.
14. Ibid., 11.
15. Ibid., 11.
16. Ibid., 24.
17. Ibid., 18.
18. *Polityka* no. 48, 1996. Quote after Tittenbrun, 2007, 37.
19. Wujec, 1993.
20. Quote after A.K.K., 1992.
21. Andreff, 1994, 293.
22. Błaszczyk et al., 2001; Błaszczyk, 2002.
23. *Gazeta Wyborcza*, December 10, 1993. Quote after Tittenbrun, 2007, 19.
24. Krajewska, Krajewski, 2002, 97.
25. Błaszczyk, 2002, 214.
26. Bochniarz, Wiśniewski, 1999.
27. Ibid.
28. Błaszczyk, 2002, 203.
29. Błaszczyk et al., 2001, 44.
30. Błaszczyk, 2002, 220.
31. Baehr, 1993, 95.
32. Bukowski, 1995, 148.
33. Ibid., 146.
34. Woś, 1996, 57–58.
35. Woś, Zegar, 1999, 87–90. I present this in great abbreviation.
36. Wojtczak, 2009.

11. MORE ON ENFRANCHISEMENT AND FOREIGN CAPITAL

1. Suwalski, 1997.
2. Semprich, 1998.
3. Ibid., 117.
4. Kieżun, 2011, 209.

5. Żyżyński, 2011.
6. Bugaj, 2002.
7. Ministry of Treasury, 2002a, 41.
8. Ministry of Treasury, 2002b, 15.
9. Bałtowski, 2002.
10. Bałtowski, 2007; Żminda, Bałtowski, 2007.
11. Bałtowski, 2007a, 262, Tables 9.12 and 9.16.
12. Ibid.
13. Bielecki, 2009.
14. Ibid.
15. Dunin-Wąsowicz, 2001b, 2001b.
16. Dunin-Wąsowicz, 2003.
17. Kozarzewski, 2007, 62–63.
18. Ibid., 63.
19. Ibid., 62.
20. Żyżyński, 2011.

12. OWNERSHIP IN DIFFERENT TYPES OF CAPITALISM

1. Ostrom, 1987.
2. Szomburg, 1993, 10.
3. Balcerowicz, 1995, 121.
4. Ibid., 121.
5. Kołakowski, 2000, 215.
6. Brossio and Hochman, 1998.
7. Rawls, 1971, 303.
8. Ackerman, 1996, 15.
9. Rawls, 1971, 94–95.
10. Ibid., xv.
11. Ibid., xv–xvi.
12. Ibid., xv.
13. Roemer, 1995.
14. Rawls, 1971, 244–45.
15. Ibid., 280.
16. Balcerowicz, 1998, 98.
17. Ibid.
18. Ibid., 99.
19. Ibid., 103.
20. Rzońca, 2008.
21. Zachorowska-Mazurkiewicz, 2007, 89.
22. Beskid, in Milic-Czernik, 1998.
23. Balcerowicz, 2006.
24. Lindert, 2007, 4.
25. Bruno, Squire, 1996.

26. Ibid., 56–57.
27. Stiglitz 1994, 279, italics added.
28. Ibid., 1994, 265-66.

13. THE NEW ORDER—A CIVILIZATION OF INEQUALITY?
1.   Sztompka, 2002.
2.   Sztompka, 2000, 66.
3.   Kabaj, 2000, 2004, 2007.
4.   Kabaj, Kowalik, 1995.
5.   Kuroń, 1991, 114–15.
6.   Ibid.
7.   Kula, 1996.
8.   Interview of Wojciech Kuczok for *Rzeczpospolita*, December 11-12, 2004.
9.   Zieliński, 2008.
10. Gardawski, 2001a.
11. Ibid., 322.
12. Ibid.
13. Ibid.
14. Gilejko, 2004, 164.
15. Milic-Czerniak, 1998.
16. Domański, 1996, 124.
17. Środa, 2010.
18. Merkel and Giebler, 2009.
19. Ibid.
20. Przychodzeń, Przychodzeń, 2009.
21. Eyal et al., 1997, 60.
22. Ibid., 67.
23. Kuroń, 1997, 119.
24. Celiński, 1999.
25. Krzemiński, 1999.
26. Ost, [2005] 2007, 33–34.
27. Kamiński, 2004.
28. Innes, 2003.
29. Mate, 2003.
30. Kuroń, 1991, 114.
31. Ibid., 114–15.
32. Ibid., 115.
33. Biuletyn, 2004, 2.
34. Miller, Grow, 2002.
35. Howell, 2003.

14. TO START A DEBATE ON POLAND AND THE EUROPEAN UNION
1.   Bieńkowski, Radło, 2006.

2. *Rzeczpospolita*, March 23–24, 2002.
3. Sachs, 2009.
4. Soros, 2002, 177–78.
5. Soros, 2009, 117.
6. Boyer, 1996, 59.
7. Wade, 1996, 60.
8. Gadomski, 2009.
9. Friedman, 1997.
10. Meade, 1993, 98–99.
11. Ibid., 193.
12. Dunin-Wąsowicz, 2001b.
13. Ibid., 117.
14. Bielecki, 2009, xxx.
15. Dunin-Wąsowicz, 2003.

Index